LOST STONES

OF THE

ANUNNAKI

And
The Mind-Altering
Journey To Find Them

Also by Madeleine Daines:

The Story of Sukurru
Before Babel The Crystal Tongue

For Ian

CONTENTS

9

Preamble

There is a rope, an internal, invisible rope connecting us all to truth. We feel it in our gut where the mother's knot is tied. It snakes silently between us in the same way that mycelium strands join the trees of the forest one to the other under the ground, taking food from their roots and nourishing them in return. We are all connected by that silver thread, the unseen umbilical cord of the celestial Matriarch. There is no escaping it and why would anyone want to? Who would not want to be nourished by Her loving truth?

When it first came into being, Sumerian was a monosyllabic language. Every word was short and every word had meaning. It was and still is a unique language, one that can't be processed according to the expectations of modern grammar. Phrases were multi-layered and coded through various devices, the positioning of words, the mirroring of sounds. It wasn't designed to be easy. The truth is there for the taking but perceived only when distracting voices have been set aside, when the finger that the monkey points at the moon loses its fascination. Only then will you look up and notice that our ancestors were stringing their short words into complex games, and that they had a sense of humour. Then if you choose to listen more closely, you will hear in those founding words the sounds that we still use today. Listen more closely and hear their laughter in the distance.

As I have said before, I have no personal agenda with regard to history other than to find the truth by going back and picking up the thread at the oldest possible source. The result is not the expression of opinion or cultural, religious beliefs, but of the consultation of the Sumerian symbols themselves. They have enough to say without forcing and twisting. Coaxing is all it takes. *The Story of Sukurru*[1] stands on its own merits and offers itself in lieu of non-existent academic credentials in a language that has long since lost sight of all its teachers. There are none. That translation was the work of someone who took the time to look long and hard at the earliest pictographic forms of the language, to pull on that invisible cord and to seek out the intentions of the original scribes. A wise old monkey kindly came forward to sit on my shoulder and to whisper and point throughout.

A word of warning. If the reader of this is enamoured of existing theoretical accounts of our past through the modern prism of the Anunnaki gods and looking forward to another layer of the same, they should perhaps stop now or at the very least prepare to be disappointed in that and in me. My work is entirely grounded in evidence; no unsubstantiated conjecture about our past proclaimed as truth, no self-serving, superficial interpretations of someone else's words, and most of all no insults to the intelligence of the original scribes. They have been sufficiently misrepresented, disrespected, wronged. My only agenda is to set the record straight concerning the Sumerians. The words 'given meaning' are used abundantly to indicate orthodox dictionary entries. My own relatively few added offerings are justified as fully as possible. No twisting of words unless twisted by the scribes themselves - only the truth revealing itself through the study of this, the oldest written language in the world. To those who are interested in moving forward and getting to the truth, whatever it might be, hold on to your hats. And bear in mind that this is a rollercoaster of a Sumerian language book, not a ride through Disneyland.

Climb Aboard

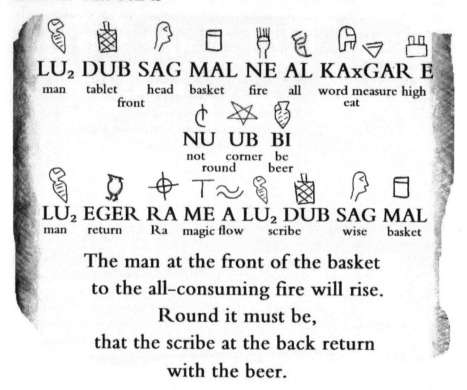

LU₂ DUB SAG MAL NE AL KAxGAR E
man tablet head basket fire all word measure high
          front   eat

NU UB BI
not corner be
     round   beer

LU₂ EGER RA ME A LU₂ DUB SAG MAL
man return Ra magic flow scribe wise basket

The man at the front of the basket
to the all–consuming fire will rise.
Round it must be,
that the scribe at the back return
with the beer.

(...) and thus the boats are made, without either stem or stern, quite round like a shield. (...) Their chief freight is wine, stored in casks made of the wood of the palm-tree. They are managed by two men who stand upright in them, each plying an oar, one pulling and the other pushing.[1]

At first glance, the wording of this riddle[2] found on a tablet dated to the Old Babylonian archaeological period of ca.1900-1600 BC is easily matched to the description made by Herodotus ca. 430 BC. They both refer to the round woven-reed coracles covered in animal skins and used to navigate the rivers of Mesopotamia, bringing proof of continuity over the millennia. But the Sumerian references to circular journeys in round boats with beer at their hearts go far beyond the physical aspect of a river boat. They spiral up and out, into the cosmic realm. Nothing is superficial. Take nothing for granted. Welcome.

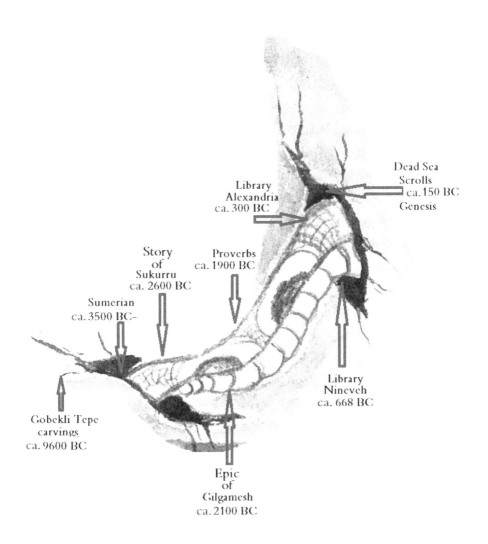

Dead Sea
Scrolls
ca. 150 BC
Genesis

Library
Alexandria
ca. 300 BC

Story
of
Sukurru
ca. 2600 BC

Proverbs
ca. 1900 BC

Sumerian
ca. 3500 BC-

Library
Nineveh
ca. 668 BC

Gobekli Tepe
carvings
ca. 9600 BC

Epic
of
Gilgamesh
ca. 2100 BC

3

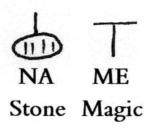

NA   ME

Stone Magic

What's In A Name?

What does your name mean? And how do you kn[ow]
Joanna, it might be that it harks back to John the Ba[ptist]
of Mesopotamian fame but that will provide not[hing but]
examples of its use. It won't tell you how the name
once meant… what concept, what story lies behind ... ___ . _
question rarely if ever arises. We were given a name at birth for any one of a
number of sometimes superficial and often closely personal reasons, and that's
all there is to know. But was that always the case?

Who discovered that Sumerian names had no more inherent meaning than
we attribute to most of our names today? Who sat down and worked out that

those names were both meaningless
and composed of more than one
syllable, just like so many names
today? Was the information laid out
somewhere in the fine print of a clay
tablet labelled "Sumerian Grammar
and How to Use it"? If so, where is
that important tablet now? Has
anyone seen it? Ever?

One tablet of great importance that
we do possess, and which is
brimming with multi-syllabic names
is the famed Sumerian King List[1], the
first forty lines of which cite the five
cities and their eight rulers during an
antediluvian age of extreme
antiquity. That portion of the overall
text is thought to have once been
separate from and potentially
considerably more ancient than the
rest, re-used to provide awe-inspiring
ancestry and endorse the legitimacy
of succeeding kings of much later times. The translated antediluvian section[2]
ends abruptly on line 39 with:

Then the flood swept over.

Below are the given names of those rulers as they currently appear in the

...anslation. The original cuneiform signs transformed into alphabetic ...ents (the transliterations) demonstrate that, despite appearances, the ...t antediluvian rulers of the five cities incorporate a total of about thirty-...x untranslated words/signs into their meaningless names[1]:

Alulim (3 symbols)

Alalgar (3 symbols)

En–men–lu–ana (6 symbols)

En–men–gal–ana (6 symbols)

Dumuzid (4 symbols)

En–sipad–zid–ana (5 symbols)

En–men–dur–ana (6 symbols)

Ubara–Tutu (3 symbols)

In the same way, four of the five antediluvian cities have names that can each be divided into three original symbols, giving twelve original words in all. The first city is left out of that equation for reasons that will perhaps become evident. Twelve plus one. All of those symbols are individually imbued with meaning according to orthodox Sumerian lexicons – but apparently not when they are found side by side or integrated one into the other as lengthy proper names. That is the way in which the entire Sumerian corpus has always been translated; through the lens of an agglutinative language where many of the individual 'syllables' are counted as elements of grammar as we know it, functional rather than inherently meaningful. Large numbers of them are not even that. They are simply ignored.

Meaningless names are nothing new. We're told that, around 270 BC, Berossus, an author living in Babylon in southern Mesopotamia, transcribed the Sumerian King List in Greek[2]. His original writings long since gone, it's presumed but obviously not proven that he did so directly from one or more Sumero-Akkadian tablets. Akkadian is the name given to a late form of Sumerian, presented as a separate language making use of the old symbols. Later copies of his version of the King List are still with us and have been compared to the information on the recovered Mesopotamian tablets. There are disparities; ten rulers for Berossus rather than eight in the reconstituted copy that we have in hand, and the sounds of most names... A lot of ink has been spent discussing the differences. In the meantime, that second or thirdhand Greek account provides silent confirmation of the meaningless nature of the original names. No ink lost on that subject. And that, it seems, is why none of the thirty-six plus twelve plus one symbols on that immensely important historical document have been probed more deeply for their information. Apparently, nobody gave it a thought.

The Sumerian King list is cited here as an example of the mountain of investigative work that still needs to be done. In the process of re-translating *The Instructions of Shuruppak*, I was intrigued by the name of the first city which is given as Eridug in the transliterations and also took a closer look at Ubara Dudu/Tutu who appears as the ruler of the last city, renamed Sukurru (aka Shuruppak), at the time of the flood. I have attempted a re-translation of the antediluvian section of the King List through the monosyllabic method. Bearing in mind that there may have been many alterations to the long-lost original source documents and that I'm not infallible, the result is open to debate. I have done my best (p.243).

It may be that we are missing whole swathes of Sumerian writings carrying additional mentions of the eight antediluvian rulers, but only two of them have so far been found repeatedly mentioned elsewhere.[1] Ubara the Sailor appears more than once in *The Story of Sukurru*, notably in the threefold refrain which takes the form of a lament for the place at the time of a flood. Both sailor and scribe, his name there appears to correspond to the final name on the most complete antediluvian King List account. Shuruppak also appears as the last city. There can be no doubt that the King List and *The Story of Sukurru* (aka *The Instructions of Shuruppak*) refer to the same city and ruler at that same crucial time. It's proven. So what happened? Did no-one notice?

There are other mysteries hidden inside the forty lines that constitute the pre-flood section of the King List. The extraordinarily long lifespans of the eight rulers appear to be elements in a mathematical riddle. I am not the first to suggest that the numbers given there might not refer to lifespans at all – perhaps some astronomical information. Is it important? Who knows? (p.71)

What's In A Nickname?

Because he came second in every branch of learning to those who had reached the highest level, he was nicknamed Beta.[2]

Beta, second letter of the Greek alphabet, doesn't sound like an affectionate nickname, more of an insult. Nevertheless, it appears that Eratosthenes was up there with the best when it came to the diversity of his discoveries. A Greek mathematician living in Alexandria, Egypt, in the 3rd century BC, he was chief librarian presiding over the famed centre of learning where all the knowledge of the ancient world had been gathered.

Among numerous other accomplishments, he is famous for having devised the method by which it was first shown that the Earth is round. It was Eratosthenes who discovered that the circumference of our planet could be calculated from shadows created by two distanced pillars measured at the same

time of day.[2] In fact, the man was credited with so much wisdom in such a wide range of subjects that his position as chief librarian in Alexandria must surely have come to the minds of jealous peers whenever he dumbfounded them with some new idea of genius; Alpha as wisdom and Beta, the copier of it, the second best. While it seems most likely that 'those who had reached the highest level' referred to the learned Greeks of immediately preceding generations such as Pythagoras or Plato who died around 347 BC, it is equally plausible that more ancient knowledge from considerably older works was inferred in that barbed comment on the work of Eratosthenes. With all the manuscripts gathered from around the globe and placed under his supervision, the broad range of his insights might be quite easily explained – perhaps even those of the earlier intellectuals also, some of the findings of Pythagoras for example. He too had an eclectic range of ideas and discoveries to his name. The truth of the matter is that there are no known original works of either Eratosthenes or Pythagoras in our possession and even if there were, plagiarism is only provable when originals are still in the public eye or memory. We have only second-hand, thirdhand, and in some cases, even more distanced sources of information about what went on in literate, educated circles some two thousand years ago.

Drip, Drip, Drip...

The same goes for another Alexandrian inventor, Ctesibius (285-222 BC), heralded as the mastermind behind the hydraulic pump, mechanisms using compressed air, the siphoning of liquids and further sophistication of the existing water clock. His own anecdotal tale of humble beginnings as the son of a barber and himself a barber, a situation which led to him inventing an adjustable mirror with counterweights, would lead me to look more closely at Ctesibius in his role as head of the Museum of Alexandria where he too would have had access to documents of great interest. Perhaps this is unfair insinuation and I willingly admit that it is purely speculative. Nevertheless, evidence of timekeeping by means of water clocks is attested since at least the 2nd millennium BC. It's difficult to believe that the inventor of the Egyptian Karnak clock, their peers and all those who followed were not themselves capable of taking the invention to a more sophisticated level, that they were satisfied for centuries gazing at a pot with a hole punched into its side, water dripping into a lower bowl, or that nobody before the Greeks possessed the wherewithal, the 'noos' to work out more complex mechanisms making use of water and air.

Just one great body of work, the science of astronomy, was acknowledged as being that of people from a much earlier timeframe than the intellectuals of the Hellenistic era: those centuries shortly before and around the birth of Jesus. According to later accounts, knowledge of the movements of the planets and stars was first credited to the Chaldeans of Babylon in the southern region of Mesopotamia by Berossus, himself an inhabitant of the place, in his work titled Babyloniaca which he wrote in Greek. Recovered cuneiform tablets, of which the famed astronomical MUL APIN text, appear to confirm that very much second-hand information.

It's impossible to know how far back stretched the body of works collected, studied, and ultimately destroyed in Alexandria, how many documents were unique, uncopied until they reached that place, no longer existent outside of its walls…what was found and then lost there…what was copied, claimed as original, carried off, hidden elsewhere.

Fire And Clay

And ye shall know the truth, and the truth shall make you free.(John 8:32)

In the second half of the 19th century, a body of writings from an earlier time than the library of Alexandria was dug up. The tablets appeared suddenly, publicly and in great profusion. The first archaeologists of the modern era had found the hitherto unknown writings of the Mesopotamians, notably those of the library of King Ashurbanipal, a great collection, intact. Like that of Alexandria, the Library at Nineveh in Mesopotamia was quite something in its time. King Ashurbanipal, who reigned over Assyria, the northern region of Mesopotamia during the 4th century BC, had ordered all existing clay tablets to be gathered from far and wide and brought to him there. The erudite king was keenly interested in recuperating works from all sources in the process of building up his library.

19th century archaeological expeditions, picking through the remnants of what was once the capital city of a vast region, uncovered and hauled away over twenty thousand whole or fragmented tablets. Every piece of cuneiform writing from Nineveh – like those discovered at Nippur and Ur in the south – predates the known sources of both Old and New Testament texts by at least several hundred years, in some cases by millennia. The writings found in the ruins of King Ashurbanipal's palace are older than manuscripts containing the Hindu Vedic writings, more ancient than all the well-documented Greek mythological characters and their adventures, including those deemed to have been written by a mysterious figure called Homer. The Sumerian literary texts predate the adventures of Odysseus or Jason by millennia. The oldest of them all, *The Story of Sukurru*, predates the entirety of the Bible by approximately two thousand six hundred years.

Clay is a relatively durable material, particularly when burned by accident or fired by intent. Buried beneath the sands, there at Nineveh and at other more ancient archaeological sites in the Near and Middle East, the writing on it can and did survive, some for over four thousand years, from as far back as 3500 BC. These were documents which had evaded notice during the purges of the early Christian era. Their dangerous treasures had not been expunged. No whitewash had taken place. Although the language and the civilisation behind it were completely unknown to historians, the tablets could be relatively safely dated through comparison of the evolving styles of writing found on them, keys to the language discovered thanks to later equivalences, the sounds and meanings of the cuneiform signs unravelled to a large extent, finally taken right back and matched to their pictographic originals, largely thanks to the abundant Sumero-Akkadian lexical lists.

In the late 19th and early 20th century, only one remaining task separated the modern world from full knowledge of that buried treasure with its numerous literary texts and other documents – the translating process. And ye shall know the truth, John said – but only if the translator gets it right. And how will ye know that? Because they tell you so…unless, of course, you decide to go back to the source and investigate for yourself.

Nabi Yunus

For just as Jonah was three days and three nights in the belly of the great fish, so will the Son of Man be three days and three nights in the heart of the earth. (Matthew 12:40)

The ruins of Nineveh consist of nothing more than two large earth-mounds, one of which named Tell Nabi Yunus. (Nabi is Arabic for 'prophet'.) Both Muslims and Christians once maintained a shrine there for the figure better known to many as Jonah, central character of a particularly strange tale. Jonah is forever associated with a giant fish, very much in the same vein as Oannes, the fish god mentioned by Berossus. The slight physical difference between them is that Jonah was not part fish, not a merman. Nevertheless, they have an extraordinarily fishy tale in common.

According to the Book of Jonah, one of the texts of the Hebrew bible, the prophet had been ordered by God to curse the city of Nineveh, clearly an unpleasant task and one that he was unwilling to undertake. Instead, Jonah defied God and boarded a ship headed in the opposite direction to a place called Tarshish. To teach him a lesson, God cooked up a terrible storm over the sea and, after much debate among the sailors as to the cause of their catastrophic situation, Jonah was thrown overboard. He was swallowed by a great fish, usually understood to be a whale, and spent three days grovelling for forgiveness in its belly before being vomited up unharmed on a beach. After that, he walked back to Nineveh, a trip that took another three days, and delivered God's new message of impending doom to its inhabitants. So far so good but the story doesn't end there. Jonah was more than a little annoyed to discover that, thanks to the rapid reaction of the ruler of the city to his predictions, God had changed His mind and decided not to follow through with His threat. Clearly, that made Jonah look a fool, belying his prophecy and undermining his reputation. So angry was he that he walked off once again and sat down exhausted to think about things. At that point in the story, a plant, given in Hebrew as kikayon, grew up over the poor hard-done-by man, providing welcome shade but, just as he was getting comfortable, it was nibbled on by a worm and withered away. The story ends there with his bitter complaint; *"I am angry enough to die!"* and a stern lesson from God on the subject of priorities and anger management.

The full meaning behind Jonah's strange adventure has not yet been explained in any logical manner that doesn't require blind faith in God. The original thread of meaning has been successfully cut, either deliberately or as part of a larger cull, leaving no obvious trace of its source; the remaining fragments nothing more than a mound of earth and a shrine to Nabi Yunus, alongside a story without discernible head or tail, whether human or fish, and an unidentified plant called kikayon. The only absolute truth to be gleaned from their continuing existence is that Jonah was once a big deal in Nineveh. That there also exists a Book of Jonah within the pantheon of biblical writings is further confirmation of his prestige. Even Jesus mentioned him by name (see above from the Book of Matthew). And yet, the translations of texts found in Mesopotamia, many of them in Nineveh itself, and written in Sumerian, the language of that land, don't mention Jonah or any element of his strange experiences at all. There are no whales, no names that might lead us to him, no accounts of that dramatic sea voyage, no prophets even…unless by other names.

Because of the presence of the shrine at its summit, Tell Nabi Yunus had not been fully explored when Islamic extremists partially destroyed the construction there in 2014, unwittingly leading to the discovery of an earlier Assyrian palace. Something always lies beneath.

Where Have They All Been Hiding?

…then Ammenon the Chaldæan, in whose time appeared the Musarus Oannes the Annedotus from the Erythræan sea. [1]

The earliest known reference to Oannes, the fish god character who appeared out of the sea to teach his wisdom and skills to a primitive people, was also apparently written down by Berossus during the 3rd century BC. No-one knows at what period Oannes lived or if he existed at all, but at least we can be sure that his fame dates back to before the beginning of our era and that many images of a fish-god[2] were produced over time, confirming that there was common knowledge of such a figure in deep antiquity.

In direct contrast, none of the ancient writings and translations in any language (Greek, Arabic, Latin…) from any time before, during or after the 1st millennium AD mention a group of beings called anything sounding even vaguely like Anunnaki despite the fact that the name is profoundly anchored in minds and regurgitated in numerous books, blogs and videos as that of a founding group of very special beings, of gods. There are two modern sources for that premise: the various academic translations of Sumerian and the best-selling books of Zecharia Sitchin.[1] But was the name Anunnaki already documented elsewhere before clay tablets were first pulled out of the sands of Mesopotamia in the 19th century? Again, to my knowledge, none of the ancient texts written in or translated to those languages that refer to the region, history and culture of the region mention them. It seems that the Anunnaki appear as such for the first time in modern-day interpretations of the Mesopotamian tablets.

Zechariah Sitchin, like all those before him, took Sumerian to be an agglutinative (multi-syllabic) language. He also took the name provided by academia (with a choice of spelling between Anuna, Annunaki or Anunnaki), and latched on to existing translations explaining them away as gods. Replacing the religious mindset with an extra-terrestrial context, he effectively took control of the Anunnaki bandwagon, adding the bells and whistles necessary to bring them to the attention of a far wider audience. The sensational news that they were in fact figures from outer space and the original founders of humanity was extremely well received by the public back in 1976 and still today. Sitchin had and still has fans and little wonder. Reading dry, disjointed and often downright nonsensical literary accounts of a bunch of lacklustre gods could not compare to the announcement that ET is real and has visited. Even impending doom from the mysterious planet X is more fun than the academic versions of that literature.

There is an abundance of information swilling around the internet and elsewhere embroidering on the subject of the Annunaki, all taken from that one fundamental 'truth'. Whatever the theory put forward concerning the nature of their being and their activities, it goes without saying today that the name 'Anunnaki' – however spelled - was well-attested, in existence since time immemorial, and that any detailed mention of Sumerian culture would be incomplete without the presence of its Anunnaki gods.

However, unless someone somewhere comes forward today with proof in the form of some ancient document bearing their name, this investigation moves forward with the following in mind; it is possible that the Anunnaki as a group of beings never existed under that name and that it was the result of erroneous translating methods in modern times. I will assume that the symbols – found numerous times together - were not intended to be read as a multi-syllabic meaningless name but as something else, something more, perhaps even several other things. My investigation must necessarily bypass all of the existing translations of both Sumerian and the later Akkadian names - the list is long – unless they are transcribed alongside images on artefacts, or I find them for myself in the texts, or they are found repeated in documents in other languages pre-dating the 19th century. As far as I know, apart from some phonetic similarities found for the antediluvian kings, only the noble but frankly weird Gilgamesh is confirmed by a mention in Greek. He also appears in the King List but at a considerably later post-diluvian point on line 112.

The Memory Stick

To be fair, there remains the possibility that all record of the Anunnaki gods after the Sumero-Akkadian era has been lost to history somewhere along the way, either voluntarily suppressed at an early date, or destroyed in some natural catastrophe. The degree to which our knowledge of the past has been dilapidated through the effects of time, of misunderstanding or deliberate, methodical suppression of certain types of material cannot be understated.

Human nature being what it is, certain types of text - alchemical, pagan, heretical - would not have been destroyed without first being eagerly poured over and thoroughly digested by those who had them in hand, the most revelatory copied and squirrelled away in secret places. Much too tempting. The idea of a purely oral tradition becomes more difficult to swallow in times when the written word was a possible, private choice. Then again, censorship has always existed for the masses; not the few. No doubt, it was once relatively easy to stifle public knowledge of teachings of the Gnostic type, to put an end to extensive, detailed awareness of pagan cultures in existence in the pre-Christian era, to hide the true significance of important seasonal rituals carried out long before the story of a Christian saviour took hold at the beginning of our era.

For the purpose of channelling large populations into one manageable belief system, two parallel methods: destruction of all openly available written texts accompanied by obfuscation of the teachings. Burn the books and distort the information provided to future generations, a tried and tested combination that has morphed in its style but continues to exist. Transcendental knowledge gathered and documented in the period before the advent of the Christian church has always represented a threat to religious dogma. Controllers have only words and punishment in their bag of tricks. They are no match for spiritual revelations of a purely personal kind. At the same time, humans being naturally inquisitive, the important nuggets of transmitted information were surely eagerly examined behind closed doors, smuggled out of here and there, smuggled into this place and that, not destroyed but kept close, extremely close. A fascinating thought.

It is equally fascinating to consider the total absence of curiosity about the ultimate source of the words we use so unthinkingly today. I have yet to come across an etymological dictionary entry stating: 'from Sumerian'. However, there are thousands of words sourced from Greek or Latin and given as ultimately deriving 'from PIE root'. PIE is the acronym for proto-Indo-European. Through overuse, it has taken on a life of its own, appearing to have morphed into a language called PIE, needing no further explanation or investigation. In truth, it's nothing more than a reference to a massive statistical experiment which has taken languages from across the board and compared them for sound and meaning. Most importantly, PIE has no basis whatsoever in any ancient document. It's nothing more than a theory, whereas the matches that can be made between monosyllabic Sumerian and later languages are too numerous, too exact in both sound and meaning, too obvious to be ignored. Yet that is what has happened. Sumerian has long since been declared an isolated language by those who had the subject under their control. It came and went, we are told, alone in the world, no cousins other than the later Assyrians who simply re-used the signs in the manufacture of a whole new writing system known to us as Akkadian. No-one has yet debunked that altogether bizarre and unproven allegation, and a lot has since been built on that thoroughly unstable premise.

When John Marco Allegro (1923-1988), a reputed philologist, wrote *The Sacred Mushroom And The Cross* in 1970, he made the case that a fertility cult was at the origin of all religious worship. The theory was that God manifested as a giant phallus in the sky which spilled its semen onto the earth in the form of rain. This 'heavenly penis', as Allegro termed it, was all powerful, the source of all knowledge.[1]

He made much of the theme in his book, suggesting that the worship of the celestial male organ was gradually superseded by a less specific understanding of other-worldly influences on life, and that a deep-rooted yearning for mystical knowledge remained from that era, paving the way for the earliest forms of Judaism and Christianity. One controversial claim was that the path to enlightenment had always involved the use of mind-altering plants which contained the 'sperm of God'. That aspect of the fertility rites was, according to Allegro, kept secret from the outset; privileged knowledge of an elite few who had been chosen by God. They were to be the only inhabitants of paradise.

To my mind, the use of hallucinogens has always been the domain of an elite few purely because it took and still takes a great deal of specialist knowledge and practice to safely dose the ingredients, to prepare and administer the brew in a fitting context, to keep participants from harm while they undertake their spiritual journey. It was never a question of tossing a few mushrooms into a pot and hoping for the best. Those lessons did not need writing down. They were taught through practice. The 'elite class' of the earliest times was not enjoying privilege for its own sake and they were not alone in Paradise. On the contrary. They were - and still are - born and bred shamans offering their unique skills and services to their communities, while carefully passing on their knowledge to future generations. They were certainly not priests keeping precious secrets close for personal reasons, not priests as we understand that term. The very sentiment of jealously guarding knowledge for oneself would be irreconcilable with that shamanic tradition, practised openly, with generosity, the natural right of all, as integral to societies then as a computer screen is to ours today, and no doubt an essential element of the initiation into adulthood. The secrecy surrounding ritual use of mind-altering substances came about by force of denigration and persecution of its wise men and women at a much later stage. Secrecy was born out of the jealousy of those who wanted power over the minds of people but had nothing to give in return. I presume that is the epoch that John Allegro was referring to, a time from which we are only now emerging.

The most scandalous element in Allegro's book was his claim that the figure of Jesus was, in fact, a coded reference to an existing name – a pre-existing Jesus – the amanita mushroom. Jesus was first and foremost a magic mushroom. His existence at the beginning of our era stemmed from nothing other than a subterfuge carried out by a heretical group seeking to hide their continuing participation in age-old pagan rituals from the heavy-handed authorities of the Roman Empire. It was Gnostic monks who deliberately created the figure, gave him the name which had always been used to describe the much-revered mushroom and attributed to him its magical powers.[1]

According to Allegro's version of events, the joke was on them. Their own invention was turned against them by astute Romans bent on destroying the unruly monks once and for all. Jesus was morphed from a newly created myth into a new-born reality, becoming the central hero of a dominant cult installed for the purpose of control. Those are the bare bones of events put forward in the introduction to his book. He offers as proof an analysis of Hebrew and Greek words in relation to their Sumerian origins. John Allegro points to the fact that Sumerian has a multitude of close links to later languages and that it is, in fact, the source. The original heavenly penis was Sumerian!

It is important to remember that he had previously been held in high regard as a philologist within academia and even chosen in 1953 to be a member of the team studying the extremely precious, recently discovered Dead Sea Scrolls which had been hidden in caves - presumably by a persecuted Gnostic sect - some two thousand years earlier. I am presuming that he perceived something of importance in those documents that led to the writing of the book and to the crediting of the Sumerian language. But Allegro's Sumero-Greek and Hebrew interpretations did not convince his peers and *The Sacred Mushroom* was discredited, disregarded, forgotten. Nothing has since been offered up to confirm or disprove any part of his theories. Fifty years have passed.

As John Allegro pointed out in his book, Sumerian had long since morphed into the alphabetic writing of the Phoenicians and others when it was rediscovered in modern-day Iraq. On that we can agree from the outset. In truth, the use of hallucinogenic plants in rituals such as those carried out in the Amazonian jungle and elsewhere still today had already existed for several millennia by the time persecuted desert monks hid their writings in the Qumran caves on the shores of the Dead Sea. That tradition also gives the source of the very name by which we know them: Gnostic. It can be discerned in the written word from as long ago as the 4th millennium BC.

As for the sacred name of Jesus attested in the New Testament stories, it is more than time to re-test a theory which has lain dormant since 1970. Was Jesus once a mushroom and, if so, who else acquired their name from the earliest known written language?

At least some of the hundreds of short 'proverbs' recorded on tablets dating to the Old Babylonian era of ca.1900-1600 BC would be better termed as riddles, and it is my understanding that a good number of them served to perpetuate information in coded form from the earliest times. A couple of the lines found in the text of *The Story of Sukurru*, one fragment of which dated to ca.2600-2500 BC, are repeated in those tablets, demonstrating that the age of the clay is not a trustworthy indication of the age of the word. Was the purpose of those riddles to maintain secrecy within an elite group or to amuse and to educate in the same way as a relatively complex crossword puzzle might do today? Why write them down without providing the keys to those who might want to read them? Sumerian riddles were not meant to be easy.

But neither were they meant to be impossible. The keys have been mislaid but they must be around here somewhere...

What secrets might a fresh look at the Sumerian corpus expose? Is there any sign that Zechariah Sitchin got it right about extra-terrestrials and ghostly planets? Was John Marco Allegro correct in his understanding of Sumerian as the source of a 'Jesus' mushroom? Two completely different perspectives on the same language, neither of which agree with the officialised translations. I offer a third which results from keeping an open mind, employing the heretical monosyllabic method of translation, and following the trail in whatever direction it leads. There may be dead ends. There may also be secret doors to otherworldly places. Magic and truth go hand in hand. Together they spiral upwards.

SEAL OF THE FATHER

Roll the greenstone cylinder seal along a lump of moist clay and discover five of the 'Anunnaki gods' as they were perceived around 2300 BC[1]. Freshly imprinted, the images with their identical multi-horned headgear give them away. On the British Museum notice accompanying this artefact known as the Adda seal, the figures are named as the goddess Ishtar to the left of Ea, he of the shoulder water, also known elsewhere as Enki. Shamash, the sun god, is cutting his way out of a cleft in the mountains, and far right, Usimu, the two-faced servant, holds his arm up to connect with the flow of water. The left-hand character with bow and arrow is unnamed. As a group (but not in the British Museum's text), these are identifiable as the elite members of the Anunnaki clan.

The images on this famous seal have been much discussed, but the four accompanying words – presumably meant to explain or, at the very least, to add valuable information – not so much, if at all. Written in the style of the times and read from top right to bottom left, they are no longer pictograms, but not yet entirely abstract cuneiform, still somewhat recognisable. Here below their equivalent pictographic forms show the symbols (read in the modern order from left to right) as they might have appeared some one thousand years earlier:[2]

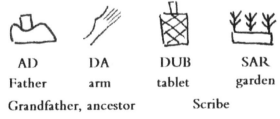

AD	DA	DUB	SAR
Father	arm	tablet	garden
Grandfather, ancestor		Scribe	

The first piece of solid information gleaned from this seal's inscription is that we are in the presence of ancestors – unless of course the ancestors were also gods as we understand that term today and that the Father was indeed God. But that's not what the inscription says. AD, also ADA/AT/ATA, has the given meanings of both 'Father' and 'bead', this last presumably a reference to the round stone cylinder seal on which the words are written.

DA has the given meanings 'arm' or 'side' and 'next to'. It can also be understood as the 'side' or bank of a river. AD-DA together have the given meanings 'father' or 'grandfather' and explain my added mention of 'ancestor'. They might read 'In the presence of the Father', 'By the Father's side', 'Father by the riverbank' or alternatively 'By the arm of the Father', 'The Seal of the Father', 'The Ancestral Seal'.

DUB, the 'tablet' or 'seal' seen top left, has SAR, the 'garden' below it. Taken together DUB-SAR result in 'scribe' according to the lexicons: the scribe of or in a garden scene (p.98).

AD-DA 'By the side of the Father' and DUB-SAR 'on the tablet to write'. It is feasible to translate the four words to 'Scribe of the Father' and imagine that the seal belonged to someone with specialised writing skills, someone who had the ability to tell the oldest tale, the story of the ancestors: The Tablet of the Father. Then again, it might have had a more religious connotation, a pierced cylinder seal threaded on a fine gold chain and worn around the neck of a cult member. Who knows? And what more can we find out about the Father and the writing of the scribe?

To my knowledge, there are no known inscriptions accompanying any Mesopotamian seals, bas-reliefs or any other artefacts from any period that might provide written proof of a direct association between the name Anunnaki and these figures. Nevertheless, it isn't a huge leap of faith from one to the other – from image to name - if those gods have been firmly established in the texts, of course.

Lord of Lords

AB

Father of Oceans

AT

Father of Writing

EN

Lord between Sky and Earth

E₂   **A**

Temple of the Flow

The central male figure is given on the British Museum's notice as Ea which stems from E_2-A, the 'temple' or 'house' with 'water' or 'flow', 'water house', 'the temple on the water', 'a flowing house', 'temple of the water', perhaps a levee, an embankment to control the flow and to irrigate the land. It's not a stretch to understand it as a riverboat. The Sumerian vessels took on a variety of names and forms. Ea as a title describes a construction of some kind, potentially personified on the seal image but not an acceptable name for a human figure per se.

To call him Enki might not be entirely false, but Enki comprises three words: AN-EN KI. EN, given in Sumerian lexicons as 'Lord', comes between AN, 'sky', and KI, 'place' or 'Earth', potentially giving 'the Lord between sky and Earth' which, once familiarity has set in, can be shortened to EN, the Lord. EN sounds like a suitable name in the context of a monosyllabic language. One visual observation can be made with regard to symbol EN: it varies quite a bit from tablet to tablet, but some of the early versions look similar to the so-called Anunnaki headgear sported by all five figures on this seal.

Another word, AB which has the given meanings 'Father' and 'elder' along with 'sea' or 'ocean', is the best linguistic fit for the figure with water pouring from his shoulders. 'Father' and' sea' together give 'the old man of the sea' he who became Greek Nereus and was portrayed by the Greeks as a human-fish hybrid, the ultimate fish god. AB is the source of the prefix in words such as 'abyss' and 'absent'. There are numerous cases of AB with BA, 'below' or 'without', giving combinations such as 'Father below' or 'Fatherless'. Together AB-BA is given in the lexicons under the same category as AB/ABA. He is 'father', 'elder' and 'an old person'. This is the source of Greek abba, the father, who became 'abbot'. Abba, the patriarch, is an epithet of Saint Anthony of Egypt (p.187) who has a curious knack of popping up from time to time in the study of this language.

The connections between Sumerian EN, the Lord, AB, the ocean, and E$_2$-A, the water temple, with Greek Nereus, also Greek Poseidon, later gods of the ocean, and with 'abyss', the watery underworld, quickly become obvious by observing the scene. The central figure on the Adda seal and on numerous other artefacts is firmly positioned between the sky and the land with indications of water flowing either from above him or from his shoulders, and below his feet, sometimes directly from pots held out in front of him and flowing into other pots. He appears to be the 'god' of the oceans and all other water sources on Earth but also the rivers and oceans of the skies, omnipotent AD/AT/ADDA/ABBA, the Father who walks on land and on water. And he continues to exist through words we use today. Whether also a god or not, the stone seal text tells us firmly that he was one of us. It is adamant.

Lord BA-AL

The character digging his way down into the cleft in the mountains is given on the notice as Shamash which is simply one phonetic form of UD, the sun. UD has a wide variety of interesting phonetic values which can be matched to other names (p.140) but the symbol itself doesn't vary. Since there is nothing in the accompanying inscription to indicate the true name of the cutlass-wielding figure and since he is quite obviously digging, Baal springs more easily to mind than Shamash. Here with the lexicon-given meanings.

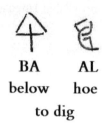

BA   **AL**
below   **hoe**
to dig

Baal is an epithet of the Sun god worshipped by the Phoenicians and Canaanites and it was a title applied to gods in diverse religious contexts, the origin remaining unknown. Hitchcock's Bible Names Dictionary gives Hebrew bal as 'master' and 'Lord', a title which translates to Sumerian EN rather than UD. Confirmation of that association is found with the Akkadian phonetic form 'belu' which has been said to correspond to the Canaanite Baal but which is simply another, later sound given to the Sumerian word EN, the Lord. Baal, the digging lord. Belu is also linked to LUGAL (p.260). Something of a mystery surrounds the Lord Baal. There appears to have been some twisting going on…

John Allegro believed that Baal's name originated with the two Sumerian words[1] BA-AL which he proposed in his book as the source of the word 'phallus', an idea based in both the sound and the meaning 'dig' and fitting into his general theme of a fertility cult. But there are many ways that the word 'dig' can be interpreted and the action understood. For example, pigs forage for truffles and people hunting for clues to enigmas also have to dig. Context is key, a wise old monkey once told me.

Another perspective on the notion of Sumerian BA-AL is that of Zechariah Sitchin. BA-AL as 'dig' and another given meaning 'excavate' fits into his theory of Anunnaki gods modifying humans to create gold-mining slaves. That's an idea that doesn't sit well with this particular cylinder seal evidence where the 'god' is doing his own dirty work. In fact, he might be preparing the ground for the planting of a young tree, the root bundle of which can be seen in the hand of so-called Ishtar just above his head. This is a garden scene as identified in the inscription by the word SAR. Is the group of 'gods' preparing the place for a second Tree?

24

And, if so, would that serrated cutlass be an ideal tool for gardening? Another possible activity for the figure comes to mind. It involves the cutting of material known as bitumen or tar, a black, sticky petroleum that seeps from rocks, widely available in Mesopotamia and utilised for a variety of purposes including waterproofing of boats and mummification. Tar comes from Sumerian TAR/KUT which has the given meaning 'to cut'. Perhaps the 'god' is busy cutting into the bitumen for the purpose of waterproofing a celestial boat, a round coracle that will carry him down to TAR-TAR, which became Greek Tartarus, the underworld, a dark pit where sinful spirits wallow after death. Baal to Tartarus? (p.37) In *The Story of Sukurru*, the fool waterproofs the door to Noah's ark – from the outside.

Back And Forth

The two-faced character on the right of the Ada cylinder seal is best known as Isimud in the Sumerian texts. In this case, it's of more interest to first consider the meanings associated with the two-faced Latin Janus of Rome in the 8th century BC than to rely on a reconstruction of the meaning of his Sumerian ancestor's name(s), particularly as nothing proves that either Usimu or Isimud is correct. Janus looked both forward and back. He was a god of time, of past and future, of beginnings and endings. The similarity can't be denied. This was also the distinguishing feature of the figure on the Adda seal,

two-faced, not duplicitous, but looking left to the past and right to the future and, for some unexplained reason, keeping physical contact with the flowing waters of his Lord.

There is another way to consider the two-headed figure; as the alchemical Rebis which derives from the Latin term 'Res Bina' meaning 'double matter', in which opposing qualities are united. This concept is symbolised through the image of the double head on the single body and might be taken as metaphor for the physical purification of base metals but is above all a philosophical theme. Contrary to common belief, we must look to the Sumerian writings for the true beginnings of Hermeticism, Paganism, alchemy, Gnosticism, Christianity,

Taoism, Sufism… Janus/Isimud was a symbol of duality, of pairs, of opposing elements, of the passage of time.

In this illustration from *The Theory of Hermetic Philosophy*,[1] the double-headed figure holds the compass and square, instruments of measurement, of architecture, of masonry, and rides on a fire-breathing dragon in turn perched on a winged and measured globe. That illustration puts a whole new level of meaning into the Sumero-Roman Janus on the Adda seal. He isn't holding a compass or square, but he is shown touching the living waters of

SAG/RES

head

sage

AD which, I suggest, had equal significance. Latin res is given as 'matter' or 'thing' while Sumerian RES has the meaning 'head', also an alchemical reference.[2] This symbol can be read as SAG or SAN, source of 'sagacity' and the 'sage', of 'sanity', words not suggested by orthodox lexicons. 'Sage' is said to be a convoluted form of Latin sapere, 'to be wise' in turn from an unknown PIE source. With the variations showing similarity with both mushroom (p.158) and snake (p.184), symbol SAG shows itself to be a word of great importance in the Sumerian scheme of things. But one thing at a time.

Who then is the character on the left of the Adda seal? The British Museum notice doesn't offer up a name, but his bow and arrow-sling give him away. Here we have the oldest image of pagan Pan, the hunter.[3] The Sumerian figure carries the name of his bow, Sumerian symbol PAN. But he can also be discerned in PA, the 'wing', where the source notion of 'pan-' as 'entirety' can also be found, another symbol of great complexity and importance (p.125). His arrow carries the name TI/TIL, another reference to expanse and to time. Pan on the Adda Seal fixes the entire scene firmly within the timeframe of the founding Mesopotamian Pagan culture. A complete index of symbols (p.265) can be used to revisit the intertwining threads between these and other symbols and the subjects discussed in this book. Take a piece of string along. Don't get lost in the maze.

What's In Another Name?

My purpose here is not to dismiss or undermine in any way the value of the phrase that has become known as the Anunnaki. Whether a name or not, there are numerous examples of these conjoined words within the Sumerian corpus of texts, ample proof of their importance. My goal is to get as far as possible to the bottom of it. Not having anywhere to look for Zechariah Sitchin's reasoning and concluding that his was a straightforward borrowing from the academic versions. I began by looking at an example found in the text curiously named '*Enki and the World Order*'[1], the intention being to match the name given as 'Anuna' to the alphabetic equivalences of the original script, from which it had been translated, and then to go back to their source and analyse the original symbols through the prism of a monosyllabic language. Line 8 of the translated text there begins:

Enki lord of plenty of the Anuna gods

The original cuneiform signs that became 'Anuna gods' in that particular translation are transliterated into alphabetic form as: d – A – NUN – NA - KE$_4$. The original pictograms and their phonetic forms might once, at the very beginning, have been read and seen as:

The five signs here above are shown as they might have appeared (but have not been found all together) in the pre-cuneiform writing of the 4th millennium BC. Lower-case 'd' is an academic convention to indicate symbol AN, the sky (from phonetic 'dingir'). This is understood to be a prefix meaning 'god' and is left silent in orthodox translations. The first two symbols AN-A show 'sky' and 'water' which can be presumed to also translate to 'flow', a flowing movement, and even 'sky water' meaning 'rain'.

The three middle symbols A-NUN-NA, lumped together and with one 'n' removed, form phonetic Anuna: the Anuna gods. As already mentioned, no attempt has been made to translate the words other than as a multi-syllabic meaningless proper name. In this case of 'Anuna', the final symbol KID disappears into the mists of time and without explanation. It is true that the phrase also exists elsewhere without the addition of symbol KID, but not in the above example. KID has one given meaning of 'mat' and I have more than once taken this to indicate a ruler, and the place where mats were laid down in order to worship the sun. It's possible I was wrong. But the symbol is considerably more complex, difficult to pin down and more thoroughly investigated in a later chapter (p.190).

Applying modern rules of grammar to these old texts is, in fact, comprehensible and useful once it has been firmly established that the language is agglutinative. Conversions into multi-syllabic names cover the extreme difficulty of properly translating all the original words, and then fitting all of them together within a logical context. Unfortunately, every word/symbol ignored has been, at the very least, a nuance overlooked. Another example shows line 248 of *Enki and Ninhursaga*[1] beginning with the same group of symbols. There they are taken to be singular and feminine. It's written somewhat intriguingly:

The Anuna (slipped off her garment)...

As the saying goes, the proof of the pudding is in the eating. Do the texts that result from applying these rules of grammar generally make sense or are they largely nonsensical? That is a valid question in my view... one which does not appear to have cost a lot of ink over the past century or so. There is only so much nonsense that can be written off as resulting from the weird and wonderful ways of the ancient world. Does the emperor have his clothes on or not?

The Oldest NUNs

NUN is one of the oldest symbols in the Sumerian language and the central element in the Anunnaki group. NUN is the original name if there is a name to be found in that phrase. It's also a symbol that has remained frustratingly difficult to pierce despite appearing more than once in *The Story of Sukurru*. If NUN is the name of a person or group of people, then the given meaning of 'prince' might apply, but only if the accompanying connotation of ruling dynasties, of earthly kings and queens, is acceptable. From a modern perspective, it rules out the notion of any godly attribute.

A useful clue comes from the combination of NUN with ME which together have the given meaning 'sage' and are also given as phonetic ABGAL. That phonetic form, derived from matching words on Sumero-Akkadian lexical lists, translates to Great Father. NUN.ME, where ME is given as 'spirit' and 'magician', translates to the 'sage and magician'.

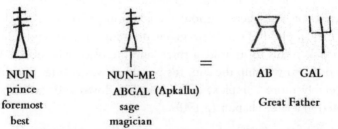

NUN	NUN-ME		AB	GAL
prince	ABGAL (Apkallu)	=		
foremost	sage		Great Father	
best	magician			

Making use of entirely conventional lexicon meanings, the figure commonly known as Apkallu is best remembered as the Great Father who was a wise magician. A good start.

Given as 'prince', 'foremost' and 'best' along with 'metal object' at a later period, NUN is one of very few pictograms appearing on the earliest known inscribed tablets dated to the archaeological period known as Uruk V, ca. 3500-3350 BC. So few words have been found on tablets from that time period that its presence there is significant, particularly as it appears at least twice.

The extremely early version of NUN [1] shown here is very different from later

versions and potentially more informative of the original intention of the scribe who devised it. It takes the form of a three-tiered construction, shaped like an obelisk, with what appears to be a wing projecting from one side and a needle-like object pointing up from its apex. The wing is well executed and of particular interest. To my knowledge, this is the only example of NUN with that feature (if it is indeed symbol NUN rather than a hybrid form or another word). A wing might be the original element that became the more easily executed horizontal stripes found across the top of all later versions. It also sits well with the notion of the Anunnaki as winged figures. Between the given meanings of 'princely' and 'metal object', the image of the wing and the collocated symbols of AN-A indicating something flowing through the sky, the extra-terrestrial theory promulgated by Zechariah Sitchin appears less far-fetched. That said, there are multiple ways in which the story might evolve. No conclusions can be drawn from that one unique feature taken alone, devoid of any helpful context and unrepeated on later tablets.

Globally, the different versions appear to indicate some form of obelisk on which was placed a pointed element. The needle is suggestive of a lightning rod, also fitting with symbol NUN as 'a metal object' at a late date. By the time of the next archaeological period known as Uruk IV, ca.3350-3200 BC, NUN had already morphed into a less detailed sign with no evidence of the three pairs of parallel lines dividing up the main body and no wing.

Another unique image of NUN, read as either NUN-A or A-NUN, appears on a tablet from the slightly later Uruk IV period.[2] This one is significant in that it shows symbol A, the water, as an unusually long and snake-like form which extends up and around the broken tablet to the left. It ends abruptly on the right under a significantly smaller NUN than might be expected. In this case, it goes far beyond the usual short rendering of the symbol for water. This is an entire river, a large waterway weaving around the tablet, and it attaches to the underside of NUN as if the flow is on or under the ground.

Confirmation of the importance of the long waterway linked to NUN comes on another fragmented tablet from the same period,[2] this time accompanied by EN, the Lord, on the left. Between them is a symbol given as AN, the sky, but which doesn't correspond to the habitual eight-pronged star symbol. To my mind, it's an unknown but no doubt important element of the story there.

But what river is it? Further investigation reveals that there are two rivers which can be safely associated with symbol NUN; one is the earthly Euphrates and the other the celestial Eridanus.

City Of The NUN

One text of major importance where symbol NUN is understood as a name in its own right is the antediluvian Sumerian King List. That fact is not immediately apparent to someone discovering academic transliterations of the language for the first time. NUN appears incognito, undercover of 'eridug':[1]

2. /eridug\ki nam-lugal-la

3. eridug ki a2-lu-lim lugal

8. eridug ki ba-šub

Eridug is just one phonetic value given for the same original symbol NUN. In my work, every word is peeled back to its source symbol and given one main alphabetic equivalence. This one is always stated as NUN in order to avoid the catastrophic confusion that the use of multiple phonetic forms for the same original word/symbol within transliterated texts (and sometimes within the same lines of those texts) can and has created elsewhere. Using capital letters for the earliest phonetic forms is an academic convention and has nothing to do with shouting... But then again, sometimes it's necessary to raise one's voice in order to be heard.

This is what NUN-KI/eridug ki might once have looked like in an early version of the antediluvian King List if such a tablet had existed before 3000 BC:

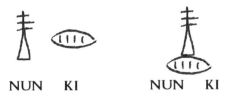

NUN   KI   NUN   KI

NUN-KI appears numerous times in texts other than the King List and is found on at least one of the proverbs/riddles in tablets from ca.1900–1600 BC. Still unsure of the best way to translate it in the context of a long and difficult riddle, I took the easy way out and left it as both 'otherworld' (p.197) and 'City of the Nun'.[1]

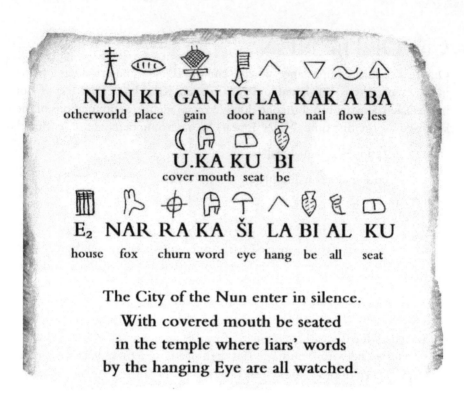

NUN	KI	GAN	IG	LA	KAK	A	BA
otherworld	place	gain	door	hang	nail	flow	less

U.	KA	KU	BI
cover	mouth	seat	be

E₂	NAR	RA	KA	ŠI	LA	BI	AL	KU
house	fox	churn	word	eye	hang	be	all	seat

The City of the Nun enter in silence.

With covered mouth be seated

in the temple where liars' words

by the hanging Eye are all watched.

There are various ways in which these words and their combinations can be understood. For example, NAR, the fox, is also a musician and is given here as 'liar' to better fit the context. NAR is the eternal trickster of various mythologies (p.110). The implications of his name are far reaching. The first five words might also translate to '*Through the suspended door to the otherworldly place*' followed by KAK, the nails of truth and founding syllable of 'acacia' (p.129).

A deep sense of a long-lost mystical setting accompanies this riddle/proverb. The four words U.KA.KU, translated literally to 'With covered mouth sit', are given as 'monkey' in lexicons. This is one of the clues to the overall meaning, a reference to the 'mind monkey' found in later philosophies, sitting on shoulders and whispering distractingly into ears.

Symbols U.KA, the 'covered mouth', are given together as 'skull'. Here we have the hitherto unknown source of the three seated monkeys who hear no evil, see no evil, speak no evil. The two words are also given as phonetic ELE in the later Akkadian versions. I wonder if the source of the secretive Greek Eleusinian (p.169) mystery school is to be found in them.

Fishing

Around

Traces Of The Lost Fish

Unless hardened by fire, clay is still a somewhat fragile material and time has done its work on even the most precious of tablets. Many of the Sumerian texts that we have in hand today have been reconstituted from more than one fragment. Those fragments were not always part of the same original tablet even if they were inscribed with sections of the same identifiable text. In other words, even if they were not found side by side, texts could be reconstituted, fitted together in the manner of a jigsaw puzzle, from pieces scattered around the land. However, those pieces were not necessarily written within the same timeframe or copied from an identical source and sometimes they contain revelatory variations on the same theme.

In that regard, there is an important clue concerning the name of the first city on one of the King List tablet fragments. Referenced as W-B 62, that fragment gives a different name[1]. NUN-KI is replaced by HA-A-KI:

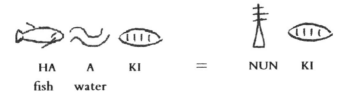

HA	A	KI	=	NUN	KI
fish	water				

It brings proof that NUN and HA-A in the context of the Sumerian King List are either synonymous or, at the very least, both representative of the main characteristics of the first city. The plot thickens when we discover that the two symbols HA-A, the fish in water, the flowing fish, the swimming fish, are found together in Sumerian lexicons as phonetic ZAH_2 in which case they have the added given meanings 'to disappear', 'to withdraw', 'to be lost' and 'fugitive'.

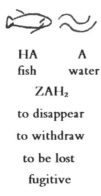

HA	A
fish	water

ZAH_2

to disappear

to withdraw

to be lost

fugitive

The lost first city? The lost city in which fish swim? The City of the Disappearing Fish? Is this Oannes, the fish god, who appeared out of the sea, who took no food and then disappeared, withdrew at night back into the water according to the account attributed to Berossus? His city?

This Being was accustomed to pass the day among men; but took no food at that season; and he gave them an insight into letters and sciences, and arts of every kind. He taught them to construct cities, to found temples, to compile laws, and explained to them the principles of geometrical knowledge. He made them distinguish the seeds of the earth and showed them how to collect the fruits; in short, he instructed them in everything which could tend to soften manners and humanize their lives. From that time, nothing material has been added by way of improvement to his instructions. And when the sun had set, this Being Oannes, retired again into the sea, and passed the night in the deep; for he was amphibious. [1]

The being in question was clearly wise and extraordinarily well informed. He fits the description of ABGAL, the Apkallu, (p.28) who is also a NUN: Great Father, Sage, and Magician – and disappearing fish... Another conclusion drawn thanks to that precious fragment of the antediluvian King List is that AT/AD/ATA, the inscribed name on the Adda seal, where the central figure has both fish and water as his attributes, can be firmly linked to NUN via the alternative and descriptive HA-A:

| AT | = | HA | A | (KI) | = | NUN | (KI) |

Father   fish   water

                to be lost

                to disappear

                        The First City

                        The Lost City

Atlantis?

Above or below? Fish in the sky or city below the seas? Metaphor or physical? Or both? The combination of the first city in the Sumerian King List with disappearance, with loss, with fathers and fish, with the sound of symbol AT, leads first and foremost downwards to the ocean floor and to the great enigma of the sunken city of Atlantis. The story written down by Plato in the 4th century BC is controversial. Did he intend it to be read as myth or as fact? Was it told to his ancestor Solon by an Egyptian priest who in turn had knowledge of it from an old cuneiform tablet or two?

The detailed account of Atlantis and its sudden disappearance found in Plato's texts doesn't fit with the more obviously fictional style of Greek myths and this analysis of the name of the first Sumerian city tends to demonstrate that he was not inventing the tale of a first city lost beneath the waves. Whether mythical or not, the above analysis of Sumerian NUN-KI provides some evidence of his having taken the story of Atlantis from a more ancient Sumerian source.[1] Line 38 of The Story of Sukurru was translated with Plato's account of Atlantis in mind:

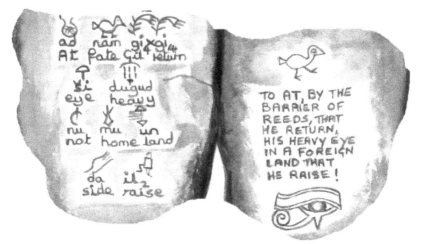

AD/AT is collocated numerous times with GI$_4$, the whirling reeds, which can be understood as the dynamic movements of the reed stylus across moist clay, the writing, but also translatable as 'to return'. The first four words of this line might even read, according to context, 'On the seal, the recurring fate is written' where NAM is 'fate'.

Line 38 was also translated within a broader context. The preceding line 36 refers to the head of a musician hanging around a female neck. That description involving the cord of a musical instrument brings Greek Orpheus, who could charm even stones into movement, firmly to mind. Orpheus is mentioned in numerous ancient texts including those of Plato. He is credited with having ventured down into the underworld in a failed attempt to rescue his wife, Eurydice. The following line 37 confirms the presence of Orpheus through KA-ZU, the word-knower, translated as 'poet', and of his fate in Tartarus through the original double TAR-TAR, 'to cut and cut'. According to the legend, Orpheus was murdered by the women he had disdained. For the Sumerians, the musician was NAR/LUL, the fox (p.110).

THE MUSICIAN'S FATE; WITH THE CHORD OF HIS GRINDING LYRE, HIS HEAD FROM A FINE NECK WILL HANG.

The only female in the Greek pantheon who wears a head around her neck is Athena, goddess of wisdom but also of war, protector of Athens and inventor of many things: both names with AT at their heart. Bearing in mind that these words were written thousands of years earlier than the well-documented but equally complex Greek myths, Athena and Orpheus had ample time to morph and yet elements of their essential features are unmissable here; jumbled together but present nevertheless. How to disentangle them if not by pulling on the oldest thread and working forward?

In these three lines 36 to 38, there is a play on the theme of words that are sung, the music of NAR, the narcotic specialist and trickster who appears to be Orpheus, and words that are written. The hero is a 'word-specialist' and on AD, the bead, the story will be inscribed. This takes us circling back to the Adda seal in the British Museum, an example of that theme which we still have in hand. There can be no doubt that, on one level, line 38 translates to 'On the seal the back and forth of the reed stylus', under the 'heavy eye', the surveillance of the Father. The heavy eye, if only the eyeball, can be understood as a stone 'bead'. Note the presence of both AD and DA, found side by side on the Adda seal, in this line. What is the content of that important story? Is it that of the lost city of the Father?

In the notes to *The Story of Sukurru*, I made the case in some detail for this being by far the earliest reference to Plato's Atlantis and I maintain that claim. Symbol AD/AT is the Father, and the seal on which the story is inscribed, and it is source of Atlantis, probably also of Athena, Athens and of Atlas, the Greek hero who balances a heavy celestial sphere on his shoulder, the heavy bead. It is source of Greek adamas, meaning 'inflexible', 'unbreakable', fitting description of the stone seal, the 'bead' of the Father. The text of *The Story of Sukurru* is multi-layered and fascinating. Does it confirm the existence of Atlantis, whether real or mythological, before Plato's account over a thousand years later? Was Atlantis the first city, also known as the City of the NUN and of the disappearing fish? Did it exist? The reader of this must look closely and decide for themselves.

Lord Of The Waves

On page 73 of *Star Names and their Meanings*, Nunki is given as the name of a bright star in the constellation of Sagittarius. The author, Richard H. Allen, cites the work of German Assyriologist Peter Jensen:

And he claims it as one of the temple stars associated with Ea or Ia of Eridhu, the Lord of the Waves, otherwise known as Oannes, the mysterious human fish and greatest god of the kingdom. [1]

It is probable that Jensen arrived at his celestial link through his study of the Babylonian astronomical text known by its incipit as MUL APIN. The suggestion of an astrological link for NUN-KI takes the subject - which was heading into the depths of Earth's oceans – up and out into celestial waters. [2]

The trouble with fish is that they are difficult to pin down. They all disappear if not closely guarded, they come in many sizes, and they are everywhere; in oceans, lakes, and rivers, at all depths, swallowing men or joining with humans as mermaids and mermen, as prestigious fish gods. They are found swimming up the sides of the awkwardly named Ea, himself often depicted as part fish, and they once flitted around in the dark, watery skies as elements of an ancient cosmology. Then again, having observed – as so many have also observed in modern times - unexplained glinting metallic objects of different sizes and shapes moving at great speed through the sky, did our distant ancestors choose to categorise those phenomena as the strangest of all cosmic fish? There have been enough sightings now openly declared by 'official' sources to consider the possibility that the unidentified flying objects were known, openly or secretly discussed, and mentioned in texts thousands of years ago as celestial fish. It's a possibility, neither proven nor disproven: a possibility. There have even been reports of unidentified objects sinking down into the oceans and moving at phenomenally high speeds under water. Who knows?

Separated By The Sky

And God said, "Let there be an expanse in the midst of the waters, and let it separate the waters from the waters." And God made the expanse and separated the waters that were under the expanse from the waters that were above the expanse. And it was so. And God called the expanse Heaven. And there was evening and there was morning, the second day. (Genesis 1:6)

Did the Sumerians call the night sky a 'dome' or perhaps 'heaven' in the sense that we give to the word today? Or did they look up to a dark cosmic ocean, mirroring the world below, its steadily roaming planets and twinkling stars likened to different types and sizes of fish swimming in circles, its consistency sometimes likened to the colour and texture of their beer?

The celestial voyage by boat of the hero in *The Story of Sukurru* is one indication that the skies were understood as something other than a dome. This was not an earthly Noah buoyed up by earthly flood waters. In the earliest version of the story of the Ark, the journey that began on the banks of a river in a round vessel carrying beer and bull continued far beyond the boundary of Mesopotamia. Sumerian Noah sailed upwards on a celestial river, an unseen flow taking its source in an otherworldly sea, joining Earth and sky. He was to be found hanging up there at night, anchored near the moon and caught off guard by the rising of an angry and cursing sun god.[1] At some unknown point in time, he merged with Homer's Odysseus, with Jason of the Golden Fleece, was potentially father to the disappeared children of Greek Medea, specialist of the poisons, and fought for his space with another specialist of cursing identifiable as biblical Ezekiel. My conclusion has been that the original sailor was a universal figure on a galactic ocean. Unless a number of different figures have become muddled together which is not impossible. There are breaks in the tablets and I am not infallible. Line 30 of *Enki's Journey to Nibru*,[2] which comprises nine words, begins:

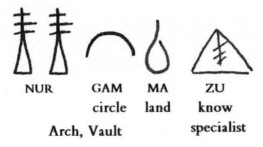

NUR	GAM	MA	ZU
	circle	land	know
Arch, Vault			specialist

Architect And Astronomer

NUR-GAM-MA is given as 'arch' or 'vault' at a late period in Sumerian lexicons, NUR being one phonetic value of the double NUN, to which is added the pyramidal symbol ZU 'to know', indicating a specialisation. In this case, MA-ZU might - rather awkwardly - be written 'the land specialist'. It would be reasonable to further translate to 'surveyor', a person who measures plots of land for the purpose of designating boundaries.

The presence of the overall given meaning of 'arch' and 'vault', 'the vault of the land' in such an ancient context indicates that the specialisation should be understood as that of a mathematician or architect, perhaps more broadly an astronomer/astrologer. That doesn't necessarily imply that the ancient culture had a firm belief in the sky as a closed vault or dome. It more logically indicates that someone somewhere, at the time when those words were first inscribed, was measuring distances, rounded distances, those of a globe.

The image and given meanings of GAM, 'circle' and 'to curve', 'to bend', are eloquent. GAM-MA, 'gamut of the land', became Greek gamma, third letter of the alphabet, which also represented the number three in the ancient counting system. The two symbols are also the source of Latin gamma, the musical range, the gamut. Without further context, this phrase NUR-GAM-MA-ZU can be read:

The vault encircling the land to know.

A considerably enlarged, more daring and unashamedly heretical translation based partially on the visual aspect of the words:

The specialist who calculates the curve of the land from pillar to pillar – and who is himself/herself a pyramid…

The full line of text in *Enki's Journey to Nibru* includes a bull, a horn and the verb 'to lift'. This is the first phase of the hero's celestial journey in that text and my more reasonable offering of the nine words goes as follows:

The skies to know, on the horn of the bull he will be lifted.

It seems most likely that this is a description of bull-jumping, of taking the bull by the horns and vaulting as famously portrayed on the wall of a Minoan palace. The given meaning 'vault' might be used as a verb. There might also be an astronomical reference, the positioning of the bull's head in the constellation of Taurus. Then again, it can't be ruled out that we are in possession of a line from the original book of Enoch who was said to have been lifted into the skies. Context is everything, along with an open mind. NUN on early tablets, those of the 4th millennium BC., is shown more than once as a duo, phonetic NUR, also NIR or NER, with AN, the sky, placed between the two 'pillars':

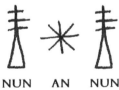

NUN   AN   NUN

Joined By The Earth

The juxtaposition shown above, where AN is not the first symbol, indicates that, in orthodox terms, NUN was not portrayed here as a god but had some form of bond with the sky. What was it then? Was the double symbol NUR a reference to structures serving to observe and make calculations, a tool of the stargazers? Another combination found at the same period:

NUR
KI

This one, where the two NUNs sit atop the symbol of 'place', might be understood as equivalent to the two NUNs separated by the 'sky' shown above. This time, they sit side by side either in one single place or as two elements on Earth separated by a distance represented by the sky. Where the first city of the King List is given as NUN-KI, this example might be given as NUR-KI. At the very least, it is evidence that NUN-KI or 'eridug-ki' was likely a more complex concept than the current status of the antediluvian portion of the King List would have us believe.

It's not impossible to understand this as a representation of a place where two obelisks or tall structures are found, either side by side or separated by some distance. In fact, the images and concept are reminiscent of the illustration on p.8, the discovery said to have been made by Eratosthenes, chief librarian at Alexandria, concerning the measurement of Earth's circumference. Other 4th millennium versions of the double symbol give:

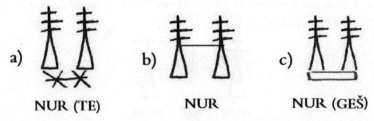

a) **NUR (TE)**   b) **NUR**   c) **NUR (GEŠ)**

All of the above indicate that the NUNs, regularly expressed as a pair, were meant to be understood as separate elements linked one to the other by air, by earth, perhaps by time.[1]

So Far To Travel

A brief summary of the main points concerning symbol NUN and its positioning within the Sumerian language, its potential synonyms and collocated signs:

NUN has the given meanings 'prince', 'foremost' and 'best'. It appears with symbol KI as the name of the first city in the antediluvian Sumerian King List. It is replaced by HA-A, 'fish', 'flow', and 'lost' on one fragment of that list, suggesting synonymity between NUN, 'disappearance', 'loss' and 'fish'.

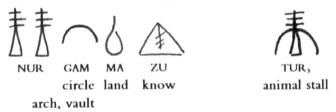

Two NUNs together were a common form, taking the phonetic values NUR, NIR or NER. They are found with both AN and KI, 'sky' and 'earth' or 'place', and other forms indicating that the two NUNs are linked together.

NUR followed by GAM-MA has the meaning 'vault of the land'. GAM-MA, gamut of the land, became Greek gamma, third letter of the Greek alphabet and represents the number 3 according to the ancient system known as gematria. Expressed as TUR₃, NUN with GAM, here on the right, is given as 'animal stall' and, considering the image, it's quite possible that this refers to physical structures, made of reed and used as stables or living quarters along the banks of the Mesopotamian waterways.[1] Nevertheless, GAM-MA-ZU suggests an architect or astronomer. A prince who is also an architect and astronomer? A wise magician with those skills? Animal stalls in the sky? Did the animals enter two by two?

IN THE

BEGINNING

WAS THE

CAMEL...

Needle Of Truth

Again I tell you, it is easier for a camel to go through the eye of a needle than for a rich man to enter the kingdom of God. (Matthew 19:24)

A parable, a comparison, a juxtaposition of two situations; on one hand the wealthy person, a successful merchant trading rare and precious goods, sending his nomadic employees out across the lands, and on the other the camel, laden with the wares, and both prevented from moving forward in their chosen direction by a needle. Why would a lofty camel faced with the eye of a needle have the advantage? Why not a more comprehensible face-off between rich man and poor in order to make a point? Something more was at play behind the words taken up in the Book of Matthew. Despite the amount of time that has been spent on it, this enigma spoken by Jesus himself has never been elucidated beyond the fact that riches are of no use when you're dead. They will not get you into heaven. But why the camel? What is the truth of the matter? Whose needle was it? Has anyone asked that question?

Around 2600 BC. a Sumerian scribe sat down to write – or to copy from a more ancient tablet - the text of a play, the underlying theme of which was the importance of truth, a concept first conveyed there through the two symbols A and ŠA₃, meaning 'the flow from the heart' and, by inference, the blood, the essence of life. That text is known today as *The Instructions of Shuruppak*. How sad or how angry would the diligent scribe have been to see their clever wordplay lifted from the clay, transliterated into alphabetic form, then chopped up, and grotesquely transformed into a nonsensical monologue about donkeys' midriffs and fields and loose women? What became of truth? Not only the riddles of the scribe were not solved. Their very existence was lost in translation. But perhaps the scribe would have found those grotesque mistakes amusing. He was writing for his peers - not for us.

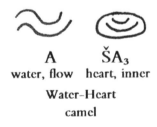

A **ŠA₃**
water, flow   heart, inner
Water-Heart
camel

ASHA
Flow of the Heart
Truth

Caravans of camels crossing the deserts between east and west, carrying on their backs the precious cargos of oils, spices, gold and copper to neighbouring or far-flung territories; those journeys were and still are only possible if the animal is adapted to the tough conditions, travelling long distances between water sources. Nothing can rival a camel on that score, hence the extremely honourable, immeasurably ancient title of that noble slobbering creature: ASHA, Water-Heart. Those two symbols became Zoroastrian Asha, a complex concept with truth at its heart, sadly lost on so many public scribes in our modern world.

Water-Heart

'Water' and 'heart', are both meanings found in Sumerian lexicons. Water extends quite naturally to the verb 'to flow'. In *The Story of Sukurru*, the lofty camel peers out more than once from under its epithet 'Water-Heart', Asha, a hitherto unrecorded name within the modern Sumerian pantheon.

Here is an example of a meaningful Sumerian name. It doesn't take a lot of figuring out but has lain hidden in plain sight for well over a century. Through the fault of an erroneous translating method and, dare I add, a total lack of imagination, no firm link has been made until now between Sumerian and Zoroastrian concepts, between a line of Sumerian text - where Asha, the camel, appears in the company of a needle - and that enduringly enigmatic verse in the Gospel of Matthew. The needle was found but no-one thought to look for a camel in the haystack.

FOR THE CAMEL,
THE BEER CASK,
AND THE VOICE
OF MIGHT A
SHARED DESTINY;
HIGH FURROW OR
LOW, LIFE UNDER
THE RISE AND FALL
OF ÇA'S NEEDLE
IT WILL BE...

The camel first enters the scene on line 16 of *The Story of Sukurru* and shows up again several times. including in the final lines of the play which are dedicated to the importance of truth, a natural conclusion. Both lines 16 and 272 comprise a riddle. In both, the farmer and his plough are involved, and an astronomical reference likely. Both are humorous but, thanks to the above analysis put side to side with the bible verse, it's probable that any serious underlying message was not lost on the audience of the play or the reader of the text.

The above is an extract from *The Story of Sukurru* showing line 16 as it might once have appeared if it had been published between 3500 and 3000 BC, peeled back to the earliest written pictographic forms before they became abstract, pre-cuneiform. The earliest known fragment of *The Story of Sukurru* dates to a time when that transformation was already under way. However presented, these are a relatively acceptable representation of the original words of that text.

Following on from ASHA on line 16, the two symbols KASKAL, given in Sumerian dictionaries as 'beer' and GIR$_3$, seen here as a mouse and given as 'mighty', have other related meanings; 'way', 'road' for the first and 'path' for the second, while KA, the 'mouth' is also read as 'word' or 'voice'.

Considering the scribe's words to contain an underlying riddle, the heart becomes a central element. Thus, there is another way to look at the first three symbols of this line. Symbol ŠA$_3$, the 'heart' or 'inner body' is placed between A and KASKAL, symbols of water and beer.

A	ŠA$_3$	KASKAL
water	heart	beer

Beer Heart

The positioning of water and beer on either side of a central pump indicates that there is a choice to be made, as does the image and meaning 'journey' given to KASKAL. There is a crossroads, a place where nomadic traders and their camels will stop to rest and drink. There must be a weighing up of two possibilities, a choice to be made as to the right path to move 'through the eye of the needle'. There is another word for beer in the Sumerian lexicon: BI. It also appears more than once in juxtaposition with the heart, notably on line 94 of *The Story of Sukurru* (p.58). A second name can be deduced from that pairing:

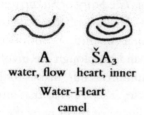

A	ŠA₃	ŠA₃	BI
water, flow	heart, inner	heart, inner	beer

Water–Heart   Beer–Heart
camel   Sabian

The merits of water over beer or vice versa was one of the themes in this and other texts. Which path was better and what kind of beer is not so obvious.

Who wrote the Sumerian texts? More specifically, who wrote *The Story of Sukurru*, a piece of literature studded with humour and riddles, sprinkled with references to cosmic figures, with mention of a great flood, of Noah, precursors of biblical stories?

Harran is among the most important places in the history of Mesopotamia, linked through ancient texts to a unique tribe of people, said to be famed astronomers and followers of the teachings of Hermes Trismegistus who was otherwise known as Egyptian Thoth.[1] Harran lies some forty kilometres from the archaeological site of Gobekli Tepe, a game-changer in terms of dating the beginnings of civilisation. The people who lived around that area in 9600 BC possessed an organised culture. That is proven beyond any possible doubt. There is one name that came to mind along with the increasingly obvious wordplay between water and beer in *The Story of Sukurru*, a name made famous by its connection to Harran: Sabian.

No-one knows at what point in time the region of Harran, in the south-east of modern-day Turkey, became the headquarters of a group of intellectuals and stargazers known as the Sabians. Greek and Arabic texts dated to the 1ˢᵗ millennium AD tell us that the name was adopted at a late stage, purely as a ruse to deflect the threats made by Islamic overlords. That suggestion, like all the information about the Sabians, comes from an ancient but late and religiously biased source. In other words, it is far from trustworthy. Truth or lies? Better to look to older sources. Better still to look to the contemporaneous writings in the language of that region ca.2600 BC.

It is my understanding that the Sabians took their name from SHA-BI and from their fame as brewers in the region of Harran, a well-known Mesopotamian trading post for desert merchants. I suggest that, from at least the early 3ʳᵈ millennium BC, Harran was equally famous for its wise astronomers, its magicians and prophets, and its beers which were transported by river in those round woven-reed coracles (p.2). It goes almost without saying that monosyllabic Sumerian was the language of that region and those people. I can't prove beyond all doubt that my offering concerning their name is the truth, but it is well supported by the evidence of a Mesopotamian text in existence ca. 2600 BC. I propose that this evidence has as much weight as can be given to anything written about them in any other language since. In fact, it has considerably more weight. What types of beer would magicians of great renown choose to brew?

Magicians Of Harran...

From the reign of Nabonasar only are the Chaldæans (from whom the Greek mathematicians copy) accurately acquainted with the heavenly motions: for Nabonasar collected all the mementos of the kings prior to himself, and destroyed them, that the enumeration of the Chaldæan kings might commence with him. [1]

The writings of Berossus are said to mention Mesopotamian records being deliberately destroyed during King Nabonasar's reign over Babylon from 757 to 734 BC. At the same time, according to another fragment of text which also attributes the information to Berossus,[2] there existed 'written accounts' carefully preserved at Babylon dating back over 'fifteen myriads of years' in which 'histories of the heaven' had been recorded. Unless I have missed something, there is a contradiction to be found in those quotes; that 'histories of the heaven' had been recorded by people who existed long before that jealous king and yet knowledge of 'heavenly motions' began only in his time.

One thing is sure. Nabonasar did not destroy documents without first extracting the useful information contained in them, presumably the methods by which the skies had long been monitored, the calculations, the means to create the records. Who would destroy such precious information? What would be the point in jealously destroying the 'mementos' of preceding rulers if they contained nothing but a list of Chaldean names? These excerpts imply that the precise astronomical data said to date from the period of his reign, the famed Babylonian astronomical records, might already have been in existence for many hundreds if not thousands of years. There was continuity in the knowledge of the 'histories of the heaven'. The only hiccup along the way was in the attribution of that knowledge to a usurper. A discreet hiccup. It became Babylonian knowledge, born there and the pride of the place.

The oldest existing MUL APIN text comprising the famed Babylonian astrological expertise is dated to 686 BC, no doubt a copy of considerably older material. Another quote attributed to Berossus appears to confirm the great antiquity of the Chaldeans:

AFTER the deluge, in the tenth generation, was a certain man among the Chaldæans renowned for his justice and great exploits, and for his skill in the celestial sciences.[1]

'After the deluge...' How to calculate that date? When did the deluge in question take place? Ten generations of people beginning after the deluge or before, and with what typical lifespan?

The name Chaldea is given in lexicons as stemming from Greek Khaldaía, Hebrew Kaśdim and/or Aramaic Kaldo. Some internet sources mention that the original Akkadian name was Kaldu, potentially formed from Sumerian symbols KA-AL-TU, or Kasdu. They were purportedly a nomadic tribe living in the marshlands of southeastern Mesopotamia from around 900 BC. who briefly took over and ruled Babylon – quite a feat!

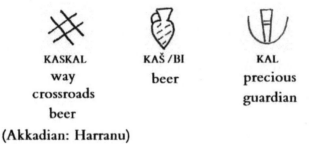

KASKAL	KAŠ /BI	KAL
way	beer	precious
crossroads		guardian
beer		

(Akkadian: Harranu)

The more ancient and therefore more relevant Sumerian tablets offer a new perspective on the name. I found no trace of Kaldu/Kasdu there. What I did find was something quite different and important. A number of entries in the Sumerian lexical lists make the direct connection between both symbols KASKAL and KAŠ/BI, the crossroads and the beer, and Harran in northern Mesopotamia, place of the churning millstone of the sky.[2]

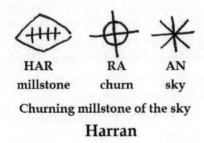

HAR	RA	AN
millstone	churn	sky

Churning millstone of the sky

Harran

Those references strongly suggest that the source syllable(s) of the name Chaldean in all three languages, Greek, Hebrew and Aramaic, stem from KASKAL and/or KAL with a further link to symbol KAŠ/BI, the beer, and that the name is firmly connected to Harran's celestial and earthly millstones. In fact, KASKAL is given as Akkadian Harranu. Further proof of the connection to Harran and its astronomical observatory comes with the lexical link between Harran and KAL, one of a group of three most noteworthy Sumerian symbols in terms of their relevance to the ancient methods of calculating the passage of time (p.67). At the same time, KAL is linked to the beer through KASKAL. Beer and time, an interesting combination.

Add to that the presence in the Akkadian lexicons of a phrase from the Old Babylonian period, ca.1900-1600 BC, which reads HAR-RA-AN-KAL, and is translated to 'fortress' and 'stronghold'. Harran is indisputably connected to KASKAL, KAŠ and KAL. Harran is connected to Chaldeans, to beer and to the sky. By extension, the beer is connected to the sky…[1]

North To South And Back Again

In terms of acknowledged histories, that poses a problem. The region of Harran is in the north of the land between the two rivers Tigris and Euphrates, close to their source in the Taurus mountains, while Chaldea is said to have been at some point the name of the region in the south where Babylon was founded. Berossus, whose writings have been a common source of information, was a native of Babylon.

The place in which they built the tower is now called Babylon, on account of the confusion of the tongues; for confusion is by the Hebrews called Babel.[2]

Did the name Chaldea come into being in the north of the region between the rivers Euphrates and Tigris where HAR-RA-AN and KAL are given as 'fortress' or in the south? Harran was a crossroads for trade from the second half of the 3rd millennium BC but also, according to the biblical accounts, the place where Abraham migrated with his family after leaving Ur, a city in the south. The dating of that episode is a complete unknown. The archaeological site known as Ur is situated along the banks of the Euphrates and includes an impressive three-tiered mudbrick 'ziggurat' constructed in the 21st century BC. It is interesting to note that the chapter of Genesis in which Abraham is moved to Harran by his father begins with mention of a unique language that existed before the tower was built at Babylon. It was in Babylon that confusion was introduced. It also gives Haran as the name of Abraham's youngest brother. Just coincidence or did the writer insist too much?

Terah took his son Abram, his grandson Lot (Haran's son), and his daughter-in-law Sarai, his son Abram's wife, and they set out together from Ur of the Chaldeans to go to the land of Canaan. But when they came to Haran, they settled there. (Genesis 11:31)

Why did they stop in Harran if Canaan was their destination? It doesn't say. There appears to be a tug of war for possession of those famous names, Abraham and Chaldea, between northern Mesopotamia and south. It strikes me as more likely that Abraham was first linked to ancient Edessa, now Sanliurfa, situated close to Harran in the northern portion of Mesopotamia, where there is a long-held tradition of it being his birthplace. Bible dictionaries give 'Haran' as both 'mountainous region' and 'mountaineer'.

Give Them Back Their Name

And Noah began to be a husbandman, and he planted a vineyard: And he drank of the wine and was drunken; and he was uncovered within his tent. (Genesis 9:20-21)

Beginning on line 97, there is a raucous, joyful drinking scene in *The Story of Sukurru*, following the opening lines of the instructions given to Noah:

The reference to the Sabians through ŠA₃-BI on line 94 (p.58) leads to the suspicion that Beer-Heart was an epithet which also applied to Noah, a suspicion largely confirmed by the Old Testament story making mention of a drunken Noah seen naked by his sons.

Was Noah, proprietor of a vineyard and survivor of a flood, a Shabi, a Beer-Heart, a Sabian? Did the NO-A epithet come about because he kept his feet and backside dry in his boat or because he chose the beer over water?

54

NU   **A**
not   **water**

Noah

Taking it all one step further, was this Ubara Dudu, the sailor of the antediluvian King List, final ruler before the flood swept over? Translation of this section, including line 97, was one of the most rewarding of the entire text thanks to the discovery of the earliest reference to Noah's ark and confirmation brought about not only by numerous similarities but also by the name barely hidden there. This is the only mention of Noah as such throughout the 280 lines, but what a context for it! How to churn the oceans without getting wet. Which waters would that have been? Those raining down on Earth, the relentless floods, those tamed by resourceful wisdom teachers for the purpose of sustainable agriculture or those perceived in the sky by indefatigable stargazers? Beer or water?

Also of interest in this section is the presence of GA, the 'milk', in the same phrase as BI, the 'beer', and A, the 'water', potentially indicating a choice between not two but three possible paths to follow. Was that deliberate? Line 99 continues this section:

Give beer to the man churning the ocean with a thick virile straw.

There are multiple possibilities to be considered in the translating process, not least the presence of riddles. The final clincher must be contextual.

Our Virile Father

And Abraham was an hundred years old, when his son Isaac was born unto him. And Sarah said, God hath made me to laugh, so that all that here will laugh with me. (Genesis 21:5-6)

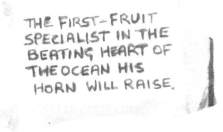

THE FIRST-FRUIT
SPECIALIST IN THE
BEATING HEART OF
THE OCEAN HIS
HORN WILL RAISE.

Line 14 of *The Story of Sukurru* comprises a relatively complex riddle involving the original names of Abram and his wife Sara. It might serve to explain why she found the situation so funny. In context, it's a reference to the phallic pagan god Pan who is also Bacchus and who can equally be found under the guise of the most indiscreet of them all, Greek Priapus. Here we find a strong hint of the founding fertility cult omnipresent in John Allegro's work. The translation to 'in the beating heart of the ocean' came about through the presence of the following three symbols which can be read from inside out, from left to right and from right to left:

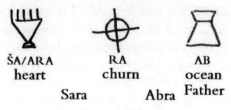

ŠA/ARA   RA   AB
heart   churn   ocean

Sara   Abra   Father

Sarah and Abraham

As with ŠA₃ (p.49), this different symbol ŠA means 'heart' and 'inside'. It is also phonetic ARA, source of the name of the constellation, and 'altar' of the Greek gods. Both the Sumerian word's image and sound are identical to the considerably later depictions of Ara as the smoking altar, place where incense was burned. What kind of incense? Or is it a brewing pot with rising steam? RA in the middle is the 'threshing, beating' movement and epithet of the sun god Ra, the same as that of his Egyptian equivalent. AB on the right is 'ocean' and 'Father'.

The following enigmatic verses in Genesis confirm that, at some point in time, there was an attempt made to muddy the waters concerning these names, perhaps to thoroughly cover up Abraham's connection to the original Sumerian pagan figure. The reason for the name change is obscure to say the least but why would God need to explain Himself?

Neither shall thy name any more be called Abram, but thy name shall be Abraham; for a father of many nations have I made thee. (Genesis 17:5)

And God said unto Abraham, As for Sarai thy wife, thou shalt not call her name Sarai, but Sarah shall her name be. (Genesis 17:15)

AB is identifiable in this riddle as AB-RA, reading from right to left, while ŠA-RA, from left to right, the churning, beating heart, became Sarah. They met in the middle et voilà! The scene is a celebration of fertility in both plant and human form, a harvest festival, a contemporaneous description of the fertility cult proposed by John Allegro. Confirmation of the wordplay on the churning of oceans comes in the form of a riddle from the Old Babylonian era, ca.1900–1700 BC in which the symbol of the phallus appears twice.[1] It translates to:

By day, the virile sinking and rising, the ocean churns. Heartless death he created. With his reed, the ocean harnessed by the Lord.

In conclusion, my suggestion is that the Chaldeans were originally far more than mere kings of Babylonia in the south. They were the same people as the group known as the Sabians, both names steeped in beer, the types and composition of which have yet to be established. They were engaged in production of great quantities of the brew, selling it to the nomadic traders who passed not only through Harran but the entire region of Mesopotamia, shipping it out in the round coracles described by Herodotus. They date back to at least the period of the tablets containing *The Story of Sukurru* ca. 2600 BC.

The renown of the Chaldean brewers and astronomers was not limited to the southernmost region of Mesopotamia but was well established in the northern region of Harran, perhaps throughout those lands and probably further afield over thousands of years... until one day a king of Babylon decided to steal their knowledge for himself and to usurp their illustrious name.

Horns To The Sky

You are to take with you seven pairs, a male and its female, of all the clean animals, and two of the animals that are not clean, a male and its female, (Genesis 7:2)

There are two mentions of a passageway, a journey to be made, within the first four symbols of line 16 (p.48). GIR₃ the 'mighty' and the 'path', is shown as a mouse peeping out of its hole in the bilingual format, a choice made in my early days of translating and based on an existing drawing,[1] but it is found on tablets from the early archaeological period of Uruk IV, ca.3350-3200 BC, as the profile of a bull's head with prominent horn; here on one of the most beautifully executed tablets from that era.[2] The visual aspect of the symbol makes it difficult to argue that it does not also carry the meaning 'bull' or, at the very least, 'bull's head' or 'bull's horn'. Never forgetting that these images are part of a written language, the basket can be easily identified as the well-documented woven reed 'bag' carried by the Mesopotamian 'gods'. On the information provided with the tablet, the bag is given as DUB, which has the given meaning 'tablet' (p.21). If correct, it is the earliest and most compelling link between that godlike figure and his mission. The bull and the reed basket, a celestial sailing vessel, are associated in Sumerian lore and, according to more than one source text, the mission involved taking notes (see the riddle p.221).

GIR$_3$ is also given as 'via' and 'by means of' in Sumerian lexicons. The bull's horn', 'by means of' and the 'path' are all aspects of one story. 'Via the horn of the bull', the basket/vessel will be tossed into the sky with its foolish ego-ridden sailor whose ride will be less than comfortable. This is the oldest tale, the oldest version of a journey into the unknown, the Sumerian voyage to the place of death and rebirth. The bull's horn is the way. The basket is the vessel. The tablet will tell the tale. The story of baby Moses found in his floating basket comes to mind.

Lines 94 to 96 of *The Story of Sukurru* have two bulls as spouses, a pair of passengers in the great houseboat to be built by Noah. This is a hitherto unrecognised account of the Old Testament story, by far the earliest written reference to a great flood. At the heart of the vessel not only the beer but also Beer-Heart, the Sabian, the cosmic voyager. Although the symbols of his name occur in the text at this point, he doesn't appear in the translation of that line, preference being given to the beer and the bull. But his presence must not be ignored. It is there in the symbols, underlying everything. Thus, it becomes possible, inevitable even, to identify Noah, another epithet also appearing in *The Story of Sukurru*, as a Sabian.

Another of the novelties in this version of Noah's ark is the evidence of Sumerian DAM as the source of 'dam', a word still in use today with the same meaning: 'animal mother', the 'female parent of a quadruped'. In Sumerian, this is the 'spouse' and the lexicons give it as the quality of 'trust', no doubt a reference to the moral contract inherent in marriage. She is the dame and the dam, the female, the cow, spouse of a bull who shares his space with the beer... what could possibly go wrong?

Horns Of Perfection

Imagine wearing a pair of large heavy horns, where one of the two is slightly

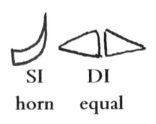

SI **DI**
horn **equal**

larger and somewhat heavier than the other. Out in a field, head down, trying to create a straight furrow with the plough, but always that steady pull on the head to one side. Left to your own devices, you find yourself walking around in circles. And you won't be of great use to the farmer. It might not end well. Or imagine wearing a pair of perfectly matched and impressive horns but finding yourself facing up to another bovine with an equally well matched but considerably larger and heavier pair...

Here is one of those age-old subjects of interest that have escaped our notice through misunderstanding of the Sumerian writings. SI, the horn, paired with DI, symbol of 'division', 'equality' and 'judgment', the 'equal horns' are found more than once in the texts. DI also has the given meaning 'lawsuit' and 'legal decision' in Sumerian lexicons. Who would want to be tried by a judge with mismatched horns?

Sanskrit has Siddhi as 'perfection', a term used to group together a set of accomplishments which would include the attainment of such magical powers as walking on water, becoming weightless, disappearing into thin air, travelling through time… all of these requiring the basic skill of equilibrium. No chance of any of that with disparate horns on your head. Too much beer wouldn't help either.

Never Forget Me

Symbol SI, the horn, has other important given meanings, of which 'to remember'. The logic is easy to find. When a lion is seen lurking on the outskirts of the town, a horn is sounded. Don't forget the danger. When the city council is due to meet to discuss affairs or to pass judgement, the horn sounds to call the citizens to the place. When the men and women of Harran are standing by their kneeling camels waiting for the ritual signal to mount and to set out on their pilgrimage, the lingering, mournful sound of the horns will journey with them. It will remind them that they will not be forgotten by their loved ones during the long journey to Egypt and to the ancient site of Giza where their forefathers gathered the knowledge of the world, their legacy, for all to study and understand. That will be my only flight of fancy. Did it happen? The reader of this must decide for themselves.

Then again, the horn has its uses as a drinking vessel, and from there comes the meaning 'to fill' also found in the dictionaries. Beer and horns go together by all accounts. Even the Sumerian snakes have horns, an attribute they share with certain representations of biblical Moses. It's more than likely that the native horned viper was used as model. Horns have gained an unfortunate reputation, an association with devilish behaviour, in relatively modern times. Worn with equanimity, their magical powers used with moderation, that was not always the case, quite the contrary.

Cogs Within Cogs

Marduk By Any Other Name

As Moses approached the camp and saw the calf and the dancing, he burned with anger and threw the tablets out of his hands, shattering them at the base of the mountain. Then he took the calf they had made, burned it in the fire, ground it to powder, and scattered the powder over the face of the water. Then he forced the Israelites to drink it. "What did this people do to you," Moses asked Aaron, "that you have led them into so great a sin?" (Exodus 32:19-21)

Given as the Statue of Marduk, an Akkadian deity, and dated to the 9th century BC, the Babylonian seal image (p.61) is described as *standing in victory on the watery body of the vanquished Tiamat on the occasion of the Babylonian New Year festival.*

I propose to disassociate the Akkadian name Marduk from that image, a relatively modern pairing added on to an age-old theme, and to look more closely at the origin of the name by breaking it down into its components.

Marduk, given just twelve times in the corpus of proper nouns offered up by academia,[1] stems from AN-AMAR-UD. Strangely, that combination doesn't sound much like Marduk whichever way you try to bend it, whichever phonetic forms of the symbols are used. In a predominantly monosyllabic world, it translates to far more informative and exciting titles: 'Celestial Son of the Sun' or 'Celestial Golden Calf'. 'Golden' is not one of the meanings

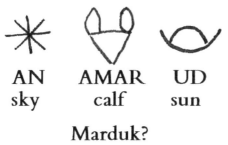

AN   **AMAR**   **UD**
sky   calf   sun

Marduk?

The Celestial Golden Calf

given in orthodox lexicons for UD, the sun, but it can hardly be denounced as unlikely or irrelevant.

Nothing explains why the image of 'Marduk' is covered in a series of spheres, cogs, the wheels of a machine, or how the notion of 'vanquished' is being displayed. The figure and the horned snake-cum-dragon are riding the water and they strike me as being complementary rather than opposed. No obvious antagonism. I suggest an alternative explanation. This is another portrayal of the central figure on the Adda seal (p.21) often shown above a flow of water, and it should be named through the symbols A-NUN (p.30). (The story of Marduk's name continues to unfold on p.162).

Image Of Lamma

There is one female Mesopotamian goddess for whom we possess both the image and a potentially well-connected name: Lamma is a baked clay statuette

dated to ca.1900 BC.[1] Along with her multi-layered robe, it's her distinctive horned hat or helmet that connects her to other 'Anunnaki' figures throughout the ages, from the earliest cylinder seals of the third millennium to the later bas-relief and high-relief carvings of the Mesopotamian region. Both wings and helmet connect her not only to the image given as Ishtar on the Adda seal (p.21) but equally to the giant statues that once stood on either side of temple doors. Her name, LAMMA, found as a written cuneiform word on the accompanying inscription, can be taken back to its earliest Sumerian equivalent phonetic form: KAL.

KAL/LAMMA at some point became Akkadian 'lamassu', thus adding a layer of written proof binding all the members of her family to those winged guardians of gates, part bull, part man, part bird, on display in museums, sadly detached from their temple settings. Today, we stand and stare at the great lamassu without so much as a 'By your leave'. Without a great gate to guard, they no longer require that we call out our names as we wander by.

The earliest images of symbol KAL are found in the Uruk III period, ca. 3200-3000 BC and come in a couple of quite different forms. This is a word which visually, like NUN, doesn't give anything much away:

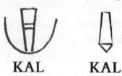

KAL   KAL

The large range of meanings attached to it in the dictionaries help to confuse the investigation into the KAL side of the Anunnaki family. It can mean 'rare' and 'valuable', 'outstanding', 'strong' and 'massive', 'good', 'sweet' and 'beautiful' but, at a later period, is given as a 'vessel' and as 'haughty' and 'arrogant'. There is nothing there that is not slightly vague. Apart from the fact that KAL became the Akkadian lamassu bull-men corresponding conveniently to the 'strong', 'massive' epithets and certainly to 'haughty', only surrounding context can help in getting to the truth of the matter. Fortunately, KAL, linked to both Chaldean and Harran (p.52), does appear on more than one occasion in *The Story of Sukurru* in interesting company:

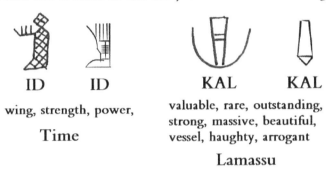

ID	ID	KAL	KAL
wing, strength, power,		valuable, rare, outstanding, strong, massive, beautiful,	
Time		vessel, haughty, arrogant	
		Lamassu	

Although not named as such, ID is a composite symbol which, as shown in the drawings taken from rare early depictions,[1] incorporates symbols DU, the 'foot' below, with what appears to be a sign of the four cardinal directions at the summit and perhaps a wing to one side, reminiscent of the early NUN (p.29). In the second computerised example to its right, copied from another damaged tablet[2] from the same era, ŠU, the raised 'hand' sticks straight out above, and a pared-down version of NUN is enclosed in its centre. ID has given meanings which include 'wing', 'strength', 'power' and 'wage'. It's also given as 'time'.

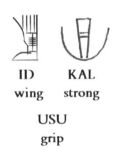

ID KAL
wing strong

USU
grip

USU, the composite phonetic form of ID-KAL is found three times in *The Story of Sukurru*.[3] The two symbols begin line 110 in the context of the building of Noah's ark, a humorous take on the age-old story and translate there to:

The strong arm/wing of Lamma (acquire)...

Both ID and KAL have given meanings related to physical force, 'strength', 'might', 'power', with USU given as 'grip'. The phrase on line 110 implies that the great bull man is being hired to do the dirtiest of all the jobs involved in preparing the ark which, in this instance, takes the form of a round woven reed coracle. He is tasked with calking the vessel; that is to say, waterproofing it by means of a mixture of sticky black bitumen and straw.

Bearing in mind that *The Story of Sukurru* is, at its most superficial level, a comedy, KAL/Lamassu is being portrayed as a useful idiot, a fool. With the deceitful promise of becoming the ruler on Earth once the door to the ark has been carefully waterproofed from the outside, he will be left behind in a land destined to be wiped out by the flood.

An Ancient Greek Beauty

If not for the given meaning 'beauty', it would be difficult to equate KAL,

the handyman of *The Story of Sukurru*, to the Ancient Greek kalos with which it shares that meaning. Nevertheless, a translation of ID KAL as 'the beautiful wing' is as acceptable as 'the strong arm' thanks to the numerous given meanings, and some illustrations next to the name on Greek pottery show 'kalos' to be a beautiful and winged youth – once again, the coincidences are too great to be ignored. According to historians, the name applied to both male and female but the presence of suffix 'os' in the Greek signifies a male name (p.143).

The Greek kalos are portrayed in situations where the 'strong arm' is in evidence, either supporting a wounded figure or, as in this illustration, demonstrating strength in some other way. The inscription on the artefact from 515 BC[1] reads 'ho pais kalos', 'the boy is beautiful'. The bull's head in profile shows him to be as strange as he is beautiful. As a direct descendant of the Mesopotamian KAL/lamassu, it's the given meaning 'strength' that best defines him here. Note that his two feet tread the circumference of an orange-coloured disk. Is he turning like a giant hamster on the wheel of time?

Only Time Will Tell

The repeated use of ID-KAL-TUK in *The Story of Sukurru* leads to the understanding that KAL was regularly 'called upon' in situations requiring a strong arm – or a wing. USU, 'on the strong wing to call', is source of our verb 'to use' through Latin usus which is given as 'use', 'custom', 'practice', 'employment', 'skill', 'habit'.

Sumerian KAL is source of Greek kallein and Latin calare which gave us 'to call' and of Old Norse kalla also meaning 'to summon, to name, to call by name'. Collocated with ID which is 'time' and its upward pointing hand, taken from ŠU, a symbol pronounced 'show', there can be no doubt of the time-keeping status of KAL.

KAL is also the ultimate source of 'calendar' through Latin kalendae which was the first day of the lunar month in Roman times, a date on which priests climbed a mount and called out to the population to announce the new moon. Both the Greek and the Roman calendars based their months on the phases of the moon.

The Canonical Hours

When daybreak came, all the chief priests and the elders of the people plotted against Jesus to put Him to death.(Matthew 27:1)

And about the ninth hour Jesus cried with a loud voice, saying, Eli, Eli, lama sabachthani, that is to say, my God, my God, why hast thou forsaken me? (Matthew 27:46)

At some unknown point in time, a decision was made that day and night be separated into four divisions of three hours each, ultimately arriving at the twenty-four hours used today. Then someone at the heart of the nascent Christian faith chose to order prayers according to this no doubt pre-existing method of counting time. The hours of a day began from the moment of dawn. Night was a separate affair. The daylight hours within that religious sphere were known as the Canonical Hours and served to rhythm the lives and prayers of the monks and nuns within their monasteries.

The names used to indicate the third, sixth and ninth hours of the day were 'terce' corresponding to 9 a.m., 'sext' to 12 a.m. and 'nones' to 3 p.m. These three were considered more important than the other hours of the day, set aside for more specific prayer. The hour of Nones, like the nones of the month, stems from Latin nonus meaning 'nine', the ninth hour of the daylight, and it has added gravitas in that this was said to be the time at which Jesus died.

Canon comes from Greek kanon, with the meaning 'a straight rod or bar', a 'measure of excellence'. This is the bar against which everything else is measured and that measuring tool stems from Sumerian KA-NUN, the 'voice of the Nun', 'word of the Nun'. Using given meanings, it translates to 'the most excellent words', 'the foremost voice' and 'the words of the Sage (ABGAL/Apkallu)'. KA-NUN are found together numerous times in the lexical lists.

KA   NUN
word guide

Canon

'Noon' is also given as deriving from Latin nonus, source of 'nine'. At first glance, 'noon' and 'nine' are unrelated. Bear with me. It gets complicated. Nonus corresponded to the Roman liturgical time of three p.m., the ninth hour of the twelve hours counted from dawn, a very different notion from the common understanding of noon as 12 o'clock, the time when the sun is at its zenith. Noon at 3p.m.? It seems that the shift in this timing of prayers took place in the 12th century for an obscure reason. I discover along the way that the word 'noon' was also used as a reference for the middle of the night, i.e. 'noon' was the equivalent of the 'mid' in midday and midnight. If there is anything bizarre to be found in any of the above, I suggest that it is the lack of a satisfying explanation for the shift that brought Latin nonus to mean both 'nine' and 'noon'. But that is just an opinion. I have probably missed something.

Chaldean Wings Of Time

As seen above, KAL, an element in the name of the Chaldeans, gave rise to both the calendar and the verb 'to call'. It was the first expression of that age-old necessity to count, source of 'calculation', the possibility to prepare schedules, to make precise plans, to be forewarned of cyclical events. The notion of calculating and calling out in the context of a lunar calendar is evocative of the first people who would have observed the night skies and established the method by which to record and understand the cycles, by which to count time in terms not only of hours and days but of months and years, millennia even; a tradition followed by the astronomers of Harran who were said to worship the god of the moon given as SIN, a phonetic form of the Sumerian word for 'three'.

For the Romans, the first day of the lunar month was the kalends. The ides came in the middle of the month, at the time of the full moon, either on the 13th or the 15th day depending on the length of the month. The remaining day of reckoning was that of the nones, ninth day before the ides, a backward calculation that included both the start day (15th or 13th) and the end day (7th or 5th).

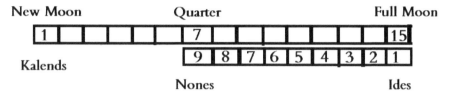

Again, nones comes from Latin nonus meaning 'nine', falling on either the seventh day following the new moon or the fifth in a shorter lunar month. It was a complicated system of looking forward and then counting backwards. No wonder Janus needed two heads. It resulted in the days from the 16th onwards being referred to as a subtraction from the following month. For the pleasure of further muddying the waters of time, below is a wholly unorthodox illustration, blending Sumerian symbols with Roman methodology:

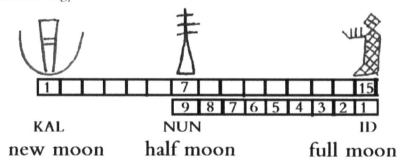

If these are indeed the source symbols of the Roman system, NUN is associated with the two quarters of the moon's cycle, between new and full, at the time when the moon displays just one half of its surface, the other half hidden in the shadows. To call it 'quarter' is somewhat misleading. Visually, it's a half-moon at a quarter or three quarters of its complete cycle. This is the waxing moon as it increases in size and the waning moon as it begins to disappear again, a halfway house, neither one nor the other, coming or going.

One - Not One - Knot Of The One

With NUN as an indicator of time, its parts, NU-UN, found as such in the lexical lists, correspond to 'not one', or 'none', the caveat here being that the only meaning found in orthodox lexicons is 'not'. My addition of 'knot' for NU stems from the sound, from contextual use and even to some extent from its visual aspect. It's an extremely important part of the Sumerian puzzle and must regain its position of power. UN given as 'land' and 'people', also KALAM (p.242), can quite reasonably be extended to 'unite as one', particularly as the symbol appears to take the form of an emblem:

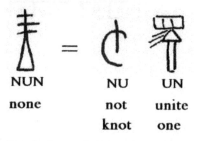

NUN	NU	UN
none	not	unite
	knot	one

At noon on the dot, the shadow of the sun on a sundial can't be quantified because it no longer exists. The sun is still there but its shadow has disappeared. It will exist again once the sun has moved on into the after-noon. NUN gives a starting point in terms of counting time. In this context, it is the none, the nothing between two somethings. It becomes 'otherworldly'.

Was NUN a halfway house in mathematical terms, between nine and ten, or between nine and a return to one? Not a fraction, not a number at all, not 'one' but 'none'? I am no mathematician - far from it - nor well versed in the mechanics of astronomy. Where the door should spring open, a fog descends. For the moment, I can add nothing to the above except that I believe Sumerian NUN to have signified both 'none' and 'noon', based on context, and that it was intimately linked to 'nine' at some extremely early point in the history of our languages, which would signify that the earliest date for the mathematical concept of 'null' or 'zero' extends back into the 4th millennium BC. And if the NUN-KI, the Lost City of the Sumerian King List was that 'none place', it might indicate a starting point in the form of a void before a long-forgotten journey. A circular journey?

In need of a tutor to better understand the mechanics, it becomes reasonable to seek out another NUN, source of Latin nonna, the 'elder' and teacher, the 'Lord of Noon' and even 'Lord of the Nine', the being who first arrived on a scene of great chaos and set about re-educating the few who had survived -

if the stories are to be believed. We find ourselves looking around for the original wisdom teacher known as Oannes in the Greek account and as Hermes or Thoth in the alchemical writings. He is not 'noon'. He is the teacher of such things, absent and present, appearing and disappearing, anonymous, bringing knowledge of mathematics, astronomy, and the written word. He is NUN.ME, the sage and magician whose emblem is the T-shaped symbol ME and who we know as 'Apkallu' (p.28). Where is he when he's needed?

What's In A Number?

At a superficial level, it seems reasonable to say that the number nine, even if it corresponds to the number of completed cycles of the moon during pregnancy, is of no more overall importance than, for example, the number twelve, the established yearly cycle of time. Not having a direct link to the Great Sage, I turned to the work of Randall Carlson[1] to gain some basic understanding of the potential greater importance of nine in the order of things.

He points out that numbers used to measure time but also space and geometrical figures can be broken down 'cabalistically' to the single digit 9. For example, the circumference of a circle equals 360 degrees, further dividing into 21,600 minutes of arc and so on:

$$3 + 6 + 0 = 9$$

$$2 + 1 + 6 + 0 + 0 = 9$$

He refers to the recurring nature of those numbers; one square foot equals 144 inches while a 24-hour day equals 1,440 minutes: 1+4+4=9. A five-sided figure known as a pentagon has 5 angles of 108 degrees adding up to 540 and again reducible to 9. Given that the earliest known image of the pentagon comes in the form of the Sumerian word, UB/UP, proposed in Sumerian lexicons as 'corner' and 'recess' from which it is possible to deduce further meanings of 'angle' and 'point', that is not an inconsequential piece of information (p.289).

UB/UP

Randall Carlson also points to the importance of 108 as a lunar number and mentions the possibility that the antediluvian portion of the Sumerian King List was a mathematical riddle. I took a closer look. In seven cases out of eight, the numbers quoted as lifespans of the antediluvian kings can be reduced to number nine, either through the so-called cabalistic addition method or by division. It is noteworthy that line 17 gives the number 108,000, a multiple of the lunar number mentioned above, as the total lifespans of three kings, three being another number closely associated with the moon. Line 7 gives the total of the first two kings as 64,800 which – minus a zero - corresponds to a division of the Great Year into four 'seasons' of 6,480 years.

The King List has been copiously cited as written proof of dynasties of kings stretching back so far that our imaginations can't follow. Some see the tremendously long lifespans of its first eight rulers as gross exaggeration while others strive to explain the anomalies in other ways. But all, except perhaps a few that I have missed, accept the basic premise that they were meant to be read as human lifespans. I share Randall Carlson's opinion that there is likely another way entirely of considering the numbers in the list.

Kings Of Old

From this are and do come admirable adaptations where of the means is here in this. Hence I am called Hermes Trismegist, having the three parts of the philosophy of the whole world.[1]

According to academia, Sumerian was an agglutinative language. Thus, as mentioned earlier, the thirty-six symbols of the eight listed kings and the twelve-plus-one symbols of the five cities have never been individually translated. Neither have the two final symbols of line 36: ME-EŠ where number three is given in cuneiform EŠ/SIN. They follow on from KI and are left unmentioned.

This image, not part of a King List, appears on a tablet dated to the Uruk III period, ca. 3200-3000 BC,[2] written much earlier than existing copies of the King List. It reads top down as KI, the place or Earth, over ME, the 'spirit', the 'magic' or the magician, giving KI-ME and bearing a remarkable resemblance to the Egyptian ankh symbol. Possible interpretations of KI-ME-EŠ without further context:

> *Place of the Three Spirits/Magicians*
> *Place of the Three Ships*[3]
> *Three Magic Places on Earth*

Cuneiform elements of lines 36 and 37 shown here below are borrowed from the transcript of the King List tablet which dates from the Old Babylonian archaeological period of ca.1900-1600 BC and is held at the Ashmolean Museum.[1] I have added the corresponding transliterations. The drawing brings proof – if needed – that the antediluvian King List has never been fully translated or, alternatively, that the orthodox agglutinative language in which it

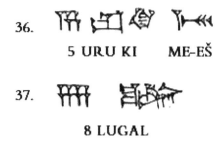

36.

5 URU KI   ME-EŠ

37.

8 LUGAL

is said to have been written included a number of completely redundant signs/words, perhaps added in as flourishes…?

ME   EŠ

Magic of the Three

Arguably the most important meaning of ME is 'measure'. That is not a meaning given in the Sumerian lexicons, but it is nevertheless the source syllable of words such as 'measure' and 'metre'. The lexical lists add an intriguing layer to the mystery of the magical three. They are found there as MEŠ$_2$ and opposite ME. In other words, the 'threesome' is inherent in symbol ME. Three is in the magic. The magic is in the number three:

ME   EŠ   =   ME

MEŠ$_2$

Magic of the Three

Trisme?

Hermes Trismegistus, the three times great Magician, takes part of his name here.[2]

It is possible that errors were introduced accidentally or deliberately into both the early composite example of the King List and the considerably later Greek offering attributed to Berossus. If code there was, it might no longer be possible to find it, let alone break it. Whatever the case, it certainly will not be me who gets to the bottom of the numbers on that list, and, in the meantime, I am grateful to Randall Carlson for the clarity of his more general explanations.

Is he right to suggest a mathematical riddle? And what do the numbers match if not lifespans? Do they refer to astronomy, to celestial bodies and their movements, to measurements of space or time? In order to clarify the situation to some extent, if that is still at all possible, and to make it easy for others to consider the options, the numbers are laid out according to their original positions in a new and utterly unorthodox translation of the antediluvian King List through the monosyllabic looking glass, given here (p.243) and followed by relatively copious notes.

Apart from the strange case of ME-EŠ, there is one other unmentioned triple occurrence in the antediluvian King List which leads me to strongly suspect the presence of another age-old Sumerian riddle. There is always more.

PERPETUAL
GENESIS

Riddle Of The Generations

Genesis: 'birth', 'origin', 'creation', from Greek genesis, from PIE root.

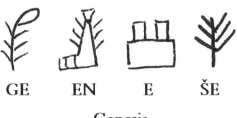

GE   EN   E   ŠE

Genesis

In the beginning was the riddle. Genesis began life as a four-word riddle. At least, that is the way in which it must be viewed to fully comprehend the extent of it, the gift that goes on giving. It has a beginning and an end. But at its centre, Genesis is endless. Where does any family tree begin? Where did the word 'begin' begin?

Found together more than once in the Sumerian tablets, the collocation of these four symbols into phonetic 'Genese' cannot be dismissed as coincidental. It all began here. At the beginning was the reed and at the end the seed. Or is it the other way round?

The Reed

GE, shown here with its given meanings, is the stylus used to write the first word, the staff with which to establish all the laws of nature. More explicit examples of the pictogram show it as an ear of wheat or similar crop, the grains of which are collected and ground down to become one of the staple foods of humans: bread.

GE   GE   GI₄

reed, green, to turn, to return, to establish

As 'turn' and 'return', Sumerian GE/GI refers not only to the spinning of words onto a lump of clay but also to cycles of time, the returning sun after the winter solstice, the greenery at the spring equinox. At the winter solstice, the sun is at its most easterly point on the horizon, hesitating there for three days before beginning the return journey westwards, the return of life on Earth. This is the much-celebrated moment heralding rebirth. Symbol GE indicates all new beginnings including that of mankind. The reed is the first stage of the tree.

Three Branches

How many branches does it take to make a tree? One alone is a stalk, splitting into two as it grows upwards. Two branches might be the promise of a tree, but only when they are offshoots of one common stalk. Two branches can't be a tree without that generating stalk which is the third element. It takes three to make a tree. The GE of Genesis is an essential element of the Tree. One lexical entry sums it up:

GE   X   EŠ   =   GEŠ

Branch times three equals tree.

Once again, we find the symbol for 'three' seen above as EŠ which is also SIN, the name given to the much later moon god Sin. The number three represents the three phases of the moon, orchestrating the rhythms of growth.

Those three words show the complexity and simple logic of this most ancient of writing systems. They take us back to the originator of it, Hermes Trismegistus, whose own name comprises a riddle - perhaps the first - and the source of our understanding of the word 'hermetic'. They also demonstrate the importance of analysing the symbols through the prism of the lexical lists, tablets from the Akkadian period which provided matching lists of words, monosyllabic Sumerian to the later Akkadian, in much the same way as modern dictionaries.

The lexical lists have always been seen as illustrations of the different sounds to be given to those multi-syllabic words, their interest deemed purely phonetic. Pens have waxed lyrical and with amusement at the propensity of Mesopotamian scribes to make endless lists and yet we do the same. Their reasons were the same as ours. They wrote etymological dictionaries offering a considerable amount of information about the connections between the source meanings of their words through the ages, not just the sounds. So much has been missed as a result of that one fundamental misunderstanding.

There is another way to understand the above breakdown

GE   X   IŠ/SAHAR/ISIS   =   GEŠ

Reed and soil equal tree.

For a reed to become a tree, there must be soil. Another way of composing
the sound of GEŠ is given in the lexical lists, this time replacing EŠ with IŠ,
the soil. This is also the source symbol of Sumero-Egyptian Isis, and can be
read as both ISIS and SAHAR, fittingly the source of both the deity and the
name of the Sahara desert.

The Miracle Of One Only Thing

That which is below is like that which is above and that which is above is like
that which is below to do the miracle of one only thing.[1]

If present day records are anything to go by, EN, given as 'lord', 'master' and
'ruler', was one of the most inscribed symbols at the earliest Uruk IV period
of writing ca.3350-3200 BC. 271 instances on 218 separate tablets or
fragments of tablets are shown on the CDLI website for that period, a huge
number compared to most, if not all, other pictograms. For comparison, GEŠ,
the tree, is found there over the same period 20 times on 18 tablets. Visually,
the writing of pictographic EN varies quite a bit but overall it's the only word
that in any way resembles the headgear of those figures on Sumerian artefacts
understood to be the Anunnaki gods.

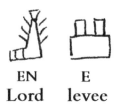

EN   **E**

Lord   **levee**

EN, the Lord, with E, the 'levee', 'high' and
'rising', give 'the levee of the Lord'. A levee is a
natural feature or artificial construction to regulate
water flows. Together EN-E form the mechanics
of the endless generating
process, the energy of the

engine, death and rebirth, the 'Risen Lord'. The
words 'end', 'new', 'energy' and 'engine' are all from
unknown PIE sources. Another more obvious way
in which this process was shown comes through the
mirroring of symbol EN with NE which has the
given meaning 'fire' to which I add 'end' and
'renew'.

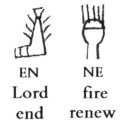

EN   **NE**

Lord   **fire**

end   **renew**

Adjectives given in Sumerian lexicons for EN are 'exalted' and 'strong'. EN with NA, the 'stone', is given as 'until', 'up to' indicating that this combination is a reference to time. EN-NA the Lord and his stone, the Lord of Stone, the Stone Lord who we will meet again at a later stage (p.231). Symbol EN is also given with the phonetic value ENA.

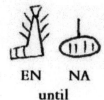

EN   NA

until

Lord of Stone

From there it isn't a great stretch to consider that EN-NA was one epithet of the ancestor of Greek Hermes, god of boundaries and of boundary stones. 'Until' implies that there are limits placed, the meaning not confined to earthly measurements of fields and property rights, but also taking time into consideration. The Lord of Stone measures and delimits far more than might be imagined while EN-E is Lord of Endings and Beginnings. Lord of Energy, of binding and boundaries of all that exists, seen and unseen.

The Architect

I am the Alpha and the Omega, the Beginning and the End," says the Lord, "who is and who was and who is to come, the Almighty. (Revelation 1:8)

This circular riddle was no doubt destined to be studied by those who had some background knowledge. Unfortunately for us, the mystery has deepened with the passage of time, but some clues might still be found by taking a closer look at SAG, the 'head'. Sumerian SAG is shown here through two different versions of its relatively numerous known pictographic forms, both taken from the oldest tablets. One of them appears to be a mushroom (p.158).

John Allegro saw multiple allusions to mind-altering substances in the Sumerian texts, as do I, but that might not have been the only subject of importance to whoever wrote the following word game. The meaning of SAG, the 'head', varies according to the context. It's also used to indicate the prow of a vessel, and opposed to EGER, the stern, in that situation – apparently nothing to do with mushrooms there (p.2). But hallucinogens come in the form of both food and drink, and EGER takes the form of a walking beer pot. Then again, both riddles can be read more simply in the context of the constantly completed circle of the year, the constant renewal of life on Earth, the return of the grain harvest and the beer, that of the Chaldeans.

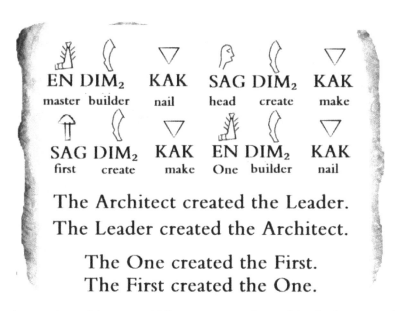

EN DIM₂   KAK   SAG DIM₂   KAK
master builder   nail   head   create   make

SAG DIM₂   KAK   EN DIM₂   KAK
first   create   make   One builder   nail

The Architect created the Leader.
The Leader created the Architect.

The One created the First.
The First created the One.

Another version of the same riddle gives TI in place of the final KAK on both lines. SAG with TI gives the source of Hindu Shakti, the divine and feminine cosmic energy. TI has the meanings 'arrow', 'to approach', 'to be long lasting', 'to be old', 'to live'. Both TI and TIL, a closely related symbol, have the meaning 'to be complete'. TIL is source of 'until'.

Note that there are four DIM₂, visually an ox leg, with given meanings 'to create', 'builder' and 'architect'. That symbol can be visually matched to its Egyptian hieroglyphic counterpart, also placed at the centre of the Dendera zodiac, and was perhaps the Sumerian astronomical equivalent. EN-DIM₂ gives the source of Greek Endymion (p.257).

KAK, the 'peg' or 'nail' and 'to build' also appears four times. See KAK in the context of the snake biting its own tail and its presence within symbol DUR as the 'nail of truth' (p.127) for a deeper dive into the never-ending, circular Hermetic riddle. As much as I would like to keep these explanations simple, the Sumerian mystery tends to spiral outwards and to deepen with every step. It might well be bottomless. The reader must decide for themselves whether to plunge or not. All the layers are equally fascinating.

The four nails of this riddle can be perceived in one version of a Sumerian word: EZEN. EZEN, source of Greek piezein,[2] is the first step in a mighty ladder of interlocking words and meanings which bring a hitherto unnoticed dimension to the people who created this language (p.254).

Lord Of Fire

This image is a drawing taken from the central crossed 'tenet' carved onto a

curious stone inside a huge cave above a gulley known as the Galamus Gorges in the French Pyrenees.[1] It is a particularly eloquent example of the Sator square, also known as the Templar Square, with its four inwardly pointing Ts and its central N taking on the form of M and/or W. Other examples of the palindrome don't possess those features and it's my suggestion that this one was carved by people who either had knowledge of the Sumerian origin of the riddle or who were blindly copying from an extremely ancient version of it.

The two central symbols of 'genesis' can be read indifferently as EN-E or E-NE, mirrored sounds. That is also the case for the central pattern of the Sator Square analysed in *Before Babel*, and which can be understood as a circulating energy confined by the crossed tenets. Words that begin 'en' such as 'engage' and 'enable', the firing up of the central engine from an unseen, endless, enduring source, take their source here… in the Hermetic 'One'.

The Sator Square can be visualised as a three-dimensional pyramidal form or octahedron where the central N of ENE becomes both the highest and the lowest central point. The energy circulates below and above, to left and to right, from north and from south according to the way in which the palindrome is viewed.

It has never been solved simply because the Sumerian key has never before been inserted. Was it originally designed to reflect the four KAK pegs in the Sumerian never-ending riddle? Did the people who inscribed it on a wall at Pompei around 79 AD know the origin and meaning or was it simply perpetuated as a talisman from a distant past with a reputation for warding off evil by binding the spirits or bringing luck?

The Seed

Beginning with the sprouting reed and ending with the seed becomes more logical if GE is understood as metaphor for the phallus, instrument of male fertility joining with ŠE, the equally important mechanism of female fertility and regeneration. Allegro considered the phallus to be quasi-omnipotent in the Sumerian texts, seeing there the obvious central symbol of an all-important fertility cult. My own understanding is more muted. In some circumstances, it is central but not the whole story.

Final ŠE of GE-EN-E-ŠE is the complement of GE and, if grammar were to be taken into consideration, would represent the verb in final position; 'to seed'. The reed and the seed come together as the seed and the seeding. GE with ŠE: 'to establish the seed'.

ŠE
seed

Pronounced SHE, this is the symbol that provides an inarguably logical origin for our word 'she'. Apparently, English 'she' appeared during the 12th century but, as with so many of our words, the origin cannot be clearly stated. 'From PIE root' remains the bog-standard answer. Consideration of Sumerian as something other than an isolated language would greatly clarify enigmas of this kind.

At first glance, the pictogram is simply a stalk with branches on either side. However, it can also be understood as an ear of wheat if the image of symbol GE is taken into account (p.77); in which case, the seed becomes identifiable as the wheat grain that gives the flour.

There exists a tablet from the Uruk III archaeological period, ca. 3200-300 BC, in which symbol ŠE is combined with another symbol NINDA₂ in a particularly significant manner. That combination shows that it was – at least in the mind of one scribe – meant also to be understood as the regenerating mechanism of the female body. In fairness, other examples of the word from the same period are less obviously feminine.

Symbol NINDA₂, comprising the outer two vertical lines of the female midriff and thighs on this tablet,[1] is given in Sumerian lexicons as 'seed funnel'.

Staff Of The Lord

This is what the LORD says: By this you will know that I am the LORD. Behold, with the staff in my hand I will strike the water of the Nile, and it will turn to blood. (Exodus 7:17)

Moses is offered a magical staff and tasked with putting the fear of God into an Egyptian pharaoh. That well known story appears in the section of the Bible known as Exodus, the exit of the Israelites from the land of Egypt. But the staff has its beginnings in Genesis as does the Lord. EN has the given meaning 'Lord'. GE-EN can be read as a possessive: The Staff of the Lord.

GE   EN

Staff of the Lord

Where did the word 'begin' begin? Etymological dictionaries give 'gen' as an essential element of many words: gene, gender, generate - words derived from genesis.

Good Genes

Within the fair-paved court of Jove, he and the gods conferred
About the sad events of Troy: amongst whom ministered
Blessed Hebe, nectar.[1]

Analysis of the founding symbols of Genesis demonstrates the perpetual motion of the central EN-E. However, from left to right, reading in the manner to which we have long been accustomed, the story of Genesis continues to unfold with GE-EN, the staff of the Lord, a magical instrument by all accounts. A search that includes the two symbols GE-EN gives numerous examples of the following:

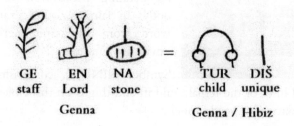

GE	EN	NA	=	TUR	DIŠ
staff	Lord	stone		child	unique
	Genna			**Genna / Hibiz**	

Here again, the ancient tablets known as 'lexical lists', provide further information. According to the entry shown above, GE-EN to which is added NA, the 'weight' and 'stone', are the source words and sounds of the Sumero-Akkadian word 'genna', equating to TUR-DIŠ, 'the unique child'.

Elixir Of Youth

TUR-DIŠ together are given with the meanings 'young child' and 'red':

TUR   DIŠ

Genna / Hibiz

Unique Child

Red

Thus, an investigation into the make-up of Genesis leads from indications of fertility to a unique child. But that isn't the end of the story. Founding symbol of Genesis, GE, the reed, has a little-known sibling. In fact, they are little short of twins, the difference between them being nothing more than a few short parallel strokes added to ZI, symbol of life and source of Zeus. Taking their pictographic forms quite literally, these are the ears of the wheat which will become the bread of life:

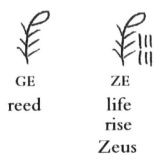

GE   ZE

reed   life

rise

Zeus

Straying somewhat from the original analysis of the four symbols of 'genesis', it is interesting to follow the trail established by the association of GE-EN with TUR-DIŠ.

The lexical lists inform us that HIBIZ, an alternative phonetic form given with GENNA, stems from HI-BI-IZ:

HI   BI   IZ

mix   beer   tree

red

Hibiscus

HI/HE with the given meaning 'mix' followed by BI/BE, 'beer' and 'bee', 'mixer of the beer', is the origin of Greek Hebe, goddess of youth, cupbearer to the gods. It was Hebe who mixed and served the drinks at the bar of the gods, a more than respectable position and an indication of the unacceptable arrogance of her suitor in the Sumerian tale called *Enki's Journey to Nibru*[1] (p.88).

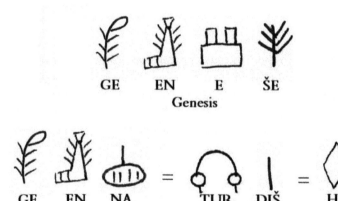

GE   EN   E   ŠE

Genesis

GE   EN   NA   =   TUR   DIŠ   =   HI   BI   IZ

Genna   **Genna / Hibiz**   **Hibiz**

Unique Child

Red

HE   BE
mix   beer

Mixing the Brew

Greek Hebe

The Ingredients

that Hebe with her lovely hair might again mix the cups,[1]

Pronounced either 'hibiz' or 'hibis', this is the origin of the hibiscus, a plant found in a variety of colours in gardens where the climate is sufficiently mild and sunny. Bearing in mind that the combined symbol HIBIZ means both 'young child' and 'red', it is interesting to note that the dried petals have been used for millennia to concoct a drink with a distinctive red colour. Perhaps there was a different reasoning behind the association of youth and the colour of the brew; a potion to increase fertility perhaps. Who knows?

Apparently, hibiscus is a potential hallucinogen. The medical information states that there have been unconfirmed reports of hallucinations which might (or might not) be the result of overuse, in that hibiscus consumption has the effect of lowering blood pressure. It seems unlikely that the dizziness resulting from low blood pressure would be likened to a state of altered consciousness such as that from recognised hallucinogens. But again who knows? Perhaps it was a metaphor for some other red brew... Whatever the truth of the matter, there is surely a direct connection with Hebe who mixes and hands out her unique brew to the gods. She is also given as daughter of Zeus.

It is not a stretch to suggest that the honey beer served by Hebe had mind-altering properties. We have entered the linguistic realm of a tradition that gave birth to the Greek Eleusinian mystery school where an 'elixir of youth' was originally served. What did the rejuvenating drink contain? The analysis of words having their source in Sumerian monosyllabic origins does not easily extend beyond one or sometimes two syllables. However, the IZ of HI-BI-IZ signals the presence of GIŠ, the tree, under one of its phonetic guises.(p.101) Perhaps this refers to the hibiscus as a tree or shrub.

The Limits Of Being

Line 17 of *Enki's Journey to Nibru*[2] tells part of a pre-Greek story which to some extent matches the wooing of Greek Hebe. Full of his own importance, the hero, who is rising to the skies in his basket, appears intent on showing off his beer-brewing skills while complaining bitterly about his overall condition, perhaps a reference to the flood. Seeking to impress Hebe on her own turf, he is supremely unaware of his foolish arrogance.

He has also been charged with writing down the story of his celestial journey[3] and, along with the beer which was apparently a central element of the ship, has taken a large amount of 'clay of the land' on board for that purpose. In this section, we find a telling link to another Sumerian text, the complaining of Momus in *The Story of Sukurru* (p.141). There is surely a moral to their stories. Does it have to do with fools and their bitterness? The bitterness associated with the beer? Bitter beer?

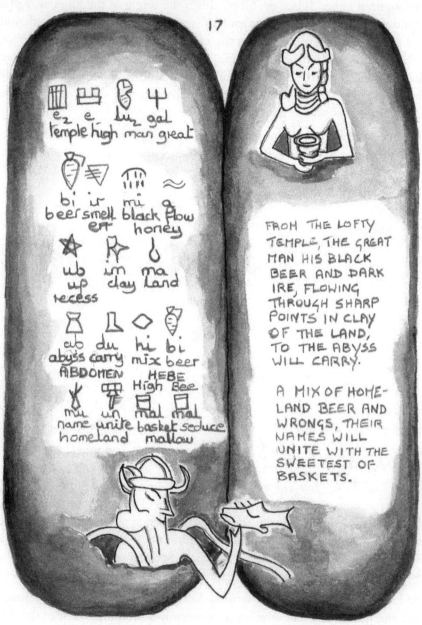

17

 e₂ e lu₂ gal
temple high man great

bi ir mi a
beer smell black flow
er honey

ub im ma
up clay land
recess

ab du hi bi
abyss carry mix beer
ABDOMEN HEBE
High Bee

mu un mal mal
name unite basket seduce
homeland mallow

FROM THE LOFTY TEMPLE, THE GREAT MAN HIS BLACK BEER AND DARK IRE, FLOWING THROUGH SHARP POINTS IN CLAY OF THE LAND, TO THE ABYSS WILL CARRY.

A MIX OF HOME-LAND BEER AND WRONGS, THEIR NAMES WILL UNITE WITH THE SWEETEST OF BASKETS.

As with *The Story of Sukurru* (aka *The Instructions of Shuruppak*), *Enki's Journey to Nibru* was written in the Sumerian monosyllabic language. The overall theme of the hero jumping into his cosmic vessel, also understood as a basket – no doubt modelled on the Mesopotamian coracle - is still present and I believe these to have been the earliest sources for Noah's ark and also the voyage of Enoch and the Homeric journeys of Odysseus and Jason. The texts contain astrological/astronomical references, indicating that Sumerian was a language of seafarers.

Whatever the truth, *The Story of Sukurru* and *The Path to Sky-End* (the title chosen for the ongoing re-translation of *Enki's Journey to Nibru*) are the products of people with the same sense of humour and, in both cases, it's clear that the female will have the last word, will make the decisions. Her raised voice, overruling the noisy virile warfare below, has been likened to the sound of a thunderstorm.[1] This was the language of a matriarchal society.

An Egyptian Genesis

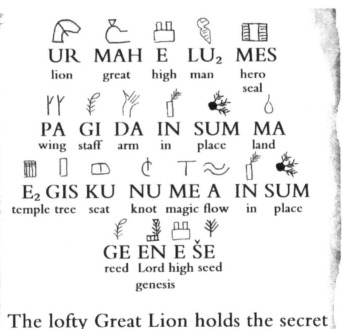

UR MAH E LU₂ MES
lion great high man hero
                         seal

PA GI DA IN SUM MA
wing staff arm in place land

E₂ GIS KU NU ME A IN SUM
temple tree seat knot magic flow in place

GE EN E ŠE
reed Lord high seed
genesis

The lofty Great Lion holds the secret
seal of man under its arm.
The Temple of GES was founded
to give the genesis of the Magic Knot.

There exists a series of Sumerian proverbs beginning with the words UR MAH E, translated to 'Great and Lofty Lion'. It's possible that they all refer to some reputed but long-lost Mesopotamian lion. However, a few contain references that fit surprisingly well with tales told elsewhere about the most lofty of them all, the Great Sphinx of the Giza Plateau in Egypt. The rumour of a secret archive hidden somewhere below the Sphinx suggests that it contains the origin of mankind and the translation of the above riddle[1] was carried out with that in mind. But it did not involve or indeed necessitate deliberate twisting of the meanings to fit that narrative.

In the four words LU$_2$ MES PA GI we find the hitherto elusive link between the Great Lion and the name of a great man. Lexicons give him as a hero and his emblems here are PA, the wings, and GE/GI, the rod or staff.

The name Hermes Trismegistus, the three times Great Magician, is analysed in *Before Babel The Crystal Tongue*[2] and broken down into its original Sumerian monosyllabic components of which ME, the magic and the Magician, a word attested in conventional lexicons. MES, given as 'cylinder seal', 'sealed tablet' and 'hero' among others, is broken down in the lexical lists in several ways, of which ME-AB/EŠ$_3$, the 'magic of the Father'. It can also be examined through ME-EŠ where the number three was hiding. ME-EŠ appear together (but are ignored and left untranslated, forgotten) in the antediluvian Sumerian King List (p.72), never forgetting that EŠ, meaning 'three', is also SIN, moon god of the Sabians. ME-GIS, the Magician and the Tree. GES/GIS, the tree, is discussed in other sections of this book.

PA, the 'wing', is the founding symbol of pagan Pan. PA takes this fundamental mystery back to a far earlier source, and to the most ancient of all known archaeological sites: Gobekli Tepe. PA is analysed through its phonetic form HENDUR and in the context of the bird on pillar 43 (p.125). In fact, PA is arguably the most enduring of any written word. It is my contention that PA was once carefully laid out in front of the greatest of the three pyramids of Giza, known as Khufu's pyramid. That message from the past – consistently ignored but magically enduring - takes the

PA/ENDUR
wings
tutor

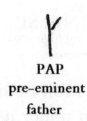

PAP
pre-eminent
father

form of Sumerian PAP and constitutes one wing of PA, shown here with a couple of the given meanings. This is not cherry picking. All of the meanings attached to all of the symbols are of interest and discussed as fully as possible here or elsewhere, but these are the most relevant to the matter in hand.

90

In front of the main entrance to Khufu's pyramid, covering almost the whole extent of its eastern flank, lie two massive boat pits carved out of the bedrock. With a third pit of equal size dug at an angle by the side of the causeway, there can be no denying that together they take a form surprisingly close to that of the Sumerian word PAP, the 'winged father'. No-one to my knowledge has offered an alternative explanation for the presence of three great ghost ships in this most prestigious location, arranged along the eastern façade, the side of the rising sun.

The pilgrimages of the Sabians of Harran into Egypt are flimsily documented and difficult to prove beyond doubt. Nevertheless, they are said to have made regular journeys to Giza and another great monument there tends to confirm that account. Alternative names for the Sphinx are Hor-em-akhet and Horakhti, names firmly associated with the monument thanks to the inscription on a nearby stela placed there by the pharaoh Amenhotep II (1427-1401 BC).[1]

I propose that Hor results from Sumerian HAR/HUR, the celestial millstone and root symbol of the name Harran (p.52). I also propose that HUR-SAG, the 'top millstone', commonly translated to 'mountain', can be read as a reference to the head of the Great Sphinx and to its twin, the millstone in the sky (p.106). It wouldn't be the first time that an Egyptian head has appeared on a Sumerian tablet.[2] Here with the relevant lexical list entries:

HU	UR		HAR/HUR		HA	ŠI	RI
flight	dog, lion		millstone		fish	eye	gather
	HUR						AR
							HAR

AR, through ŠI-RI and without any twisting, reads 'the eye of the bird' and, I suggest, gave both the name Sirius and the AR of 'Archon', biblical name for the Watchers.[3] Would that be the eye of Egyptian Horus, the falcon, or are these all simply phonetic coincidences? The watching fish or watching the fish? Greek arkhein with the meanings 'be the first' and 'begin from' is a fitting element in a title applied to the Great Sphinx of the Giza plateau.

Again according to the lexical lists, there is another possible breakdown of HAR. This time, the two symbols that together give AR are replaced by just one word given as AR$_2$ and corresponding to UB, the earliest known image of a pentagram. UB/AR$_2$ has some intriguing given meanings, of which 'corner' and 'recess' and extended to 'angle'. This is the word used in the

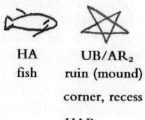

HA	UB/AR₂
fish	ruin (mound)
	corner, recess

HAR

proverb on p.2 with NU, the negative, giving NU-UB, 'no corner', 'no angle' and from there translated as 'round'. Below HA-AR₂ is another of its given meanings 'ruin' which, according to ePSD, can be extended to include 'mound'. Again, it might be said that 'ruin' and 'mound' applied to the rocky outcrop that became the Sphinx stems from nothing more than a coincidence. A recess in an ancient mound? In a fish?

Returning to the riddle in question, IN-SUM gives the source of Latin insum: 'to belong to'. IN has the given meaning 'straw' and is the source of 'in' potentially through an original reference to the harvesting of crops. SUM, visually the crops laid down, comes from the same reference. NU-ME, the Magic Knot, became Latin numen, the 'divine will'

Does this riddle refer to and give the source names of the Giza plateau and its lion? Does it link the place irrefutably to those magicians who used the language of Mesopotamia to weave their riddles, the Sabians of Harran? That is my conviction. The reader of this must decide for themselves. Did those great magicians travel far afield spreading knowledge of an even more ancient world, a lost civilisation? An open mind is a prerequisite for this journey back through the ages where each individual travels at their own speed, examining the evidence offered here along the way. This is not a question of believing or disbelieving. The evidence is available here and elsewhere to those who want the truth. While the words of Hermes Trismegistus are gifted to us, their meanings are hermetic and must be earned. Everything is possible to a truly great magician – even the heavy task of opening modern eyes. See Harran and the Millstone on p.289 for an overview.

THE
GARDEN

Musarus Oannes

THIS is the history which Berossus has transmitted to us. He tells us that the first king was Alorus of Babylon, a Chaldæan: he reigned ten sari: and afterwards Alaparus, and Amelon who came from Pantibiblon: then Ammenon the Chaldæan, in whose time appeared the Musarus Oannes the Annedotus from the Erythræan sea.[1]

The figure given by Berossus as Musarus Oannes was said to have landed directly onto the southern shore of Mesopotamia, an indication of the direction from which a ship had arrived. The Erythraean sea was not limited to the Persian Gulf, a body of water lying to the south of Babylon. It opens up onto the Indian Ocean and the name could once have signalled the entirety of that expanse. It's possible that Berossus meant it that way. It's equally possible that the words written by the Babylonian were chosen with the intention to underscore the prestige of Babylon, his home, as the place where it all began.

The inference taken from that quote has been that Oannes was not aboard a sailing vessel but miraculously emerged directly from the water, a notion reinforced by the half-man half-fish images said to represent him. It is more feasible that the memory became blurred, that it was an arrival from an unknown place, potentially from the furthest reaches of the Pacific Ocean, and that his body became fused with the usual inhabitants of an unfathomable ocean, out of nowhere like a great fish, a dolphin, or a whale, jumping from

the waters only to disappear again. What is the truth? Was it out of the sea or out of a ship? We simply do not know.

And the LORD God took the man and put him into the garden of Eden to dress it and to keep it. (Genesis 2:15)

The description given by Alexander Polyhistor (105-35 BC) presents three names: Musarus, Oannes and Annedotus. Picking up the most ancient and forgotten Sumerian threads to attempt to elucidate some part of the mystery, it's the epithet Musarus that rises most easily to the surface.

The Sumerian symbol for the garden is SAR, shown here on a tablet from the Uruk IV period, ca.3350-3200 BC.[2] It's a relatively

95

straightforward image, easily understood with that meaning: 'garden'. According to the lexicons, SAR also has the meanings 'to grow', 'orchard', and 'to make splendid', again understandable within a primitive written language comprising a limited number of images for a limited number of subjects.

SAR can be heard as MU₂, linking it to another important symbol, MU, the time of year, the movements of the moon, again all necessary gardening knowledge.

SAR is a combination of ŠE, the seed growing out of a horizontal version of GIŠ, the tree. On some tablets there are only two plants sprouting. On some there are three. In other versions, where SAR is translated as 'orchard', the symbol of the tree is repeated next to it. But then, without warning, the horizons of the splendid garden known as SAR expand to

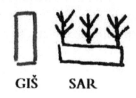

GIŠ   SAR

include the subjects of 'writing' and 'totality', 'world', 'to be numerous' and the number '3600', none of which have any obvious connection to a garden per se.

A phonetic cousin of the garden, SAR₂ is the simplest of geometric figures, a circle punched into the clay, also given with the meanings of 3600, 'totality' and 'world'. SAR₂ has other important given meanings 'to be perfect' and 'to slaughter'.

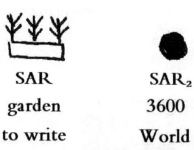

SAR

garden

to write

SAR₂

3600

World

Pictographic SAR appears over one hundred times on CDLI at the earliest

MU₂   SAR

MUSAR
garden

Uruk period of writing pre-3000 BC, and numerous times as SAR-SAR. MU₂ being another phonetic value for the same symbol, SAR-SAR has the potential to be expressed as MU₂-SAR, becoming Akkadian musaru which is also given as 'garden' from the Old Babylonian period, ca.1900 BC.

Add to this the Greek suffix 'us' (Zeus, Kronos) which was originally sourced directly from Sumerian symbol UŠ, symbol of the penis, meaning 'male', and find MU₂-ŠAR-UŠ, the male writer in or of the garden. Perhaps a scribe who also liked to garden…unless there is a better reason for linking them.

It is also possible that the Greek name was derived from a four-syllable combination MU₂-SAR-RU-UŠ

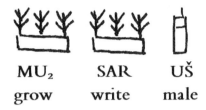

MU₂	SAR	UŠ
grow	write	male

since ŠAR-RU appear more than once together on the lexical tablets opposite LUGAL, the 'great man'[1]:

MU₂	SAR	RU	UŠ
grow	write	lay down	male

Musarus

This combination might translate to 'he who imposed the writing', where 'impose' or 'to lay down' stems from the added RU. Or perhaps 'he who brought down the writing'…? The above four words have not been found together to my knowledge but that doesn't mean that they never were. I have further identified RU as the source of 'to rotate', and French 'roue', the wheel, neither given in lexicons.

There are other more orthodox ways to read the agglutinated Akkadian version, 'musaru', of which 'inscription' from MU-SAR and even 'penis' where UŠ alone can be read as the Akkadian 'muŠaru' according to one source.[2] The path is full of twists and turns.

MU	SAR
name	write

Inscription

Renown of the Garden

The Writer's Name

Closely linked to gardens, to writing and to growth, this analysis goes a long way to confirming that the fish-god figure, if he did exist, was indeed a law-giver. A law implies an inscribed word and Musarus Oannes appears to have been the original famed scribe - Sumerian, of course.

SAR, given alone as 'to write' is also commonly coupled with DUB, symbol of the tablet, as can be seen on the Adda seal (p.21). DUB, the tablet of Musarus, or DUB, the tablet of Sar. But who then is Sar? Perhaps there is an

Egyptian link to be found here. It has been suggested that Osiris also carried the epithet Sar in The Book of the Dead.[1]

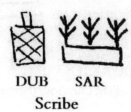

DUB   SAR
Scribe
Tablet of the Garden

Nowhere in the bible is there a reference to the origin, the invention of writing. Genesis does not bring the subject up at all. The earliest Old Testament mention of the written word comes in Exodus and in a context of control and censorship:

The LORD then said to Moses, "Write this down on a scroll as a reminder and recite it to Joshua: I will completely blot out the memory of Amalek under heaven. (Exodus 17:14)

The origin of the name Amalek is unclear. In *The Story of Sukurru*, it was AMA, the cosmic Matriarch, who called the shots. In the Bible, it was Moses who did the writing.

Welcome To Eden

EDEN

Generally shown in lexicons under the alternative spelling EDIN, the lexical entries give it as resulting from combinations of its three primary symbols: E-DI/DE-IN/EN. Those possibilities show that the name can be read in alphabetic form as either Eden or Edin, purely a question of choice on the part of the 19th and 20th century philologists. Why was Edin chosen in preference to Eden, equivalent to the bible spelling? Was it to distinguish them one from the other? Was that necessary?

With what appears to be a bizarre blindness to any possible link to its biblical sibling, Sumerian Edin, which should have aroused fervent curiosity as a far more ancient source of the biblical name, has the given meanings 'steppe' or 'plain'. Certainly not 'garden'. It is claimed by scholars to consist of the fertile alluvial area known as Babylonia and to correspond only to the southern region of Mesopotamia. However, the given meanings of the word might equally apply to the landscape between the rivers Tigris and Euphrates in both upper and lower Mesopotamia. It is altogether feasible that the entire region was known as EDEN at some point in time. There is no concrete evidence to the contrary. Or is there? I wait to be corrected.

As with all the early Sumerian pictograms on tablets dating to between 3500 and 3000 BC, word and image were likely to have been closely related in some way, the image reflecting the primary meaning to some extent if not entirely. Many, if not most, of the symbols do not give up that connection without a fight. EDEN, taken without any context, sits on the garden fence between penetrable and obscure. Nevertheless, there is some extra linguistic information to be gleaned from it.

KI/KE

EDEN incorporates a silent KI, symbol of place, at its base, confirming that this is indeed a specific place name rather than a run-of-the-mill noun as suggested by the lexicons. EDEN-KI can be compared to all the other 'city' names cited in the Sumerian King List in that regard. Given its biblical connection, EDEN-KI might even stir in us the paradigm-shifting thought that these are all 'places' where people gathered and not necessarily 'cities' as we understand that word. Then again, the name might have extended from a central place, a garden of renown, to an entire region. Who knows? Applying names to specific places without having found the welcoming sign with that specific name on it above the main gate or on the mat is not a solid foundation for truth.

Perhaps the term 'garden' once applied to large areas of fertile land which were fittingly irrigated by rivers, levees and canals measured out and carefully constructed, the land cultivated, brimming with trees and flowers, and also habitations, homes blending into their surroundings, rendered pleasant by expert gardeners. We would not find synonymity between 'city' and 'garden' today. Public gardens are enclosed within small segments of the cities, not the other way around. But that may not always have been the case.

Formal enclosed gardens were originally a Persian speciality much admired by the Ancient Greeks. Pasargadae, an ancient city close to Persepolis in Iran, translates to 'paradise', and it was there that that the first formal garden design appeared, laid out according to a quadrilateral design known as a Charbagh garden. It is tempting to find the source of 'Char' in the garden that is Sumerian ŠAR, also pronounced 'shar'.

Tree Of Consciousness And Knowledge

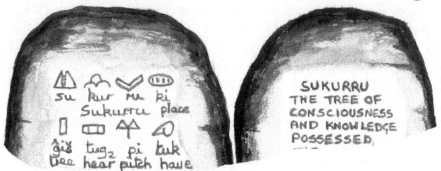

The Mesopotamian Tree, occulted in the orthodox version of *The Story of Sukurru* and seen here for the first time on line 5 of that text, has great advantages over all other ancient magical trees. It is the oldest of them all and comprises three words which open it up to further analysis. According to the author of *The Story of Sukurru*, it was present in the final city of the antediluvian Sumerian King List and lost when the flood swept over.

Visible on numerous Sumerian and Akkadian artefacts but unmentioned in all translated texts until 2017, the Tree of Consciousness and Knowledge appears three times in the opening lines and is repeated three times thereafter[1], six in all in a text of some 3,000 words. Its loss is part of the lament for the city. No other work mentions a special tree in such profusion.

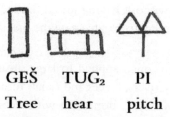

GEŠ   **TUG₂**   **PI**

Tree   **hear**   **pitch**

The most exciting aspect of the Sumerian Tree is that it can be quite extensively explored to rediscover the thought process of whoever inscribed its name onto clay. Together the three words have one phonetic value written

GIŠTUG$_2$, an agglutinated form which doesn't phonetically incorporate the third symbol PI. Nevertheless, PI is an important piece of the puzzle.

The Trunk

GEŠ, the tree, has a range of closely similar phonetic possibilities. It can even drop the initial G/J sound that links it directly to its generating reed, GE/GI:

GESH, GISH, GIZ, GEZ, GIS, GES, JISH, JESH, JIZ, JEZ, JIS, JES
IZ, EZ, IS, ES

The Sumerian tree provides a whole new perspective on the stories and figures of both Old and New Testaments, and on the properties of the Tree of Life. Shady trees were mentioned by John Allegro and are discussed on p.175-76.

Line 58 of *The Story of Sukurru* has GEŠ followed by SAR, a combination having the given meaning 'orchard' and translated there separately to 'tree' and 'grow'. The line was translated in the context of a scene in which 'kanab', cannabis,[1] and the 'spirit between the eyes' also appear (p.158).

The tree grew large and strong and its top touched the sky; it was visible to the ends of the earth. Its foliage was beautiful and its fruit abundant, And in it was food for all. The beasts of the field found shade under it, And the birds of the sky dwelt in its branches, And all living creatures fed themselves from it. I was looking in the visions in my mind as I lay on my bed, and behold, an angelic watcher, a holy one, descended from heaven.... (Daniel 4:11)

In this line, GA refers both to the cosmic Mother's nurturing milk and, in context, a more literal cloud of white smoke, becoming a metaphorical meeting of above and below: the canopy of the tree with the clouds in the sky. In the following lines, GA, twice followed by AB the ocean, is the white surf of the ocean waves, creating the 'cream of the ocean', as the waters are churned. The existence of a connection here the smoke of the ritual burning of cannabis as well as to the Hindu 'churning of the ocean of milk' is too obvious to be ignored.

Awareness

When the spirit consented, Foreknowledge appeared and stood by Forethought. [1]

TUG$_2$
forethought

In the introduction to *The Story of Sukurru*, the short fictional account was intended to conjure up something of an ambience and also provide an explanation of the translation process. It included a short analysis of TUG$_2$, the second symbol of the Sumerian tree:

He already knows the various meanings of TUG$_2$, but which one to choose here? They have their avowed origin in the textile mill. The sign could be 'garment' or the verb 'to clothe', but equally it might be 'hearing' and 'ear' from the renowned rhythmic songs★ of the mill workers as they tug at the wool to clean and soften it. Other less evident notions of 'attention', 'awareness', 'forethought,' and 'planning' may also be expressed through this symbol; the consciousness of being clothed, the awareness of being. Thus, according to context, an apparently simple sign goes far beyond the confines of any textile mill. Most of the meanings are still in use in his time, and the milling songs continue. Little is ever truly lost; only faded and misunderstood. ★Waulking songs

The meanings suggested in that introduction are all present with TUG$_2$ in orthodox lexicons. Finding a word with the meaning 'clothing' next to a tree in the context of an ancient myth links inevitably to the biblical story of Adam and Eve buck naked next to their own special tree. If it is a coincidence, then it's just one in a long list. What we have here is a Mesopotamian version of the Garden of Eden with its central tree, source of the much later Old Testament story. And I perceive it to have once been a story of considerably more profundity than the version that came down to us through the unfortunate prism of a wily snake, an apple, and an original sin to make our hearts forever heavy.

Good Versus Evil

While Adam and Eve are situated at the beginnings of guilt-ridden humanity in biblical Genesis, other writings – a few centuries before the appearance of Genesis – put a different spin on questions of right and wrong through a comparison of nakedness and clothing. The clothing is the earthly body, a notion which, if applied to Adam and Eve, would interpret the naked couple as 'unearthly', as spirits about to take on human form. Foreknowledge of death is an issue and the discussion comes at the end of life rather than the beginning. This from Plato:

Then spake Zeus : 'Nay,' said he, 'I will put a stop to these proceedings. The cases are now indeed judged ill and it is because they who are on trial are tried in their clothing, for they are tried alive. Now many,' said he, 'who have wicked souls are clad in fair bodies and ancestry and wealth, and at their judgement appear many witnesses to testify that their lives have been just. Now, the judges are confounded not only by their evidence but at the same time by being clothed themselves while they sit in judgement, having their own soul muffled in the veil of eyes and ears and the whole body. Thus all these are a hindrance to them, their own habiliments no less than those of the judged.'

'Well, first of all,' he said, 'we must put a stop to their foreknowledge of their death; for this they at present foreknow. However, Prometheus has already been given the word to stop this in them. Next they must be stripped bare of all those things before they are tried; for they must stand their trial dead. Their judge also must be naked, dead, beholding with very soul the very soul of each immediately upon his death, bereft of all his kin and having left behind on earth all that fine array, to the end that the judgement may be just.' [1]

Thus, according to the Greek account, it was nakedness in death that abolished the sin of superficiality, of artifice, and of lies; nakedness was a good thing. Life or death, clothed or unclothed, body or nobody, lies or truth….

The Greek account spoken by Zeus doesn't sit well with the following curious verse from Revelation and the advice given there. It seems that the sin of 'shameful' nakedness could be absolved thanks to purchasing powers, presumably the result of a life of riches. Any attempt at pleading one's case based entirely on a humble lifestyle would not cut the mustard with the gatekeeper in this version. Everything has a price:

I advise you to buy from Me gold refined in the fire so that you may be rich, white clothes so that you may be dressed and your shameful nakedness not be exposed, and ointment to spread on your eyes so that you may see. (Revelation 3:18)

That is a very strange verse by any standard. It suggests that the speaker was a provider of gold, an alchemist disengaging it from other lesser minerals in his crucible. Wasn't it Moses who refined gold? (p.63) And what is this ointment without which there can be no revelation?

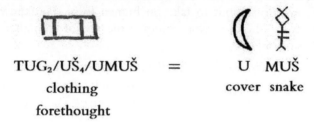

TUG₂/UŠ₄/UMUŠ   =   U   MUŠ

clothing   cover   snake

forethought

TUG₂ has some other interesting phonetic values of which UŠ₄ which links it to UŠ, symbol of the phallus, to UŠ₂, symbol of death, and to Osiris, gatekeeper of the dead. Phonetic UMUŠ is listed next to the meanings 'forethought' and 'planning'. UMUŠ is the phonetic form of TUG₂ which hides the serpent at its heart; lexical entries break it down to U, the cover, with MUŠ, the snake (p.181). One interpretation gives 'He or she who wears the snake as a head-covering possesses the capacity to foresee and prepare...'

The translation to 'consciousness' in the Tree of Consciousness and Knowledge took into account all aspects of the symbol: its most obvious link to clothing as well as to awareness and planning. I was also mindful of Plato's account of the hiding of truth under fine garments in order to deceive, to avoid the merited judgement at the time of death, perhaps to shed one's skin in the manner of the snake and to avoid death altogether. Of course, it all depends on MUSH being pure snake.

Sumerian Eve

To find the symbol for clothing and consciousness next to the Tree is one thing. Finding it collocated with the symbol for a female equates to meeting the original Eve in person:

SAL–TUG₂
The Clothed Lady

In orthodox translations, SAL–TUG₂ is given as the goddess or priestess Nin, from phonetic NIN attributed to the above duo. In Sumerian lexicons, she is 'Lady', 'mistress', 'owner' and, strangely, 'Lord'.

The word SAL has more generally been used in an overly literal, unnuanced manner, i.e. as a reference to female genitalia and sexuality rather than to any inherent qualities that might come with the female condition or form. I have added 'fine' into my own lexicon with the French term 'finesse' in mind, delicacy as opposed to brute force. It is obvious why a language seeking to reference 'male' and 'female' would have used the penis and the vulva for that purpose. That does not infer that the text in which they are found has anything to do with those body parts or the sexual act per se.

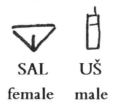

SAL   UŠ
female   male

UŠ is a word related to strength and virility, and has the given meanings 'male', 'penis' and 'to lean', to which can be added 'to thrust'. SAL is a chamber (French salle) in which reproduction takes place, the place in which consciousness might be said to take form. This is the chamber to which the sun god retires during the three days and nights of resting at the winter solstice.[1] SAL is also source of 'salvation' and 'salve', the arts of the female healer, while UŠ became the Greek suffix for male names.

A telling example of SAL employed in a superficial and even ludicrous manner comes in that salacious portion of the text known as *Enki and Ninhursaga* (p.28):

Ninhursaga hastened to the temple. The Anuna slipped off her garment, made ......, determined its destiny and .... Ninhursaga made Enki sit by her vagina. [1]

The so-called goddess Ninhursaga stems from SAL-TUG₂ followed by HUR/HAR-SAG (which together can be a reference to a top millstone, also celestial, but have the given meaning 'mountain' and 'foothills'):

SAL-TUG₂   HUR/HAR   SAG
                         HOR   head

Chamber of Awareness

The truly bizarre vagina reference stems from a repetition of SAL in the original transliteration and a contrived context. Admittedly, it is more than probable that Latin salax which led to 'salacious' does have its source in this symbol, but the key lies in rediscovering the original context.

SAL as 'chamber' is qualified by TUG₂, both 'hearing' and 'consciousness', Together they refer to the womb and to the harmonic properties of certain locations, temples, caves, places with particular acoustic properties in which it is possible to enter a state of trance, first step on the path to shamanic enlightenment.

HUR is also phonetic HAR, source symbol of the place name Harran but also origin of the word 'harmonic'. I further equate it to the main element of the ancient name of the Sphinx at Giza: HOR (p.92) which, thanks to SAG, might constitute a reference to the head of that monument: a chamber of resonance inside the head of the Great Sphinx? Without context, it is worthy of mention but, of course, far from proven. Nevertheless, there is more to both Nin and SAL, the Lady of the Mountains and Foothills, than she has so far been given credit for (also see Persephone and Kore p.169).

The Ear

Anyone who has an ear should listen to what the Spirit says to the churches. (Revelation 2:7)

In my fictional account of the scribe, TUG₂ was a reference to the musical beat that ordered the rhythmic movements of the mill workers as they passed the wool from hand to hand. But of course, it is more than that. There are numerous enigmatic mentions of the need to listen closely in coded messages scattered throughout biblical writings and also in the Norse mythologies. For example:

She knows that Heimdall's hearing is hidden
under the radiant, sacred tree.
She sees, pouring down, the muddy torrent
from the wager of Father of the Slain; do you
understand yet, or what more? [1]

GEŠ-TUG₂ easily translates to 'Tree of Hearing' and it is my contention that line 260 of *The Story of Sukurru* is a different, earlier version of that enigmatic Norse tale:

Under the flying stone, Father by the rope of the Tree of Consciousness and Knowledge, the light vessel, bear witness before Ia to multiply Her waters.

The Norse words 'Pouring down, the muddy torrent' correspond to Sumerian 'multiply Her waters' from symbols I-A. The equivalent of the Norse wager (or pledge in other translations) is found in the Sumerian 'bear witness'. The final line in the Norse text 'Do you understand yet, or what more?' indicates the presence of a riddle as does the lending of an ear in Revelation 2:7. Both the Norse and the Sumerian quotes find their counterpart in the well-attested image of Mesopotamian fish gods holding their ropes on either side of the sacred tree.

A Perfect Pitch

Greek 'ous', and 'ous' meaning 'ear' is remarkably close to one of the phonetic forms of TUG₂ which also has the given meaning 'ear':

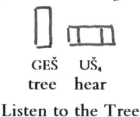

GEŠ   UŠ₄
tree   hear

Listen to the Tree

PI

WA, WE, WI, WU, YA, YE, YI, YU

PI comes with a large family of phonetic values and is represented in different ways, all corresponding to a central T-shape with either triangular forms like this one or straight vertical lines rising above. It can even be seen as a pair of 'rabbit' ears without the added vertical line.

Given meanings for this sign include 'to expand' and 'to diminish'. PI represents perfection or the search for perfection, attained through adjustment. As a musician tunes the strings of their instrument before launching into a sublime performance, so a scribe strives to generate an immaculate form of the written word, a precise meaning, a perfectly copied text. Also given as SAG-ŠU, translatable to 'the leader who shows', PI is found balanced on top of SAG, the head, in a variety of styles:

Although the above five images are given as SAG x PI, they might be seen as heads with horns rather than ears. The second image, found on more than one tablet, seems to indicate a transformation from the somewhat human form into UR, the dog. The three on the right come from the slightly later period of Uruk III. An evocative combination of sagacity and perfection.

Music Of The Pleiades

PI is found with EL, which has the given meaning 'pure', on line 35 of *The Story of Sukurru*. Together they form the basis for the name of the Pleiades, the prominent, easily identified cluster of seven stars that shine in the constellation of Taurus and figure on a number of Mesopotamian seals.

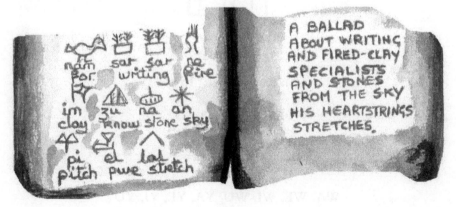

The following is written about this line in *Before Babel The Crystal Tongue*:

the hero is seduced, not by the beauty of a companion, but by a song about clay tablets and writing. PI alone might signify 'perfection' but with EL, it goes one step beyond, perhaps to ecstasy…(…) Pitch is the word I favour for the symbol. It would have had a more general sense at its origin, broader than 'musical', extended to 'resonance'.

This section of text refers to the same original story that gave biblical Moses on the mountain listening to the voice of God. In fact, the presence of the double SAR (p.97) offers the possibility that Moses and Musarus began life here as one figure, as Musar.

IM/EM, the clay, and NI_2, with given meaning 'self', are almost identical symbols and interchangeable, resulting in the underlying meaning of 'self-knowledge'.[1] That there is a reference to the Pleiades and their musical skills in line 35 is confirmed by other Sumerian writings, notably a proverb comprising seven lines in which the fine tuning of a song is carried out to seduce seven different characters. As is the case in *The Story of Sukurru*, the theme of the song varies to correspond to the individual interests of each profession, with PI-EL, the pure pitch, repeated seven times.[2]

Line 125 of *Enki's Journey to Nibru* mentions the seven houses of music through other symbols and is particularly interesting in that it also contains the words SI-DI, the equal horns, source of Siddhi, a Vedic term for perfection (p.59-60). In a context of astronomy/astrology and with a little coaxing, that line translates to:

The seven lofty houses of music (Pleiades) their perfection (SI-DI) gives the rhythm for the rotation of the land (MA).

E_2 BALAG LUL

BALAG is one of those rare pictograms which can be identified as the origin of a string instrument and 'balalaika' just by its aspect. Hidden behind a deceptive phonetic form 'tigi' in the transliteration, the trickster fox, transliterated here as LUL, source of 'to lull' and 'lullaby' but also seen slinking around as phonetic NAR, source of French 'renard', is found with his string instrument, in this case, the lyre of Orpheus. Here too is found the origin of the word 'narcotic', a drug to sooth, to lull into sleep. The fox and instrument are unmistakable through both their phonetic (renard and balalaika) and their pictographic forms, but no longer recognisable in any way on the cuneiform tablets of the much later Old Babylonian period where the line of text was found, demonstrating the importance of peeling back the layers. The lexical lists offer up an intriguing link to UB, the pentagram symbol [1], potentially giving NA-AR₂ as 'angled stone', 'the angle of the stone', 'the cornerstone':

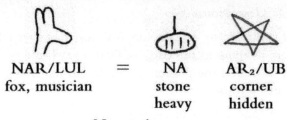

NAR/LUL	=	NA	AR₂/UB
fox, musician		stone	corner
		heavy	hidden

Nar–cotic
Lul–laby

The following brings confirmation of that correspondence between the music, the seven and the Pleiades, the only difference being that this was written in Greek:

Others say that when Mercurius [Hermes] first made the lyre on Mount Cyllene in Arcadia, he made it with seven strings to correspond to the number of Atlantides [Pleiades], since Maia, his mother, was of their company. [2]

At the same time, the Sumerian writings link the story of Moses and the Tablets of Wisdom (line 35 of *The Story of Sukurru*) to the music of Orpheus and to the Pleiades. Looking once again at the three symbols of the Tree of Consciousness and Knowledge, a more complete interpretation:

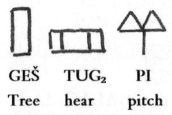

GEŠ	TUG₂	PI
Tree	hear	pitch

Tree through which to hear and to become aware of the purity of the musical pitch, and to become conscious of perfection.

But what or who is the Tree?

Mediterranean Nuraghes

Norm: "a standard, pattern, or model," 1821 (Coleridge), from French norme, from Latin norma "carpenter's square, rule, pattern," a word of unknown origin.

'Nuraghe' is the name given to the ancient conical stone towers found all over Sardinia, a large island in the Mediterranean Sea. Local tradition has it that they were built by the lost civilisation of the Nuragics and they are thought to date to ca. 1900 BC. Sardinia is home to around seven thousand of the impressive constructions, but it's not impossible that there were as many as ten thousand at some point. Nuraghes are not small buildings. They stand anywhere between twenty and thirty metres high. The reason or reasons for their existence is unknown.

It should come as no surprise at this point that 'nuraghe' is derived, like so many other words, from the Sumerian mother tongue, language of the Mediterranean islands and surrounding continents, of the Greeks and Romans. NUR is a multiple of NUN, central symbol of the so-called Anunnaki. Another derivative of NUR, Latin norma, suggests that tall structures of this type served as a means of measurement, an array of towers mirroring the patterns made by groups of stars and marking out on land the garden perceived in the night sky, a formal garden on Earth reflecting an Eden

111

above. It's a theory. The reader of this must decide for themselves how likely it is to be true.

The Italian island of Sardinia possesses a great number of megaliths and is said to be the island of the giants who once inhabited our planet, a place where huge skeletons have purportedly been found. There are ruins of Neolithic burial chambers made of large blocks of granite and limestone dated to around 1800 BC. More generally, Sardinia has a history of occupation going back to 9000 BC and the source of its name has become lost in the mists of time.

Sardinia: large island west of Italy, Latin, from Greek Sardo; perhaps named for the local Iberian people who settled there; the original form and meaning of the name is lost. A Punic (Phoenician) stelle from 7c. B.C.E. refers to it as Shardan. The oblique cases are sometimes Sardonos, etc., as if from Sardon.

Two words already mentioned in relation to Musarus Oannes (p.96) provide the most likely origin of this island's name:

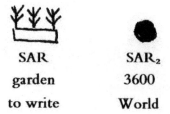

SAR	SAR₂
garden	3600
to write	World

SAR is both the garden and the writing that was once done there. If my analysis is correct, Greek sardo stems from both SAR-DU and SAR²-DU. To establish a formal garden implies first measuring out the ground plan by striding around on DU, the foot.

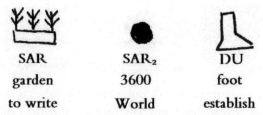

SAR	SAR₂	DU
garden	3600	foot
to write	World	establish

DUB-SAR is given numerous times with the meaning 'scribe' while DUB, the tablet, appears in lexical entries broken down to DU-UB, with the given meanings 'to establish' and 'corner', a reference to both the boundary stones of the planned garden and the angular writing by means of a stylus on clay:

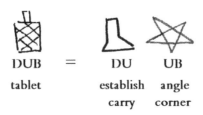

DUB = DU UB

tablet | establish | angle
| carry | corner

UB has the given meanings 'corner' and 'recess'. It refers to angles and is the source of words that begin 'ob'; such as 'obelisk' but also 'obscure'. According to the lexicons, UB can also read as 'mound' and 'to enunciate', both of them relative to the nuraghes and to the writing.

DUB is a reference to the dimensions of the original garden of Eden as noted on the tablet of the Lord. The verb 'to dub', to give a name, comes from there.

An extended translation of DU-UB might read '*enunciate the dimensions of the mound*' or alternatively '*the mound that serves to announce the corners/dimensions*'. Latin enunciatus carries several evocative meanings beyond 'enunciate' and 'speaking up'. In more occult terms, the association of a pentagram through Sumerian UB with its given meaning 'enunciate' leads on to enunciatus as 'divulge, disclose, reveal and betray'. But I prefer to keep my feet firmly in the beauty of a formal garden where the written word will openly flourish, revealing all its angles and perfect symmetry.

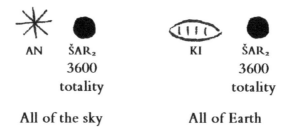

AN | ŠAR₂ | KI | ŠAR₂
| 3600 | | 3600
| totality | | totality

All of the sky | **All of Earth**

With AN, the sky, ŠAR₂ is given in lexicons as 'the entirety of heaven'. My own translation of these two together would be 'the sky as 3600 (360?) degree circle' or 'the entirety of the sky to measure'. With KI, symbol of 'Earth', it's given as 'the whole of Earth' leading to 'the whole of Earth to measure'. This is the domain of the star-gazers, those who measured absolutely everything above and below, and wrote it all down in one form or another. Is AN-ŠAR the source of 'answer'? Etymological dictionaries can't tell us. They don't have the answer to that one either.

113

If the NUN of Anunnaki was the proper name of a group of beings, then the Sardinian nuraghe appears to be the only existent name in the world that derives directly from theirs, from a multiple of NUNs to NUR to nuraghe, from KA-NUN the canon (p.68) to 'announce', and from NUR to 'norm', 'announcing the norm'. I propose that these are they, the Nuragics... and that the island of Sardinia was one of the original lands in which they worked their stones and their magic, if not the first.

Ziggurats Of Sardinia ?

In 1880, Archibald Sayce and Robert Bosanquet published news of the two Mul Apin tablets containing the earliest evidence of detailed cuneiform writings on the subject of astronomy, identifying the constellations. Since that time, it has been taken for granted that such knowledge originated in Babylon, city in the south of Mesopotamia, home of Berossus and of the Chaldean rulers, in a region called Sumer.

There are no complete tablets, only fragments that were painstakingly pieced together to reconstruct the original MUL APIN text, but there can be no doubt about the type of information contained in them. A date for the so-called Babylonian copy puts it at around the 1000 BC mark, perhaps slightly earlier or later. The British Museum copy is dated to somewhere between 1000 BC and 500 BC. If the remarks made by King Nabonasar of Babylon and reported by Berossus (p.51) are taken into account - as they must be - the truth about the original sages, the proof of their place of origin along with their original records and methods of documenting the night skies are well and truly lost. This is all we have. But absence of proof is not proof of absence.

If the first Chaldeans were not uniquely Babylonian, then the linguistic evidence points to a headquarters in Harran in the first half of the 3rd millennium BC. And before that? And parallel to that? Who were the people inhabiting the islands and the coasts of the Mediterranean Sea before 1800 BC? Were they also magicians of the skies, and related to the astronomers of Harran? Were the Nuragics of Sardinia also SHA-BI, Beer-Hearts, Sabians, or their cousins?

The mighty Assyrian Dictionary of the University of Chicago, which is now available for consultation online, has two mentions of 'ziqqurrat' under the entry 'zaqaru', 'to build high', and that's it. Nevertheless, it's the word commonly used - without the slightest hesitation - to designate mudbrick tiered towers, the Mesopotamian equivalents of the Egyptian pyramids. No trace of the word trickles down into translations of the writings of Herodotus who went into great detail about the layout of Babylon. His words in the English translations are given as 'tower' and 'temple'. What I did find was just a couple of lexical entries giving the source symbols that became the commonly used word 'ziggurat'.[1] Either I didn't look in the right place – and I wait to be corrected - or there is overuse of the word 'ziggurat' in translations of the Sumero-Akkadian texts.

Looking into translated texts which include the word 'ziggurat', it became apparent that these were not the symbols given in the majority of the original transliterations. Most translations to 'ziggurat' are not taken from symbols reading phonetic ZI-IG-GUR-RA or any other similar combination. They are taken from a phrase which includes the double symbol of Anunnaki fame: NUR. They are all based on transliterations of two symbols ŠI, the 'eye' and E_2, the 'temple' which together became phonetic U_6 and to which is added NIR/NUR, double symbol of NUN.

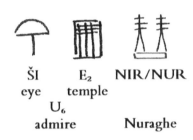

ŠI	E_2	NIR/NUR
eye	temple	

U_6

admire   Nuraghe

The given meaning of ŠI-E_2 is 'admiration', but it translates literally to 'the eye of the temple', presumably the topmost point of the nuraghe or any other manmade mound from which to admire and to collect information on the night sky – unless the eye is a metaphor for a light, representing the beam from a lighthouse. The 'eye of the temple' brings to mind the eye above the pyramid found on the dollar bill and commonly linked to an occult message of some kind. In terms of the Egyptian pyramids, it recalls the elusive benben stone, the topmost point.

In the lexical lists, U_6 is found opposite symbols that became 'ziggurat':[1]

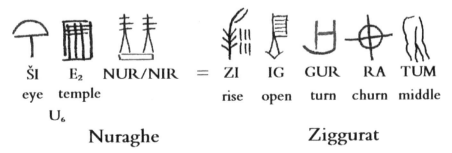

ŠI	E_2	NUR/NIR	=	ZI	IG	GUR	RA	TUM
eye	temple			rise	open	turn	churn	middle

U_6

        Nuraghe   Ziggurat

Is it possible that Mesopotamian towers were, like the Sardinian nuraghes, once known simply as 'nur' or perhaps 'unir' and that they acquired that

115

curiously rare name 'ziggurat' only in relatively modern times? Unless there is evidence of its existence in some intermediary Greek, Latin, or Arabic writings, the multi-syllabic word 'ziggurat' appears to be a modern interpretation. Granted that Sardinian nuraghes don't compare in size to what we can still see of the Mesopotamian mudbrick mounds but still...we might be closer to their original name if we were to replace 'ziggurat' with 'nur' or 'unir' − which was most likely one of the sources for Latin unire, 'to unite'.

AROUND AND AROUND WE GO O

en an nu
end sky not
year knot

dim₂
create

hu hi ra
bird round rat
wheal churn

mu un na
age land stone
moon heavy

du du du du
foot foot foot foot
sailor bring

gi eš
reed three
lum

THE END-OF-THE
SKY KNOT SHE
CREATED,

THAT THE BIRD
AND THE RAT
ON THE HEAVY
MOON CHURNING,

THE TWO SAILORS
THEIR FOUR FEET
TREADING...

THREE WILL
TURN...

117

Riddles Of The Sphinx

What goes on four feet in the morning, two feet at noon, and three feet in the evening? [1]

In Oedipus Rex, a tragedy written by the Greek playwright Sophocles, ca.429 BC, the young hero encounters the Sphinx in Thebes and is challenged with solving the riddle before being allowed to pass by. According to most accounts, the answer is 'mankind' because the baby crawls on all fours, an adult uses two feet, and the old man has a stick, making three. That answer seems logical but something of a let-down. It lacks complexity. Not overly evident but still too easy to be of great interest. It can even be seen as false in that man has only two feet at any age. And why did the Sphinx feel the need to kill itself over such a trivial defeat rather than simply stand aside to allow Oedipus to continue on to his own terrible fate? I don't know the answer but it strikes me as strange. There is more to the story than meets the eye. The following comment made by a 16th century alchemist, Michael Maier, writing on the obscure subject of the quest for the Philosopher's Stone, pours a different light on the subject:

The Sphinx is indeed reported to have had many Riddles, but this offered to Oedipus was the chief, "What is that which in the morning goeth upon four feet; upon two feet in the afternoon; and in the Evening upon three?" What was answered by Oedipus is not known. But they who interpret concerning the Ages of Man are deceived. For a Quadrangle of Four Elements are of all things first to be considered, from thence we come to the Hemisphere having two lines, a Right and a Curve, that is, to the White Luna; from thence to the Triangle which consists of Body, Soul and Spirit, or Sol, Luna and Mercury. Hence Rhasis in his Epistles, "The Stone," says he, "is a Triangle in its essence, a Quadrangle in its quality." [2]

That sounds more interesting. Line 10 of *The Path to Sky-End* (aka *Enki's Journey to Nibru*) shown above (p.117) takes the form of a riddle showing some remarkable similarities to the Riddle of the Sphinx. My sketch shows the considerably more ancient Sumerian riddle as I left it after weeks of puzzling. It isn't solved but one thing is certain; it refers to the 'ring of the year' through symbols AN-NU, 'sky' and 'knot', source of Latin annul, meaning 'to make to nothing', Latin annus, the 'year', and French anneau, the 'ring'. From that and other elements, it became apparent that line 10 of *Enki's Journey to Nibru* was likely the most ancient of the riddles attached to the figure of the Sphinx.

AN   **NU**
sky   knot

The Sky Knot

All Is One

One is the Serpent which has its poison according to two compositions, and One is All and through it is All, and by it is All, and if you have not All, All is Nothing.[1]

The serpent biting its tail is just one of a wide variety of images on the same theme of the perpetual knot of time from different cultures over millennia and the details of the 16th century illustration with the addition of four paws and the head of a crested bird used as the underlying illustration of my translation correspond quite eerily to elements of this Sumerian puzzle, perhaps an alchemical and/or geometrical formula as suggested by Maier.

The two DU.DU symbols in the Sukurru riddle translate to 'two sailors' with four feet between them. Do they also correspond to the two sailors caught up in another complicated knot carved onto the façade of the altogether fascinating church at Kilpeck in England? [2] The so-called Gordian knot, a problem solved not by disentangling but by cutting straight through, also takes its roots in Sumerian: notably with GUR, the 'twisting' and 'turning' (p.115), one syllable of 'ziggurat'. My suggestion is that, despite their spread across time and cultures, the knotted enigmas have their origins in just one source.

The name 'ouroboros', given to the snake biting its own tail, is said to stem from Greek 'oura' with the meaning "tail' or 'rear' to which is added -boros

meaning 'eating'. In fact, it doesn't appear to be the case that the name ouroboros was used by the ancient Greeks. The earliest known written mention of the beast is that of Servius in Latin in the 4th century AD and it is perhaps significant that he did not mention the ouroboros by that name, writing simply that the image existed before the invention of the alphabet and could be called 'year'.[3]

The oldest known images[1] of the circular snake were, until now, those found on the shrine enclosing the mummified body of the young pharaoh Tutankhamun who died ca.1235 BC. Two snakes encircle the figure, one around his head and the other around his feet. That Egyptian ouroboros comprises a couple of fascinating elements from a Sumerian viewpoint; two pairs of detached legs and feet facing towards him on either side on both versions – an Egyptian equivalent of DU.DU-DU.DU, the double symbol of the foot, the two sailors, the four feet – and a discreet bird next to the serpent's tail on the upper image, the Sumerian HU.

One important fact has been missed in common accounts of the serpent image. The ouroboros was inscribed on clay in Mesopotamia during the 4th millennium BC. This tablet,[2] although severely damaged and showing only a part of the scene, provides the evidence. Overall, it gives the impression that more than one snake is involved and that the knot is quite complex. They are weaving around symbol EZEN (p.81). Fortunately, the detail here showing the head biting the tail is recognisable and, although the long sinuous body is that of a snake, the head with beak looks more like a water bird, perhaps a duck or goose. Was this Sumerian ouroboros inscribed on a clay tablet by a primitive trader in a Mesopotamian world still taking baby steps towards civilisation as conventional accounts of the Sumerian pictograms would have us believe? Probably not.

Why would they? It is my contention that images of this kind are the remnants of knowledge from a pre-existing literate group of people, some of whom had the good idea of copying them onto clay from 3500 BC onwards.

The ouroboros image[2] with 'Hen Tu Pan' meaning 'All is One' written at its centre was found on a manuscript from around the 10th to 12th century AD, a copy of the work of a famed alchemist called Cleopatra of Alexandria. She is thought to have lived during the 3rd century AD. and to have been one of just four female alchemists capable of producing the philosopher's stone, whatever that might be.

The Chrysopoeia of Cleopatra comprises three mysterious sets of symbols of which this well-known ouroboros.[1] The explanation for the presence and the

positioning of the three words at its heart must surely be that Cleopatra had knowledge of original Hermetic alchemical texts or, at the very least, some precious Greek magical papyri derived from them. The papyri are documents dating to the early 1st millennium AD written in various languages and dealing with a great variety of spells and rituals. Note that she was present in Alexandria at a time when the library there was probably still in existence, even if in its final decline. What was it that Cleopatra studied there?

An Enduring Bird

This is a story of continuity, of the enduring nature of things, of ideas, of unbreakable links between people from far different times. The river Tigris, along with its twin the Euphrates, takes its source in the Taurus mountains not far from the slopes of Gobekli Tepe in south-eastern Turkey. No doubt the people of that region so close to Harran, those Lords of the Stones, were fully conscious of the precious gift that the rivers represented. Their water-carved gullies were already age-old when the masons of Gobekli Tepe first hoisted huge T-shaped stones into place there, in or before 9600 BC. They sculpted two birds onto the most intriguing pillar discovered at the site. The topmost bird was given a distinctive head; an eye, a curved beak and neck rings. The lower bird was left headless. Pillar 43 had lain beneath ground for some six thousand years when, on the earliest Sumerian tablets ca.3350 BC, the river Tigris was first referenced as the full-frontal image of a bird, sometimes with a head, sometimes without.

There are a couple of points to keep in mind before reading what follows. The first is that the people who sculpted and erected the huge stones at Gobekli Tepe had a language. Every time they heaved a block into place, there was communication which went beyond any primitive grunting and pointing. The evidence lies in the sophistication of their communal work. These people spoke. They had words – words that necessarily existed in sufficient quantity and intricacy of meaning for them to plan and carry out the construction. The second point to remember is that Sumerian was once the language of the entire region of Mesopotamia, from north to south. Whether expressed in modern textbooks as Sumerian or Akkadian, the later cuneiform version, it is the same language built from the same original pictograms. There is every reason to accept that proto-Sumerian was by far the most probable form of verbal communication between the people who built Gobekli Tepe.

GU₂/TIG

gulley

throat

GU₂/TIG, is one of three symbols comprising the Sumero-Akkadian name for the fiercer of the two rivers which became known as Tigris. It takes over from the earlier bird image. In *Before Babel The Crystal Tongue*, I posit that symbol GU₂ replicates an element on pillar 43, namely the neck-ring of the central bird, also a full-frontal image, carved in bas relief there.[1]

GU₂, has the given meaning 'gulley', a channel carved out of the mountains by running water, extending easily and reasonably to the bird's 'gullet', and more generally 'throat' or 'neck'. The same symbol is given as phonetic DUR when combined with symbol KAK, the 'nail' or 'peg' of the 'builder' at its centre. Thus, we have a symbol which, both visually and linguistically, represents a gullet, a throat with a nail or peg at its centre. KAK takes the form of a downward pointing triangle, a keystone. Presented here below as an alternative striated symbol found at the earliest period and side by side for clarity: Phonetic DUR (photo p.132) has the following all-important given meanings:

GU₂ x KAK
gullet x nail

DUR

binding, knot, bond, tie, umbilical cord, totality

123

The name given to Gobekli Tepe, the 'pot-bellied hill', stems from Turkish 'gobek' which translates to 'navel'.[1] In turn, the navel is inherently linked with the umbilical cord, the binding between mother and child. The strong links between the written Sumerian words GU₂ and DUR and that now famous bird on pillar 43 are not imagined. The Sumerian symbol for the mountain gorge or gulley leads directly to the ancient site of Gobekli Tepe at every level. It is irrefutable. The only question is 'Which came first?' A reminder:

→ The neck rings of the carved bird, unusually detailed in comparison to other bas-relief animals at the site closely correspond to the symbol, including KAK, the nail, despite the six to seven thousand years separating the images.

→ GU₂ has the given meaning 'gorge' which is synonymous of 'gulley' or 'throat', the 'gulley' carved by cascading rivers, corresponding to its position on the bird's gullet.[1]

→ GU₂ carries the phonetic value TIK/TIG, and is the middle element of the Sumero-Akkadian three-symbol name given to the river Tigris,

→ A full-frontal bird symbol - with and without a head – is given as 'Tigris' on three of the earliest Sumerian tablets. All have slightly extended wings,

→ the proximity of the region of Harran and Gobekli Tepe to the source of the rivers,

→ the corresponding meanings of Turkish Gobek and Armenian Portasar, the navel, and Sumerian DUR, the umbilical cord.

→ Sumerian was the language of Mesopotamia.

KAK is the nail in the middle of the throat of the bird, the knot of time binding Earth and the heavens. The bird is the link, the conduit.

DUR is the source of Latin durus, meaning 'hard', 'difficult' and Medieval Latin durationem, the source of 'duration' and 'during', a measure of time.

DUR is the umbilical cord binding humanity to the cosmic Matriarch at Gobekli Tepe and at all those places where the stones stand upright. This is the story of the enduring bird who has the difficult task of flying up to perpetuate that bond, the rope held firmly in its beak, the fool riding on its back. In *The Story of Sukurru*, a humorous version of an otherwise lost age-old tale, it is identified as both DAR and A-HU, the water birds, (p.211) and in one instance as DU.DU which gives the source of both the sailor and the dodo in that tale.[2]

It goes almost without saying that DUR, a peg or nail inside a gulley or throat, is a direct reference to the concept behind the age-old image of the serpent biting its own tail, the so-called ouroboros understood throughout the ages as a magical symbol, associated with Gnosticism, Hermeticism, and with the equally enigmatic concept of the Philosopher's Stone. By association, the bird on Pillar 43 can be linked to the mysteries of alchemy. Indeed, it might be said that the bird, thanks to its great age, gives the origin of all magical proceedings. Who came first? The Gobekli Tepe bird or the written word? Sumerian DUR, the 'eternal knot', or the bandana around its neck?

The HEN Of Pan

PA/HENDUR

The Wings

HEN does not figure alone as a phonetic value for any Sumerian symbol in the modern lexicons. However, it's not a coincidence that HENDUR (also ENDUR) is one phonetic value of symbol PA, root of both 'pagan' and 'Pan'. PA has disparate given meanings of which 'instructor' and 'wing'. It can also mean 'branch', 'sceptre', 'to disperse' or 'breath', the breath of life as symbolised by the pipes of Pan. The word takes the form of a pair of wings.

Phonetic HENDUR in the lexical lists takes its source in three symbols, HI-EN-DUR and, unsurprisingly, we find that the DUR of the enduring umbilical cord along with KAK, its nail, is hidden inside:

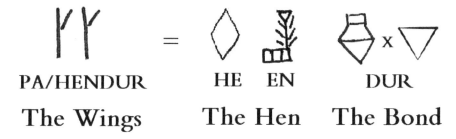

HI/HE is given as 'mix', easily identified as an alchemical term, taking the form of a rhombus, natural entrance to the spirit realm, likely the first syllable of 'heaven' and also 'hymen'. This is the original version of the rhombus surrounding the 'heavenly' Madonna in religious depictions. It's also the HE of Greek Hebe (p.86) and the place from which the hen's egg will arrive.

Given in Sumerian lexicons as 'Lord', EN is discussed in the context of Genesis (p.79). Both EN and HE-EN are source symbols of Greek 'hen', also 'en', meaning 'one'. HE, the 'mixing' of the elements, also given as 'goodness' and 'sweet', is carried out by EN, the Lord and the One:

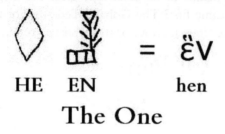

HE   EN   hen

The One

EN, the 'Lord', read as 'the One' provides a glimpse into the origins of Hermetic teachings, evidence of the existence of Hermeticism in the 3rd millennium BC, a fact fully accepted by medieval alchemists but successfully refuted in the 17th century on the grounds of lack of original written sources. Those sources had been copied and recopied – no doubt with great care and with infinite respect - but in 1614, the authoritative announcement by a Swiss citizen named Isaac Casaubon that none of the copies dated back further than the 1st or 2nd centuries AD succeeded slowly but surely in diminishing the prestige of documents hitherto understood to have been handed down from the original Egyptian magicians, from Thoth himself. That is how the destructive forces of time, perhaps coupled with ill intent and certainly with a hefty dose of cynicism, finally succeeded in damning the Great Magician to obscurity. But absence of proof is not proof of absence. Thanks to the old clay tablets, everything here above comes directly from the source with one exception. I have nothing on the HEN apart perhaps an egg… (p.132)

EN-E and E-NE, found at the heart of both Genesis and the Tenet of the Sator Square, is 'the Lord on high', 'the lofty One', 'Lord of the Levee'. This is the energy, the highest river source of the universe, the perpetual ending and beginning, another way of expressing the Gnostic serpent biting its tail. The presence of Sumerian EN next to DUR, (components of HENDUR), signals the origin of 'enduring', a quality that most certainly applies to the famous bird of pillar 43 and to the entirety of the fabulous Gobekli Tepe site:

Endure: late 14c., "to undergo or suffer" (especially without breaking); also "to continue in existence," from Old French endurer (12c.) "make hard, harden; bear, tolerate; keep up, maintain," (…) from PIE root

126

Nails Of Truth

This analysis stays firmly and unashamedly within the age-old nest of the Gobekli Tepe bird and the three offering baskets placed above it. And it is no flight of fancy. The meanings of the Sumerian words are all founded in existing lexicon entries. Further analysis of another phonetic form of KAK adds the concept of an offering into the mix. KAK, the nail or peg contained in DUR and visible on the neck of the Gobekli Tepe bird, is also phonetic HENBUR, leading to the rediscovery of BUR, the stone offering bowl. The HEN of KAK/HENBUR connects neatly back to PA/HENDUR. A reminder:

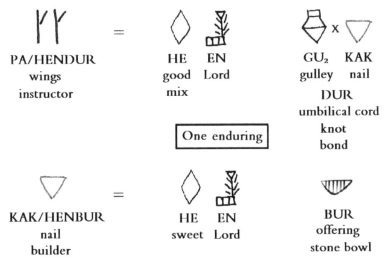

PA/HENDUR	=	HE	EN		GU₂	KAK
wings		good	Lord		gulley	nail
instructor		mix				DUR
						umbilical cord
		One enduring				knot
						bond

KAK/HENBUR	=	HE	EN		BUR
nail		sweet	Lord		offering
builder					stone bowl

BUR can also be read as PUR/POR, potentially giving the origin of the Armenian name for the site, Portasar which, like Turkish Gobek, has the meaning 'navel'. Do these connections prove that the people who carved pillar 43 were aware of the concept of the ouroboros? It looks very much that way. This sketch was made from one of the tablets inscribed during the Uruk IV period ca.3350-3200 BC. The word has the given meanings 'ring', 'crown', 'fierce' and 'bird' and is the original Sumerian name for the river Tigris. Other versions are increasingly headless. Later versions are composed of three cuneiform words of which GU₂/TIG and, by extension, KAK and DUR.

Does a sculpted bird decorated with a neck ring from 11,600 years ago in Mesopotamia correspond to a pictograph of a bird on clay tablets inscribed 5,200 years ago also in Mesopotamia? And if it does, at what point in time was the distinctive neck ring noted and used to illustrate the word that sounded like 'gu' or 'go' having the fundamental meaning of 'gorge', 'gulley', 'gush'...? Until a second bird with the same or similar markings from an intermediary period comes to light, the reader of this must consider the evidence presented here and decide for themselves.

The Word

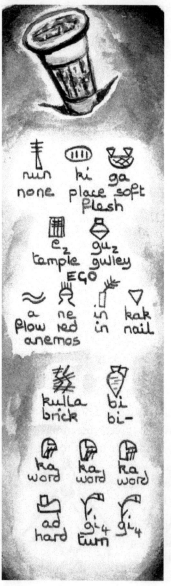

In the beginning was the Word, and the Word was with God, and the Word was God. (John 1:1)

$$\bigtriangledown = \text{KA} \quad \text{AK}$$

KAK   **KA**   **AK**
nail   word   to do

Taking the analysis one step further, the lexical lists indicate that KAK derives from KA, the 'word', with AK, the 'action', together giving 'the word to do'. KAK is the Word in action, the nail, the central peg, keystone holding the celestial construction in place.[1] I translated:

in the red hot windy gulley to nail...

The meaning behind the scribe's choice of symbols on lines 13 and 14 of *The Path to Sky-End* is reinforced by the emphatic repetition of KA, the 'word', on line 14:

$$\text{KA} \quad \text{KA} \quad \text{KA}$$

And harsh words around the cone will turn.

The bitter young hero is writing down his grievances (AD used here as 'adamant', 'hard stone'). E_2 with GU_2 as source of 'ego' stems from that overall context.[3] The four winds of the Greek Anemoi stem from A-NE, the hot or fiery flow. As for the profundity of meaning hidden in those carvings carried out shortly after the last ice age on pillar 43 at Gobekli

128

Tepe, we might look to the HEN TU PAN of Cleopatra's alchemical ouroboros sketch and consider the Mesopotamian origin of the verb 'to endure' and of 'ego'. Did the Gobekli Tepe bird seen balancing a round object on the tip of its outstretched wing represent the knot of time, the casting aside of ego before a feathered journey to the celestial Matriarch, or was it simply holding up a ball for a game of catch with endurance as a skill? The reader must decide for themselves. But first, please read the following words on the subject of KAK (also p.259 and the notes to p.128).

Plant Of Truth, Plant Of Thoth

Acacia: 1540s, type of shrub or tree fund in warm climates of Africa and Australia, from Latin acacia, from Greek akakia "thorny Egyptian tree, from PIE root(…)

A-KAK, 'the flow and the nail', and A-KA, 'flow of the word', give the origin of 'acacia', a thorny plant known since antiquity for its hallucinogenic properties. Ethnopharmacologist Dennis McKenna identified the tree carved onto a wall of the Temple of Amun[1] at Karnak in Egypt as being the acacia niotica, a tree particularly rich in dimethyltryptamine, a mind-altering chemical. KAK is more generally the source of 'cacti', all prickly plants. Symbol A is the Sumerian word for all that is liquid and flows. I suggest that the flow in this context is a reference to the use of the plant in shamanic brews and rituals. Bearing in mind the Sumerian penchant for riddles and the indication of a secret meaning (signalled by threefold repetition on line 14 above), these symbols together give a circular and potentially endless AKAKAKA.

The Teacher sought to find delightful sayings and write words of truth accurately. The words of the wise are like goads... (…) like firmly

129

embedded nails. The sayings are given by one Shepherd. (Ecclesiastes 12:10-11)

Building with nails or without posed a dilemma in the translating of line 269 of *The Story of Sukurru*. In context, a decision had to be made between 'not nail' or a 'knot to create'. In light of the above analyses, 'the knot to peg into place' would be acceptable, particularly as KAK takes the form of a keystone.

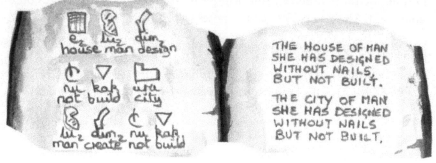

Eternal Knot Or Not?

Then the LORD said to Noah, "Enter the ark, you and all your household, for I have seen that you alone are righteous before Me in this generation. (Genesis 7:1)

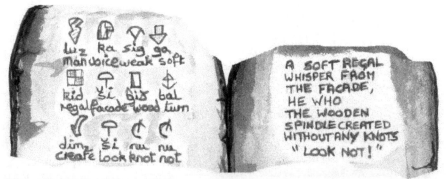

Line 65 of *The Story of Sukurru* offers the earliest known version of the instructions given to Noah for the building of his ark. It agrees with the Akkadian Atrahasis in that the message is whispered from behind a screen.

Any line of text containing GEŠ-BAL, the wooden spindle, is liable to contain a riddle (p.223). In this case, the repetition of NU is significant. 'Knot' is an Old English word of undetermined origin also found in Old Norse as 'knutr'. In context and in relation to the wood of the spindle, I found it irresistible – even if unnecessary - to use the second NU and add that the wood of the spindle was 'without any knots'. Was that the original intention of the scribe?

A perfect spindle made of the best wood is a pre-requisite for the weaving of wool and planets. But again, the reader of this must decide for themselves and perhaps before doing so, continue reading. There is more than one layer to the mystery of the voice giving instructions from behind his reed façade. The presence of GEŠ BAL tells us so.

NU is one of two symbols underlying the NUN of NUN-KI (p.70) while here on line 65 the twofold repetition turns it into an egg. The lexical entries inform us that two NUs make one NUNUZ:

NU	NU	=	NUNUZ/NUNU/NUS
knot	not		egg, bead

When is a knot not a knot? When it is an egg. NUNUZ, also NUNU/NUS, given as 'egg' and 'ovoid bead', is the symbol that figures with MI, meaning 'black' and 'night', to form GIG (p.170). We already knew that Noah was being offered life-saving knowledge of a forthcoming cataclysmic event. It may be that he was destined not only to ride out a flood in his round vessel but also to travel within the realm of gnosis.

ŠI-NU-NU in the context of line 65 offers a couple of tantalising underlying meanings: *'Don't look at the knot!', 'See the egg!'*. Is this a reference to the mycelium egg that gives birth to the amanita mushroom stalk or perhaps the elongated bead known as ergot, the wheat fungus? Is NUS source of Greek 'noos', a philosophical term meaning the faculty of understanding? Is it the stone egg held out on the wing of the bird on pillar 43 at Gobekli Tepe?

Line 66 continues the announcement of the coming flood and predicts the flight of the hero with his lofty bird (see the flying men p.148-149).

"FOR THE LEADER
IN WATER A LOFTY
DESTINY SHARED
WITH THE LOFTY
DODO, FLIGHT,
OF THE NOBLE"
—TEARS FROM THE
HEART OF THE
REED FACADE —
"AND BOTH FROM
THEIR HOMELAND
STONES ESTRANGED."

Images on clay tablets from the 4ᵗʰ millennium BC confirm that a solid connection existed between this language and the people who carved the stone circles of Gobekli Tepe. I insist. There was continuity at some level between 9600 BC and 3500 BC. These fragmented tablets dating to the Uruk III period, ca.3200-3000 BC add to that written evidence.

The symbol on the left of this one[1] is GEŠ, the tree, beside an image which has no known phonetic form but is distinguishable as an unfurled wing. To the right is DUR, the word resembling the neck markings of the Gobekli Tepe bird (p.123) and which has the given meanings 'umbilical cord' and 'bond' along with the underlying given meanings 'gulley' and 'nail' through GU₂/TIG.

Below DUR lies a faint but visible NUNUZ, the egg. I posit that these four symbols together form the linguistic representation of the bird on pillar 43 and that they stem from the same source tradition.

The combination of the tree and the unnamed wing appears on just two known and photographed tablets. Here is the other elegant and unmistakeable example from that same early period.[2] There is

the strong possibility that the wing and tree came together to form the pictogram which became both PAP and PA/HENDUR (p.90 and 127).

A Dog In Orbit

For example, an ancient belief prevailed throughout Greece that Caelus (Sky) [Ouranos (Uranus)] was mutilated by his son Saturnus [Kronos (Cronus)], and Saturnus himself thrown into bondage by his son Jove [Zeus] : now these immoral fables enshrined a decidedly clever scientific theory. Their meaning was that the highest element of celestial ether or fire [i.e. Ouranos], which by itself generates all things, is devoid of that bodily part which required union with another for the work of procreation. [2]

Aion is represented inside a celestial sphere decorated with the zodiacal signs.[3] Ouranos, partially sourced from Greek 'oura', the 'tail' or 'rear', has the meaning 'heaven' and 'sky' and, as attested by Cicero in the above extract, was the name of the first god in Greek mythology. It's not immediately obvious why a word meaning 'heaven' might have its source in 'tail' or 'rear' - if that is indeed the case – unless Ouranos is inherited from an earlier reference to the serpent biting its tail. Another name from the same source is Greek Urania, one of nine muses, her speciality being astronomy and celestial forces.

Ancient Greek 'oura' stems from UR/URA, the Sumerian word for both 'lion' and 'dog'. The symbol consists of a dog's head. It varies somewhat and here is one example. Given the Greek meaning of 'tail', the dog's head might seem an unlikely pairing...until the image of the ouroboros comes to mind. Heads or tails?

URA

dog, lion

unity

UR/URA is given as 'unity' in the lexicons, so both then. UR/URA, the dog/lion, is collocated with BI, the beer, more than once. I have surmised that the 'dog' was sometimes a euphemism for a drunk, the dog and its beer connoting the individual found slumped outside the city gates, lacking the wherewithal to articulate their name to get past the guards.

At the same time, UR/URA-BI are the founding symbols of 'orb' and 'orbit' through Latin orbis, 'circle' and 'ring'. I will stick my neck out and suggest that UR also constitutes the first syllable of Orpheus, the musician who was capable of charming everything that circled around him including – strangely - stones. Orpheus is also found through LUL/NAR, the fox and musician, the narcotics specialist (p.110).

Line 6 of *The Path to Sky-End* (aka *Enki's Journey to Nibru*) uses UR-BI in the context of the hero's preparations for his voyage to the skies where he intends to seduce the cosmic maiden Hebe with his beer-mixing skills. KAK appears again in final position. He thinks he has it nailed.

The comical figure of a dog wearing a coat of glowing orbs seen on a Minoan artefact was the obvious choice to illustrate that line. Could the strangely glowing, self-important creature presenting oil to the queen bee be a reference to that lost story? Is that a fish-skin coat covered in shining stars? And why three ears? And what exactly is in that oil of which it is so proud? Questions…questions.

IN THE NAME

OF THE

SNAKE

In Defence Of The Snake

The serpent said to the woman, 'You surely will not die! For God knows that in the day you eat from it your eyes will be opened, and you will be like God, knowing good and evil.' (Genesis 3:4)

The devious nature of the snake is borne out by its unfathomable ability to rear up without any help from arms or legs. It slides about in the undergrowth and coils itself menacingly around things. It stares us out unblinkingly. We have no idea what snakes think of us - if anything. They are unnerving creatures. But that doesn't make them evil. Perhaps fascination took hold when we first noticed their extraordinary capacity for renewal; wriggling out of an old skin and slithering away in a silky new one as if nothing untoward had happened. And then, as we humans began to pay closer attention, it became evident that some snakes had another trick up their long sleeve; they could reproduce without the need for a mate, a process known as parthenogenesis, the virgin birth…more magical than a hen's egg.

The Greek oil jar on which this Garden of Eden scene was painted ca.400 BC[1] sends the message that the serpent was once a friendly kind of beast with a penchant for sipping oil. Here it's the woman who encourages the snake to take food. Admittedly, they do appear to be communicating on some level, but neither look particularly evil. If anyone is guilty of a treacherous act of temptation in this scene, it isn't the snake.

The Genesis account of the snake as deceiver of Eve, leading to the more general small-minded branding of women as deceivers of men, came into being at a later date than this painting. And there was no mention of oil. What purpose did the snake serve in pre- and early Christian minds? Even the Old Testament doesn't have it down as pure evil. On the contrary, on several occasions the snake had its uses in a good cause.

The Serpent And The Staff

The LORD asked him, "What is that in your hand?"" A staff," he replied. Then He said, "Throw it on the ground." He threw it on the ground, and it became a snake. Moses ran from it, but the LORD told him, "Stretch out your hand and grab it by the tail." So he stretched out his hand and caught it, and it became a staff in his hand. (Exodus 4:2-4)

Then the LORD said to Moses, "Make a snake image and mount it on a pole. When anyone who is bitten looks at it, he will recover. So Moses made a bronze snake and mounted it on a pole. Whenever someone was bitten and he looked at the bronze snake, he recovered. (Numbers 21:8-9)

According to the bible, Moses was gifted a magical staff by God for the purpose of persuading the Egyptian pharaoh to allow the Israelites to leave his country. It was a veiled threat that became reality with the onset of a variety of plagues. Moses used his staff again during the exodus to obtain water from a stone. Those are not the only occasions in which snake and staff, rod or pole were conjoined or synonymous and magical. The so-called Aesculapian Snake, thought to possess healing powers, wound itself around the rod of Greek Asclepius, god of healing. Another Greek epithet for Asclepius at some point was Paian[1], the healer and the healing, given with various spellings including Paeon in Latin. Etymology dictionaries give Greek paian as 'hymn, chant, hymn to Apollo'. No mention of a link to Pan or to 'pagan' given as sourced from Latin paganus. I have my opinion. The reader of this might like to consider it.

Written MUŠ in lexicons, the Sumerian snake is pronounced MUSH but would probably not take offense if called MUS or MUZ, neither of which

are sounds already taken by other words. MUSH is endowed with a pair of oblique lines above the head, demonstrating that the word was in the image of the horned snake, a type of viper.

MUŠ   **BU**

The few early images of MUŠ shown on very damaged fragments are not helpful in the study of this pictograph. But there exists another version of the Sumerian snake - not recorded as such in orthodox lexicons. Nevertheless, there can be no mistake. BU shown here in the middle and again (on the right) on a tablet from the Uruk IV period ca.3350-3200 BC [1] is also a horned

138

snake. BU will answer to PU and would have willingly answered to BO or PO had the vowel 'O' been included in the Sumerian lexicons. The differences between symbols MUŠ and BU above are not game changers; a straight and striated vertical line and a forked tail according to the computer-generated images of MUŠ, a wavy or straight line for BU. In fact, it might be said that the differences are reminiscent of the straight staff of Moses in his hand and the writhing, animated snake on the ground. BU is unarguably a snake. Why did that not percolate through to Sumerian lexicons? When was that piece of information lost or set aside?

There are at least two Buddhist parables concerning a monk and a snake, one of which replaces the staff with a piece of rope. The monk, travelling at night, saw what he believed to be a snake, a potential danger and source of fear, lying on the path ahead of him. Finding the means to make a torch for light, he discovered that it was nothing more than a piece of rope from which he had nothing to fear. In this story and others, the snake is the educator, the wisdom teacher. The monk and staff work as a pair. The staff or rope and the snake also.

The Sun And The Snake

What was the founding story, the source of the link made by the Sumerian scribes between the image of the horned snake and the sounds of MUSH and BU? Why has BU, also phonetic PU/PO, not been recognised as the source of the Greek word 'potamos' meaning 'river'? Marrying the image of a writhing snake to that of a winding river is so obvious that it merits no more than a passing mention. And yet to my knowledge, the connection has never been made in terms of the Sumerian language, a word that matches the word for river in Greek, in the language of the region known to the Greeks as Mesopotamia, a name that translates from the Greek to 'between the rivers'…

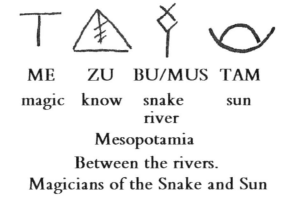

ME   ZU   BU/MUS TAM
magic   know   snake   sun
                 river
Mesopotamia
Between the rivers.
Magicians of the Snake and Sun

139

ME-ZU is the source of Greek meso- with the meaning 'between', and 'middle'. T-shaped symbol ME gives the foundation of all references to measurement. The 'meta' of metaphysical also takes its source here. Given as 'since when?' in the lexicons, the combination ME-TA translates through the monosyllabic forms to 'the magic to question', 'the question of magic'. (See p.220 to learn more magic from ME-ZU.)

Greek 'meso-po' and Sumerian BU/PU refer to the two rivers Euphrates and Tigris, giving 'Between the rivers' but also 'between the snakes' and 'Magicians of the Snakes'. This is an important point. It explains the images from all around the world showing a central figure holding a snake in each hand. He is, of course, the central figure of the Adda Seal with the two great rivers rising and falling from his shoulders.

The women of Gebal used to repair to this temple in midsummer to celebrate the death of Adonis or Tammuz, and there arose in connection with this celebration those licentious rites which rendered the cult so infamous that it was suppressed by Constantine the Great.[1]

The TAM of Mesopotamia corresponds to one of the phonetic values of UD, the sun, and as shown above, BU/PU/PO, the snake and river, can be replaced by its sibling MUŠ:

This combination of sun and snake found in the Bible as Tammuz calls to mind the Egyptian uraeus, a rising cobra representing the snake goddess Wadjet who was known to the Greeks as Buto. Her importance in Ancient Egyptian culture is also easily demonstrated by her presence on the foreheads of pharaohs. With BU as snake and UD/UTU as the sun, the origin of the Greek name Buto is not difficult to fathom; when the phonetics are taken back to their original Sumerian forms, it morphs back into its original pictographic Tammuz. Tammuz is Buto is Tammuz. A linguistic connection between the Magicians of Mesopotamia and traditions of the Egyptian dynastic and pre-dynastic periods comes back into the light of day - and everyone knows that light is a necessary element on the path to truth.

Traces Of The Serpent

Looking for later words with the sound 'MUS' or 'MUSH' which might have taken their source here and provide further clues, a few intriguing possibilities:

→ Latin mus, the mouse, appears along with one of its principal attributes, discretion, perhaps even secrecy,

→ Latin musso, 'to keep quiet' or 'to mutter' but also 'to hum'. Humming brings an insect to mind,

→ Latin musca confirms the presence of the fly; more precisely, the gadfly, an annoying creature once used as a metaphor for people who mutter discontentedly.

One of them exists in *The Story of Sukurru*. His name is Mumu and he is not at all happy with his fate. MU-MU appears on line 168 where he is taken back to his given meaning of 'time' and to a multiple of 'year'.

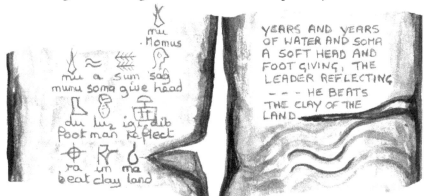

Translated from the two collocated symbols MU-MU with a dictionary-given meaning of 'name', this section of the story gave rise to Greek Momus, a secondary god whose only pleasure was in finding fault with the achievements of others:

Momus began by finding fault with the bull because his horns were not below his eyes, so that he might see when he butted with them. Next he found fault with the man because there was no window in his breast that all might see his inward thoughts and feelings. Lastly he found fault with the house because it had no wheels to enable its inhabitants to leave bad neighbours behind. [1]

Line 168 and its context also confirmed my suspicion that the undiscovered source of Vedic 'soma', elixir of immortality, is found here. SUM, 'to place' was originally the act of cutting the crops, of harvesting them, as evidenced by the pictogram showing plants laid horizontally. SUM with its given meaning 'to equal' gives the source of mathematical 'sum', to sum up. SUM as 'give' is the generous gift of nature. SUM-MA, 'gift of the land', is found numerous times in the lexical lists. Soma is not found as a meaning in Sumerian dictionaries but then neither has anything resembling the story of Momus been found in a literary text in that language – until now.

MU   MUŠ
Name of the Snake
Momus

According to *The Story of Sukurru*, the original complaint (about humans) was inscribed on tablets that Momus prepared personally during the time he was constrained to ride out the great flood in his coracle. Momus was a toady to the Great Brother and Sister. His tablet appears to claim responsibility for man's downfall – a veritable traitor then and certainly not himself a god. A snake perhaps? Or would that be an insulting comparison?

A Virile Thrust

Looking for the source of 'mushroom' in etymological dictionaries throws up the usual enigmatic PIE root. Where do mushrooms come from? Out of the ground? Out of thin air? The etymology of 'mushroom' is a complete unknown. Suggestions have been made, but there is no certainty. Linguists can't agree. French mousse and English moss have been offered up as related to 'mushroom' which is a reasonable assumption on phonetic grounds, but still that does not indicate the original provenance of any of those words. 'Moss', the green carpet that forms in moist, shady places, stems from proto-Germanic 'musa' and Old Norse 'musi'. That information provides only one or two potential stages of the word's use and not its source. It says nothing about why the sound was attributed in the first place nor by whom.

Despite appearances, moss and mushrooms have little in common. They are not of the same botanical family. The obvious link between them is that they both grow easily in damp and shaded conditions, pushing up out of the ground with no apparent stimulus, certainly not in need of sunlight. Could that be the key that binds them not only to each other but to MUSH the snake? Apparently, mosses can be dated back some 470 million years. How far back do mushrooms go? Or snakes?

Rearing Up

Another way to approach MUŠ is to look for its parts in the lexical lists.[1] This is the point at which Allegro's concept of the omnipotent fertility god, the mushroom in its phallic form, comes into view:

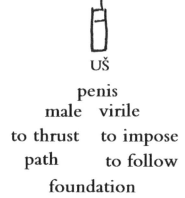

MU   UŠ   =   MUŠ

move virile   snake

MU...USH....MUSH...US...MUS...os...mos....osmos?

Osmosis is given in etymological dictionaries as stemming from Greek osmos 'a thrusting, a pushing', from an unknown proto-Indo-European source. It is my contention that both 'osmosis' and the 'os' of 'oscillate' find their source in Sumerian UŠ, symbol of the phallus.

The snake rearing up effortlessly as if by magic, with no help from arms or legs, was surely the 'virile movement' meant by this combination and the resulting name MUSH, as was the upward thrust of the mushroom, independent of any help from the sun. As a verb, 'to mushroom' with the meaning 'to expand and increase rapidly' is a fitting description for the growth of the fungus, and also applies to MU-UŠ, the 'movement of the phallus'.

UŠ

penis
male   virile
to thrust   to impose
path   to follow
foundation

And so, thanks to that virile thrust forward, we come fairly and squarely to the central symbol of John Allegro's fertility cult as described in *The Sacred Mushroom and the Cross*.[1] Here above with given meanings and the added 'virile' and 'to thrust', neither of which require further explanation or justification.

At this crucial point in the path to understanding, I am duty bound to introduce a caveat. MU is not given in orthodox dictionaries as 'move' or 'movement'. Nevertheless, it appears as 'year' many times in the translation of the entire Sumerian King List which, in terms of years, has done some serious moving. MU lies behind many interesting words: 'moon', 'month', 'music', 'to muse'... One given meaning of MU is 'name' and it has another much longer and highly intriguing phonetic form which is MEHIDA. (See the notes to p.232.)

BONES

OF

OSIRIS

Our Pagan Root

Enki, the wise one, toward Nintur, the country's mother, was digging his phallus into the dykes, plunging his phallus into the reedbeds. The august one pulled his phallus aside and cried out: "No man take me in the marsh.[1]

The above quote is yet another absurdity from the translated text referenced as *Enki and Ninhursaga.* Read it once. Read it twice. My goal is not to ridicule a translation for the pleasure - and I daresay it was written in complete good faith - but to point out all that has potentially been lost in the process. No doubt it was carried out before the arrival of the tools made available to everyone today; the online Sumerian dictionaries, the corpus of texts highlighting common collocations and enabling useful comparisons, the much-appreciated photographic corpus[2] of early tablets housed in various museums around the world, all available at the click of a computer key. Nevertheless, I struggle to see how it has ever been believed by anyone - either within academia or outside looking in - that some scribe of ancient times took up their stylus to write such nonsense. The content of that paragraph has no equivalent in, no similarity to, no back-up from any other known myth from a different source. Neither does it make any sense in any imaginable context, allegorical or factual. It is unfathomable that the word 'wise' be used for the Enki character in this context where he is discovered digging, plunging and pulling aside his phallus…into and from reedbeds. If Enki had been made to cry out 'This is how you get stuff to grow, folks!" I might be slightly more circumspect in my criticism but 'No man take me in the marsh!'… really?

It might be said that clay tablets found inside or next to the ruins of a monument necessarily dealt with spiritual beliefs, perhaps stories about gods, but that should not be taken as proven, nor used as an excuse for offering approximations that have no meaning in our modern world. Tablets found in the rubble of a temple might be the secret stash of some dissident and/or dissolute monk, the underground humour of the day, or - God forbid - the pornography of those times. Who can know unless we study what was written on them with a completely open mind and, at the same time, some expectation of logical human thought processes? Whatever the truth, it is highly unlikely that there would be nothing more than a string of quasi-incomprehensible, disjointed phrases. Insulting to the scribe, they represent a block to learning the truth about our past.

The Sacred Mushroom and the Cross makes constant reference to an ancient fertility cult and specifically to symbol UŠ, the phallus. Allegro goes into great detail about a worldview involving a heavenly phallus, its orgasm and life-giving semen. Was he right to believe that this was the sole original metaphor in which all rituals were grounded? [1] Whatever the case may be, he pointed to Sumerian UŠ in that regard.

The ithyphallic image is many thousands of years old but the earliest written mention of it is Sumerian, found on clay tablets dating from the late 4th millennium BC. UŠ is the source of the Ancient Greek suffix 'us' used for male names.: Zeus, Cronus, Herodotus....

Osiris, Bacchus, Silenus, Pan, Priapus.... Multi-cultural and linguistic complexities along with the passage of time mean that the archetypal phallic figure has taken on multiple names. In contrast, the central element of his image is inherently unwavering, and, as John Allegro pointed out, primarily a reference to fertility, whether that of the people or of the land. The earliest known ithyphallic bird-headed man was painted onto a cave wall in France, an image thought to be around 17,000 years old.[2] The figure lies below an imposing auroch, ancestor of the bull, and above a bird perched on a stick. The auroch appears to be pointing its horns towards the man, perhaps offering to give him a lift up to the skies.

The recently discovered headless ithyphallic man riding on a bird at Gobekli Tepe dates to ca.9600 BC.[1] This is the lowest figure visible on pillar 43 and corresponds to other figures also riding on birds who can be seen on several Mesopotamian seals from much later times. Is it a stretch to equate the pre-ice-age ithyphallic bird-man in France with the equally ithyphallic man on a bird some 5,400 years later in Turkey? I would say not. The similarities are too great. The possibility that the pairing of the headless man and bird in that way be coincidental are really quite small.

In the same way, the Gobekli image cannot be disassociated from the considerably later man and bird figures carved onto more than one seal from the Mesopotamian region.[2] Man and bird, ithyphallic bird-headed man, ithyphallic headless man and bird, bird and flight. There was continuity of that theme, at least twelve thousand years of it, however mind-boggling that might be. A traditional tale of feathered flight to the skies and its link to humankind was somehow perpetuated despite an intervening and all-erasing ice age.

Scene Of The Murder

Of the members of Osiris the only one Isis was unable to find was the genital member, for it had been thrown at first into the River, and lepidotus, phagrus, and oxyrynchus had fed upon it, which kinds of fish the natives scruple to eat above all others, and that Isis in its stead made a model and consecrated it, namely the phallus, in honour whereof the Egyptians hold a festival.[3]

The Greek version of the name Osiris stems at least partially from Sumerian UŠ, the phallus, which would have sounded like USH or OSH but also US or OS. Given the tossing around of body parts in versions of the Osiris myth and other ancient writings, it seems feasible that there also be a connection to Latin 'os' which has the meaning 'bone' and led to the word 'ossuary', a box in which bones were collected. The French word 'ossature' stems from Latin 'os' and has the meaning 'structural framework', used in relation to a building but also the human skeleton, the internal framework.

Yet another word of unknown origin is 'usher'. Given as also stemming from Latin 'os' (this time as 'mouth') and ultimately from PIE, its meanings through

Latin ostiarius are 'door-keeper', 'door', 'entrance'. These are equally evocative of Egyptian Osiris, this time in his major function as gate-keeper and expeditor of the dead to their well-deserved fates.

At that time," says YHVH, "they shall bring out the bones of the kings of Judah, and the bones of its princes, and the bones of the priests, and the bones of the prophets, and the bones of the inhabitants of Jerusalem, out of their graves. They shall spread them before the sun and the moon and all the host of heaven, which they have loved and which they have served and after which they have walked, which they have sought and which they have worshiped. They shall not be gathered nor buried; they shall be like refuse on the face of the earth." (Jeremiah 8:1-2)

Like those of Osiris, the bones in the Book of Jeremiah are spread to the winds rather than kept neatly in an ossuary or burial site of some kind. It is also shown in the biblical account to be an act of contempt for the dead, specifically of pagan stargazers and, I suggest, a useful indication of the destructive war waged on the knowledge accumulated by those astronomers. But at what point in time? In any event, it indicates an apocalyptic moment of great and deliberate destruction, not of the information but of those who provided it.

Considering that Sumerian UŠ, the penis, generated the Latin word for bone 'os' results in a real conundrum in that the human penis does not incorporate a bone as such. It might be argued that there are other mammals, namely whales, which do have bones in their penises. However, a more obvious reason behind the evolution of the 'os' is to be found elsewhere, in the heart of the tree…wherein lies the body of Osiris.

Heart Of The Tree

Latin 'os' has yet another meaning: heartwood, the innermost section of a tree or branch. Heartwood has more density than the surrounding sapwood. Although it is essentially dead wood, no longer transporting sap, this is nevertheless the internal structure that enables growth, the backbone, the skeleton, the upward thrust. UŠ, the phallus, gave 'os', the heartwood. According to Plutarch's account, the body of Osiris is found by Isis hidden inside a tree that had been cut away to provide a structural beam.

Proceeding thence, she learnt by inquiry that the chest had been washed up by the sea at a place called Byblus, and that the surf had gently laid it under an Erica tree. This Erica, a most lovely plant, growing up very large in a very short time had enfolded, embraced, and concealed the coffer within itself. The king of the place being astonished at the size of the plant and having cut away the clump that concealed the coffer from sight, set the latter up as a pillar to support his roof.[1]

Is it a coincidence that 'os', the sound which acquired the meaning of 'bone' but also 'heartwood', two different biological elements with the same internal structural functions, is also the first syllable of Greek Osiris? With a slight adjustment to that version of the tale, to 'cut away the clump' is to cut away the sapwood in order to expose the hard, durable heartwood. Osiris was concealed inside the coffer. The coffer was the heartwood.

One key to unlocking the truth behind the biblical story of the snake and the tree in the Garden of Eden is found in a line of a lexical list fittingly dubbed EME-SAL, the 'language of the prophetess'.[2] The synonymity of MUŠ, the snake, through MU-UŠ, with GEŠ, the tree, is demonstrated there, and it specifically refers to the Tree of Consciousness and Knowledge:

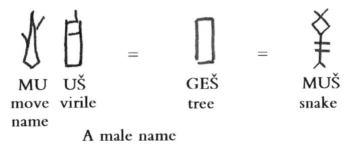

MU	UŠ	TUG₂	PI		GEŠ	TUG₂	PI
						GEŠTUG₂	

Tree of Consciousness and Knowledge

Latin 'os' meaning 'heartwood' and Greek 'osmos' 'to thrust' both stemming from UŠ, it can be argued that the Sumerian tree is also very much the Tree of Life, the ultimate symbol of growth, not least the growth of wisdom, gaining strength as it takes form. Thanks to the above lexical entry showing the synonymity of MU-UŠ and GEŠ, it becomes possible to make a further important connection, one that does not require embroidery or any giant leap of faith. Therein lies the heart of the mystery of the mushroom:

MU	UŠ	=	GEŠ	=	MUŠ
move	virile		tree		snake
name					

A male name

Give Them Their Name

And there shall come forth a rod out of the stem of Jesse, and a Branch shall grow out of his roots: (Isaiah 11:1)

What's in a name? Everything, absolutely everything on Earth if not in Heaven. The Tree of Life is full of names and, over the years, sacred books and churches have been filled with pictures of the Tree, the Family Tree.

Biblical Jesse was the father of King David, youngest of his eight sons. Taken literally, Jesse really is a tree. But a strangely horizontal version of one. The bearded figure in the Old Testament Book of Isaiah is pictured lounging on one side with a tree growing out of him, perhaps directly from his kidney since that organ was the most hidden, the most secret and of particular importance to the Jewish community long ago (p.196). This curious and unlikely image has been copied many times since the beginning of the Christian era. In some versions of it, Madonna and Child are seen perched precariously between his central branches.

Behold the man whose name is the Branch (Zechariah 6:12)

I am the root and the offspring of David and the bright and morning star (Revelation 22:16)

All in all, the images from the Middle Ages are telling us that the church was once quite happy with the idea of a man with a branch, a new tree growing out of him. But why? Why that name? What is at his root? The answer might lie in the fact that the family tree of Jesse was of immense importance in the transmitted history of Israel, demonstrating the great lineage of King David. There could be no question of leaving in the public domain the fact that Jesse was derived from the considerably more ancient Gnostic and Pagan texts and that those texts were referring to an altogether different concept and tree, potentially one possessing magical mind-altering properties.

Remain In ME

Remain in Me, and I in you. Just as a branch is unable to produce fruit by itself unless it remains on the vine, so neither can you unless you remain in Me. (John 15:4)

My theory is that the scholars who were given the task of twisting existing literature into a more acceptable mould, one with which to indoctrinate future generations, did not succeed in entirely separating the entangled man from his Sumerian GEŠ root. Like Siamese twins with just one heart between them, Jesse remained forever attached to his tree – or the other way around. It could not be undone. Another clever way to pitch the tale had to be devised. It is my guess that the whole concept of the family tree evolved out of that original conundrum: Jesse who just happened to be a reclining man with a branch growing out of his midriff.

Behold the man whose name is the Branch. strikes me as being adapted from a Sumerian riddle, designed to provoke curiosity and to be solved. Symbol GE/GI, first word of Sumerian 'genese', is an easy match for 'rod' and definitely belongs with GES (p.78).

One Sumerian word for 'branch' is PA/HENDUR which also has the given meanings 'wing' and 'instructor' and is analysed in the context of the ouroboros (p.125). Around and around we go.

Another important piece of this paradigm-changing puzzle is found in the epithet given to Oannes, the fish god, who is named by Berossus as Musarus. The horizontal tree is the foundation of SAR, the garden, the orchard and the writing. Thus, JES, the tree or beam with ŠE, symbol of fertility, rising up from it, is the founding element of that garden.

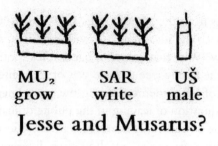

MU₂	SAR	UŠ
grow	**write**	**male**

Jesse and Musarus?

I am the root: UŠ, the phallus, is also given as 'foundation' in Sumerian lexicons. At the same time, Sumerian GES quite naturally gives the source of our word 'joist' through French 'giste', a joist being one way of describing a beam used to support a structure. The Tree, the branch, the root, the foundation, and the crossbeam. A fantastic family indeed, never forgetting that GES is an integral part of Trismegistus, the three times great.

AMA-NITA

Mon Amour

In The Name Of The Mother

According to John Allegro, the amanita mushroom had more than one secret name.[1] He noted that those names date back to ancient Sumer and that Sumerian provided a bridge between all other languages, Indo-European and Semitic. He went on to say that Sumerian provides the key to deciphering the names of gods, mythological figures both classical and biblical, and the names of plants. That extraordinary claim comes in the introduction to *The Sacred Mushroom and the Cross* written in 1970. It's safe to say that it has gained no traction whatsoever over the past fifty years. No etymological dictionary has so far had the good idea of adding the mention 'ultimately from Sumerian' onto a word. And yet John Marco Allegro was a distinguished philologist who had studied the Dead Sea Scrolls and who was thus well placed to know what he was talking about. For my part, it has perhaps been an advantage to have no extensive academia-based knowledge of other ancient languages as he did. I started where it all began, directly with the Sumerian, and my own independent discovery, after years of personal study, is that Sumerian provides the source of all of those languages.

Looking through the notes to Allegro's book today, it isn't possible for me to fathom the reasoning behind most of the Sumero-Akkadian examples given there but, whatever our differences, the overall conclusion stands: Sumerian is the way. His opening chapter delves straight into the history and importance of amanita muscaria. Here is my version of the mushroom's first name:[2]

Syllables A-MA-NI-TA, trip quite pleasingly off the tongue. Most people are aware of the name, that of the mushroom with extraordinary psychedelic properties. With its distinctive red and white cap, the amanita mushroom has long epitomised the winter solstice season. Plastic versions hang on Christmas trees and its colourful image appears in Christmas card scenes. But it was more than a brightly coloured image that brought about the association of amanita and Christmas. The marriage of the mushroom and the winter solstice celebration is said to go way back to pre-Christian pagan times.

Out of pure curiosity, we might look up the origin of the name and discover, without being much the wiser, that amanita was first coined by the Ancient Greeks: amanitai, a plural with the meaning 'a kind of fungi'. The Greeks coined many of their words, almost all of them in fact. Either that or they inherited them from somewhere yet unknown; not given as 'unknown' in etymological dictionaries but often as sourced from PIE, proto-Indo-European.

Trawling through the tablets displayed on the CDLI site led to a discovery which, in my view, goes a long way to confirming the existence of a misnamed Sumerian mushroom pictogram. Given as a version of SAG, the 'head', that symbol appears to the right of EDEN on two known tablets[1], both from the 4th millennium. A comparison with numerous other pictograms of SAG from around the same early period reveals a considerable difference between the two, the example on the right demonstrating that a naturalistic image was used for that word:

The two have little in common apart from the existence of a protuberance on the end of a stalk. Phonetic SAG, also SAN, is the source of words such as 'sage', 'sacred', 'sane', potentially 'saint'. It's given in lexicons as 'front', 'first', the head, the

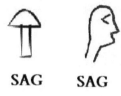

SAG   **SAG**

leader. SAG as a leader is a status shared with symbol ŠI, given as the 'eye' and 'front'. ŠI is a considerably better visual match than SAG for the mushroom pictogram above. I suspect that they were once intimately connected; the head, the forehead, and the eye.

ŠI
eye

Cannabis and the third eye are both clearly referenced in *The Story of Sukurru*[2] while line 168 suggests the presence of soma (p.141). But the mushroom is not found there in any obvious guise. Nevertheless, it is inferred by the very form of the pictograms. Cannabis or amanita mushroom? Both lead to the notion of the 'spirit eye' through their well attested psychedelic properties. It is possible to see either SAG (the left-hand version above) or ŠI as words which would have been understood as 'spirit eye' either independently or in association with symbol ME, given as 'spirit'.

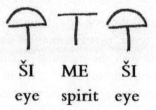

ŠI   ME   ŠI
eye   spirit   eye

The combination of two ŠI, two 'eyes', surrounding ME appears three times in *The Story of Sukurru*, of which twice in the section mentioning cannabis, and offers a visually evocative glimpse into the scribe's mindset at the time of writing.

On the understanding that the Greek language is sourced directly from Sumerian, a straightforward division of 'amanita' throws up the two symbols AMA, 'mother', and NITA, 'male', another phonetic version of UŠ, the phallus. Both of them appear on more than one occasion in *The Story of Sukurru*, but not together and not in such an easily definable context. That doesn't mean that they never did. AMA is a combination of MAL, the basket, which is also a

AMA   NITA

cosmic sailing vessel enclosing AN, eight-pointed symbol of the sky. AMA appears in all its pictographic splendour on a number of tablets during the 4th millennium BC. Seen here next to a rendering of GAN, the crucible.[1]

AMA has the given meanings 'Mother' and 'wide' as attested in orthodox Sumerian lexicons. This is the source of Latin amare with the meaning 'love'. AMA is the Great Cosmic Mother who is the container of the sky. How could she be anything other than pure love? The magnificent Egyptian Hathor at Dendera, whose wide body also contains all the elements of the sky flowing along on their boats, was surely a manifestation of the same theme.

As mentioned, UŠ/NITA has been identified as an essential element of the mushroom both in sound through MU-UŠ (p.143) and meaning; the virile, thrusting movement. For obvious reasons, Allegro placed heavy emphasis on symbol UŠ in his discussion of the ancient fertility cult. But he doesn't appear to have come across this collocation which confirms the Sumerian origin of the amanita name.

Mother And Son

The number of 'coincidences' between monosyllabic Sumerian and Greek words is too great to be ignored, and the existence of both AMA and NITA can be added to that list. However, without finding the mother and the male (the son) together on a clay tablet, that assertion would understandably be met with little enthusiasm. Fortunately, and, in my view, unsurprisingly, there is just one entry on just one ancient lexical list serving to prove that these two symbols were knowingly collocated at some point.

The entry appears on a tablet from the Old Babylonian period, ca.1900-1600 BC, discovered at Nippur.[1] How probable is it that those four syllables A-MA-NI-TA found together as AMA-NITA be totally unrelated to later Greek amanitai, the mind–altering fungi of unknown original source? Perhaps there is a statistician somewhere who can do the calculation. I would be interested in the result and, in the meantime, will add the following image into the mix. In my view, it should tip the balance even further in favour of the Feather of Truth:

Thanks to the Sumerian meanings and explanations given above, the scene on this Mesopotamian seal[2] might be decrypted using referenced linguistic sources. AMA, the cosmic Mother seated on her tree-trunk throne, holds NITA, a childlike figure who appears to have a cord sticking up from his head or perhaps a ponytail. He isn't seated on her lap but appears to float or is being held out to the figures on the left. Whichever it is, this is not mundane mother and child interaction, not a scene of ordinary comforting and nurturing. His head is turned towards her and he looks into her eyes, an indication of confidence and/or questioning. Meanwhile, his body faces the other 'brewer' figures and, most important, his hand is held out to receive their potion. This is one possible interpretation of the scene, and my imaginary caption would read, "Go ahead. Take it. Have no fear." But of course, I could be wrong.

The scene also calls to mind the mushroom symbol found on two tablets from the Uruk III period, ca.3200-3000 BC. This one below is collocated on one side with EDEN, source symbol of the biblical garden of Eden, and on the other with an unidentified symbol pretty much identical to the three vessels on display in the above seal. Unfortunately, there is no photo of the original tablet on CDLI and no stated location:

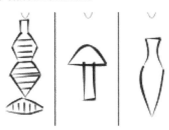

The vessel seen here on the right is labelled ZATU707, an indication that the phonetic form and meaning of it are unknown. It appears on both of the 4th millennium BC tablets alongside EDEN and SAG (given there as SAG@n), the mushroom symbol, indicating that they were meant to be read as a connected trio, that they had meaning as a threesome.

Question Of Death

But the wise ones took oil in flasks along with their lamps. (Matthew 25:4)

According to the ancient lexical lists, phonetic NITA stems from a combination of two symbols: NI, seen here on a 4th millennium tablet,[2] with TA.

NI has the given meaning 'oil' and I have also identified it as 'abundance' and 'night'. A central element of the Solstice Riddle[3] which begins on line 223 of *The Story of Sukurru*, NI appears there three times in sixth position over three consecutive lines: 666 (p.290). There was nothing haphazard about the positioning: three nights, three oils.

Given in the lexicons as 'what', symbol TA of NI-TA is both 'death' and 'question': the question posed at the moment of death, the question of life and death, the questioning of the oil when found with NI and in the context of divination, of prophecy…

NI-TA as the 'questioning at death' is relevant to the role of Osiris as the Egyptian god of both fertility and death. It is also relevant to the shamanic use of entheogens, the 'oils', and to the sun's apparent three-day hesitation at the winter solstice. Another given meaning of UŠ is 'path':

UŠ /NITA   =   NI   TA
path   oil question

UŠ/NITA, symbol of male fertility, is at the origin of Egyptian Osiris, god of fertility, of death and rebirth, along with another symbol having the same sound; UŠ$_2$ which has the more direct given meaning of 'death'.

Holy Cow

While the duo AMA-NITA appear as such only once in the context of a transliterated lexical list, the three signs that give AMA-NI-TA appear together on at least three tablets from the Old Babylonian period. There are also two known examples of the four-symbol phrase AMA-A-NI-TA, so more than one case where 'amanita' would have been an acceptable result of blending the two identical vowel sounds into one. Add into the mix that AMA-NI appear together numerous times over various archaeological periods, some with symbol A between them.

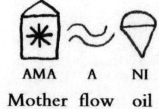

AMA   A   NI
Mother flow oil

In this case, the central A between 'mother' and 'oil' indicates flow. Perhaps an abundant flow of love would be an apt interpretation where no other defining context is available. But it could signify a flow of oil, the type of mind-altering oil by means of which to undertake a voyage in the basket of the sky.[1] Symbols A-NI give the source of Latin animus and anima; 'give life to', 'the vital principle', 'the breath', 'the soul'.

Taking it all one step further as only a monosyllabic rendering of the old texts can do, I invite the reader to return to the section on Marduk (p.63) and read it through once again, particularly the bible verses. The breakdown of the original Sumerian words translated by academia to Marduk gives a quite distinctive 'Golden Calf', a precious effigy which, in biblical terms, is the cause of the bitter outburst of Moses and the breaking of a pair of precious tablets.

The earliest versions of AMAR, given as 'to take care of' and 'calf' or 'son' appear as an unidentifiable animal head, presumably that of the son of the bull – which in turn leads to the bull being the sun, which in turn leads to the mother also being a bull or rather a cow. Hathor, is that you?

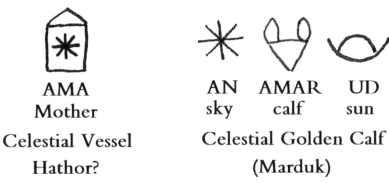

AMA
Mother
Celestial Vessel
Hathor?

AN   AMAR   UD
sky   calf   sun
Celestial Golden Calf
(Marduk)

AMA and AMAR are two distinct symbols, the first being the mother and the second her calf, her offspring which is in her care, which she nourishes with her milk. The biblical text describes a curious scene in which the calf is ground down and transformed into something else altogether, a brew that will be forced on the unruly crowd by an angry Moses. Why would he do that? Why not just walk off in a huff and leave them to fend for themselves? Instead of that natural reaction, he gets out his cauldron and starts grinding. 'Curioser and curioser', as only Alice could say about such strange behaviour.

Flies And Worms

Agaric: 1530s, an herbalists' name for a wide range of fungi, from Latinized form of Greek agarikon, name of a corky tree-fungus used as tinder, said by ancient sources to be from Agari in Sarmatia.

Taking AMA, the mother, and AMAR, the son, to be sources of later words, we find another curious mix through Latin amare which is 'to love' and Latin amarus which is 'bitter'.

The lexical lists confirm the bitterness through the breakdown of AMAR[1] into A-MAR, then on to Akkadian 'marru' given as 'bitter'. 'Parasite', 'worm' and 'louse' are three of the main given meanings of MAR. There are also lexical links to the colour red:

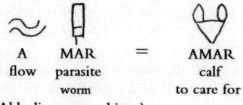

A	MAR	=	AMAR
flow	parasite		calf
	worm		to care for

(Akkadian marru: bitter)

In MAR we find the worm that ate the shady kikayon plant of biblical Jonah with its accompanying theme of bitterness and anger. Visually, MAR appears to be an inversion of symbol UŠ, the phallus, which was given by John Allegro as the 'heavenly penis', principal word in his theory of the mushroom-consuming fertility cult. Was there perhaps some sense of opposition between the two 'virile' signs. Was there a war?

The lexical lists for AMAR offer up a compelling origin for the secondary name of the amanita muscaria mushroom, the 'agaric'. A-MAR is given numerous times opposite A-GAR.[1]

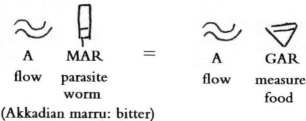

A	MAR	=	A	GAR
flow	parasite		flow	measure
	worm			food

(Akkadian marru: bitter)

Sumerian MAR is source of 'margosa', name of a bitter-tasting plant which has far-reaching anti-parasitic and curative properties, a fitting name for the loving care extended by AMA, the mother; difficult to swallow but effective.

Margosa is also commonly called neem, a name that stems from Sumerian NIM, given as 'insect', 'fly' and 'buzz'. MAR, the worm, and NIM, the fly. NIM is the fly of the fly agaric, a name acquired because amanita muscaria both attracts and kills insects. The flies are the fools in love. NIM appears in the description of an ancient ritual, just one of

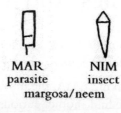

MAR	NIM
parasite	insect
margosa/neem	

the revelations of *The Story of Sukurru*. It was obvious from the outset that some form of hallucinogen was being evoked during this increasingly frenetic scene, and hence the illustration of a female hand brandishing opium poppy buds, a detail taken from a painting on an ancient Greek vase. I made the choice of using the easily recognisable name Ea, and translating NIM, the insect, as 'buzz', transforming it into a mosquito for comedic effect – fitting with the overall humour of the text. It's also the first line of the Solstice Riddle [2] (p.290). This is how line 223 of *The Story of Sukurru* was translated in context:

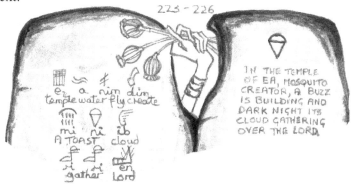

At the time of translating, it didn't come to mind that the amanita muscaria is also known as the 'fly agaric' and that the presence of MI next to NI, the 'blackness' and the 'oil', given as 'dark night' was an important reference to mind-altering substances (p.172). The fly-in-a-jar character, as I chose to name him more than once, had been identified in other parts of the text but also in at least one proverb and I took it to be nothing more than a humorous term for the incessant noise of humanity – likened to that of a fly fighting to disentangle itself from a spider's web or escape through a closed window. I was missing something. The fly is a metaphor for the fool who will be cured of his folly by a bitter treatment. The harsh but loving cure takes the form of a dark cloud through which he will have to travel in order to be reborn. The reference to hallucinogens is unmistakeable. I perceived some of it but not the full extent.

I also noted under MI-NI the words 'a toast', borrowed from the meaning of 'minni' in Old Norse: a toast to the deceased. A dead body was evidently involved as proven by the presence of TAR-A on the next line which has the meaning 'to cut the flow' and which translated quite literally to 'tar water', a cedar extract mentioned by Pliny in the context of embalming but not only:

This extract from the cedar preserves the bodies of the dead uncorrupted for ages but exercises a noxious effect upon the bodies of the living – singular that there should be such a diversity in its properties, taking away life from animated beings, and imparting a sort of life, as it were, to the dead. [1]

And so back to A-GAR, which together have the given meaning 'to irrigate' from 'the flow to measure'. They are also given opposite a late version of NUN. That version, which, in my view, does not visually differ from earlier forms, has the added phonetic value AGARGARA and the given meaning 'fish spawn'.

Shown with HA, it's also given simply as 'fish'. The description of AGARGARA as fish spawn fits rather well with the name 'agar-agar' given to the equally jelly-like substance obtained from red algae and used as a growing medium in microbiology. That etymology is Malaysian.

The central figure of the Adda seal (p.21) generally given as Ea, the water temple, was an expert in water management and irrigation. Perhaps the following entry in the Dictionary of Greek and Roman Geography written in 1854 will provide some further clues about the so-called Anunnaki:

Eth. A´GARI (Eth. Ἄγαροι), a Scythian people of Sarmatia Europaea, on the N. shore of the Palus Maeotis (Sea of Azov), about a promontory Agarum and a river Agarus, probably not far E. of the Isthmus. They were skilful in medicine, and are said to have cured wounds with serpents' venom! (...) A fungus called Agaricum (prob. German tinder), much used in ancient medicine, was said to grow in their country. [1]

That dictionary entry is precious. Therein lies the unique link between A-GAR and MUŠ, the snake, through the reference to the medicinal skills of the Agari who have a linguistic link to the NUN of the Anunnaki. This is the first direct glimpse of the ancestral culture behind the language, or at least one branch of that age-old civilisation; an Agaric known to us as Marduk with his serpent companion. Sarmatia is another name of unknown origin. The people of that name are thought to have their origin in and around modern-day Ukraine and parts of southern Russia. Sarmatia as in SAR, the garden and the written word? The SAR of Musarus, the fish god? The SAR of Sardinia?

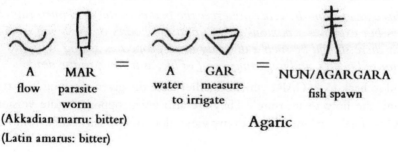

THE
SECRET
REVEALED

The Mussstery Of Gnosticism

In an atmosphere of secrecy and initiation, the rituals held in Eleusis in Ancient Greece involved the replaying of the myth of Persephone, also known as Kore, the maiden who was kidnapped and carried off by Haides, god of the underworld, while out gathering flowers on the island of Sicily. In

a far earlier Sumerian version, she is mentioned in passing by the Sun during his great outburst of bitter anger at an ungrateful young hero.

Persephone is identified there through SAL-KUR, the 'female' and the 'mountains':

SAL.KUR

female mountain

fine Kore

Persephone

The translated words 'flower collecting' resulted from a desire to connect the Sumerian maiden to her Greek descendent but it can now be disclosed that her flower was not immediately obvious (p.261). The original words RI followed by EŠ₂ had another layer. I admit to a slightly convoluted path, the only one in this book that doesn't find direct confirmation in the Sumerian lexical lists, but logical nevertheless. 'Native' and 'princess' are both given meanings of EŠ₂:

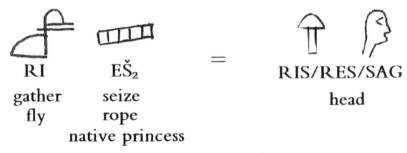

RI	EŠ₂	=	RIS/RES/SAG
gather	seize		head
fly	rope		
	native princess		

Collecting the flower

Among the words generated by the Sumerian snake MUŠ, we find Greek musterion, a mystery or secret doctrine. Mustikos has the meaning 'secret' and 'connected to the mysteries'. Did the secret rituals of the Ancient Greek Eleusinian Mystery school which endured over several millennia have their root in Sumerian culture? The snake is rearing its head and pointing us in that direction.

Discovering the work of Professor Carl Ruck[1] shortly after that of John Allegro led me to a better understanding of the role of Persephone as she appears in *The Story of Sukurru*. I can only scratch the surface of this broad and important topic that is the use of entheogens (neologism for mind-altering substances) in the ancient world. But in the process, I can confirm the importance of Sumero-Greek Persephone in that regard, adding the ultimate linguistic source into the mix. RI-EŠ$_2$ might also translate to 'flight on (by seizing) the rope' where the rope is the umbilical cord linking to the celestial Matriarch, the rope carried by the birds in *The Story of Sukurru* (p.211). As RIS/RES, phonetic values of SAG, the head, it becomes not only the 'maidenhead', the virginity of Persephone, but also the means to fly, and the magic mushroom (p.158).

The enduring mystery of the Eleusinian rites is the nature of the substance that was consumed there. A potion possessing psychoactive properties is the general consensus, but the ingredients are unknown. Professor Ruck has theorised that it contained ergot, a black fungus which infects wheat crops and causes hallucinations. In recent times, analysis of the surface of ancient vessels indicates that his theory was correct and that ergot was indeed an element of that ancient concoction.

The Greek name for the brew is kykeon, supposedly taken from the word 'kukao' meaning 'I mix'. As with 'musterion' and 'mystery', use of the two vowel sounds, U or I, is acceptable. That is particularly true in that kykeon takes the first syllable of its name – KIK - from the inevitable Sumerian source.

GIG/KIK
troublesome
wheat

Symbol GIG/KIK, is given as 'wheat', 'sick' and 'troublesome' in the lexicons, and first appears as two separate symbols MI, which has the given meaning 'black', with NUS, the egg, ca.3200-3000 BC.

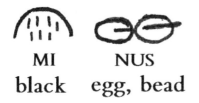

MI
black

NUS
egg, bead

As shown in the pictogram, GIG contains NUS at its base. The word can be unpacked and read – discreetly - as GIG-NUS. The egg was hidden for a reason…and it is best to tread carefully. I sense the hand of a magician, a trickster. The Great Hermes himself is an example of this hermetic game whereby the name must be unpacked to arrive at its essence. Curiosity is a prerequisite. Silence also.

KIK In Any Language

Sumerian GIG/KIK is the source syllable of both Greek kykeon, the drink of the gods, and Hebrew kikayon, the plant that gave shade to Jonah (p.11), a plant which has never been identified beyond doubt. John Allegro also gave GIG/KIK as a partial source for a plant resembling the kikayon of the Jonah story, his reasons being both phonetic and that it has the meaning 'shade'.[1] Kikayon's uneasy translation to either 'gourd' or 'ivy' was discussed by Jerome, an ascetic monk who translated texts between Hebrew, Greek and Latin, in a letter (404 AD):

It is a kind of shrub having large leaves like a vine, and when planted it quickly springs up to the size of a small tree, standing upright by its own stem, without requiring any support of canes or poles, as both gourds and ivy do. If, therefore, in translating word for word, I had put the word ciceia, no one would know what it meant; if I had used the word gourd, I would have said what is not found in the Hebrew. I therefore put down ivy, that I might not differ from all other translators.

That description, 'standing upright by its own stem', offers an evocative parallel to the analysis of MUŠ, the rearing snake. The similarity of sound between the Eleusinian kykeon and Jonah's kikayon, both names appearing in mysterious circumstances, is unlikely to be the result of coincidence.

The underlying meanings of MI 'black' with NUS, the 'egg' or 'bead', are potentially a direct reference to ergot in that the image of that fungus fits the image of NUS as 'black bead' perfectly. Ergot is known to cause severe hallucinations when inadvertently baked into bread. Used with more care, it is an ingredient of the kykeon.

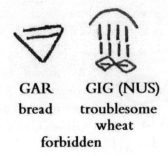

GAR   **GIG (NUS)**
bread   troublesome
wheat
forbidden

GAR, already found in the context of 'agaric' (p.166), takes the form of a bowl having the given meaning 'bread' or 'food' and also 'measure' and 'to place'. GAR combined with GIG is given as 'that which is bad, forbidden, and evil' – a meaning supposedly attached after 2500 BC. I wonder whose opinion that was. They are found together in at least one riddle (p.293).

GIG/KIK is not only the source of 'kikeon'. As GIG-NUS, it is also the founding symbol of 'Gnosis', an important term from those nebulous Pagan times before the onset of full-blown Christianism. Gnosticism might be described as the quest for truth, a philosophical mindset not far removed, if at all, from that of the first Christians. Gnosis stems from Greek gignoskein: 'to learn', 'to come to know' while Latin gigno, a word too closely connected to be ignored, has meanings which include 'to generate', 'to be born', 'to yield'. From GIG-NUS to GIG-NOS is no leap at all, nothing more than a long-lost stepping-stone to truth:

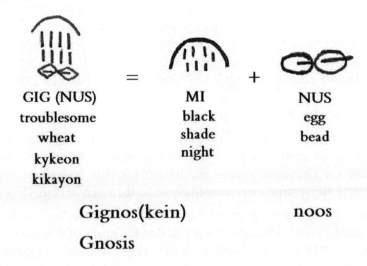

GIG (NUS)   **MI**   **NUS**
troublesome   black   egg
wheat   shade   bead
kykeon   night
kikayon

Gignos(kein)   **noos**

Gnosis

172

According to John Allegro, the Gnostics, a sect prominent in the second century AD, provide a major key to the transition from an entheogen-consuming tradition to what he termed 'the Church'. Among them were those desert monks who found their spiritual well-being through the renouncement of personal possessions, a life of solitary contemplation. practising an ascetic form of early Christianism. Saint Anthony of Egypt, (251-356 AD), famed for his terrible struggles with multiple demons, stands out in that regard. Thanks to the above analysis of their name, it becomes evident that the Gnostics were, in fact, heirs to an age-old tradition, one in which knowledge of the spirit world was enhanced through the consumption of mind-altering substances.

Accidental poisoning from grains contaminated with ergot is known as ergotism and a strange link to Saint Anthony is found, best explained by those rituals inherited from a Pagan and Gnostic world. We are told that the remains of the monk were brought to France by a certain Count Jocelin in the 11th century, and a church built in his name: Saint-Antoine-l'Abbaye which still stands. He was thereafter credited with having assisted – through the presence of his skeleton, no doubt - the recovery of people afflicted with ergotism. For that reason, the Order of Saint Anthony was founded, a community of monks and healers particularly dedicated to helping those suffering with the disease which became known as 'Saint Anthony's fire'.

Apart from that unusual story based in superstition, nothing openly connects the Egyptian monk to ergot. He is best known for his battle with demons in the desert, but, to my knowledge, no mention of hallucinogens is attached to that story in ancient accounts of it. Was it known that the ascetic and meditative life of Saint Anthony involved the absorption of a brew or food which resulted in his torment, or did Saint Anthony's name become linked posthumously to ergot because of the similarity between his experiences and the hallucinatory effects of ergot? Which came first? Around and around we go.

Gnosticism is thought to have originated around the first century AD. Yet Sumerian symbol GIG proves that the label of it, whatever form it took over the ages, was known long before then. As was the kykeon. As was the ergot? As was the magic mushroom? Did the faithful servant pig of Saint Anthony have special training in magic mushroom foraging? Were all the different types of hallucinogenic substances banded together under that one label because they were all used in the pursuit of self-knowledge?

Knowledge Of The Knot

I advise all those who wish to fry, poach or boil the Philosophers' egg to be careful that the shell does not break, for then (…) all the poison would come out, and would kill everyone nearby (…) for within it is the most evil poison in the whole world.[1]

GAR with GIG-NUS might read 'bread of gnosis' and 'measure of gnosis' but that would depend on context. It is possible that the pictographic form of NUS was an image of both the 'egg' from which the amanita mushroom grows and the 'bead' that is ergot. A reminder: NUS/NUNUZ is found opposite NU–NU in the lexical lists (p.131).

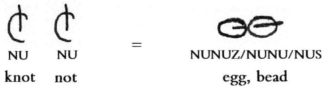

NU	NU	=	NUNUZ/NUNU/NUS
knot	**not**		**egg, bead**

The K of knot also appears in the Norse version of the word, knutr. Knot and gnosis both carry that enigmatic first letter K or G, as does 'gnomon' which is given as a 'carpenter's rule', an instrument used to count time according to the shadow of the sun. Are the words related, all extracted and estranged from their original GIG/KIK cover which gave the original Greek 'gignoskein'? Does GIG-NUS also mean 'knot'? Gnosis and the knot? Knot of time and the gnomon? To know? Knowledge of the knot of time? Knowledge of the original kikeon? Is this the secret essence of the language of the stargazing magicians of Mesopotamia whose documents concerning astronomy found their way into the hands of a greedy Babylonian king?

While John Allegro mentions Sumerian GIG in relation to Jonah's plant, he doesn't make this connection of kykeon with the name of the Gnostics, despite his book being rooted in the subject of sacred entheogens and despite mentioning their ownership of 'certain mystic writings'. I have to admit that I almost missed that vital link too. His description of the Gnostics was limited to what he knew of a sect which had supposedly come into existence shortly before our current era. No-one to my knowledge has yet imagined their existence in far earlier times, in any form or place. Nevertheless, his point that GIG was the root symbol of Greek gigas demonstrates that he understood the direct source of the Greek to lie with Sumerian, a fact that brings a fair degree of posthumous validation from an eminent linguist and scholar of the Dead Sea scrolls for all of the above. Well, that is my opinion and I trust he would have approved of my offering. *The Story of Sukurru* has GIG-GA as 'giants' on line 225. Line 184 has both GAR and GIG.[1]

The re-emergence from the darkness of the cave, out of the belly of the whale, rebirth into a world of light and knowledge, out of the egg that provides both magic mushroom and ergot, and into 'gnosis'; it all lies at the heart of the most ancient culture which once inhabited the Mesopotamian region and beyond. John Allegro was on the right track. It was a founding theme of the language of that group of people known today as 'Sumerians'. That is my analysis of it. And yet again, the reader of this must decide for themselves.

Was Jesus A Mushroom?

The ultimate reason for the almighty stir caused by John Allegro's book in 1970 was that he claimed Jesus to be a name invented by the Nabateans to cover for their ceremonial use of 'sacred' psychedelic mushrooms. Symbol MI is shown here as a pictogram on a tablet from the Uruk III period, ca.3200-3000 BC.[2]

Without a doubt, it evokes the amanita mushroom cap with its multiple dots. But the mushroom is bright red with white dots while MI has the meaning 'black' and 'night'. As image of the mushroom, the meaning surely reflects the fact that it grows in the shadow and at the foot of GEŠ, the tree. The mushroom lives in symbiosis with the tree, its mycelium, the underground, unseen strands, nourishing the roots and receiving nourishment from the roots of the tree. MI, main element of GIG, is the source of Greek mykes translating to 'fungus', another word of unknown origin. In that respect, MI/KIK applies to both ergot, fungus of the wheat grain, and to the magic mushroom. Thus, 'kykeon' and 'gnosis' stem from references to fungi in general.

GEŠ   **MI**
tree   black

JESSU
shade
protection

Coupled with GEŠ, the tree, MI is given as 'protective shade' and that combination takes on a third form. Phonetic JISSU/JESSU, might be read as ISSU or ESSU when all phonetic possibilities of GEŠ are considered (p.101). The two S blend into one. Together they present an extremely compelling candidate for the original name of Jesus. JISSU is found on numerous tablets beginning in the ED IIIa period, ca.2600-2500 BC, age attributed to *The Story of Sukurru*. Line 247 of that text refers to the fate of the young son who has been carried off to the nest of the Bird of Knowledge. It begins with GEŠ-MI, awkwardly translated at the time to: *Under the shady tree stump...* [1]

The two symbols also appear together transliterated as GEŠ-MI, (rather than JISSU/JESSU) on several tablets from the earlier Uruk III period, ca.3200-3000 BC. And so it can safely be said that Jessu existed and was hiding in the shadows as far back as the 4th millennium BC.

My analysis does nothing to detract from that fundamental claim that the original Jesus was a mushroom cap born of MI, the mycelium. On the contrary. If Allegro had been in possession of a computer and the vast corpus of Sumerian writings available to all today along with the tools for cross-referencing, I have little doubt that he would have offered up all of the above as the ultimate proof of that theory. He might have pushed further still and suggested, as do I, that the shady Sumerian tree in question not only sports the original name of Jesus but that it is visually taken from the image of an amanita mushroom cap to be found in the shade of a mighty tree.

It was under a shady plant called kikayon that the Mesopotamian prophet Jonah sat down to meditate in a state of bitterness on the traumatic events of his life. From those strange elements of his story, we might deduce that JESSU and GIG-NUS, his difficult bitter journey and gnosis, are both referenced there through symbol MI. This Mayan figure sculpted in symbiosis with the mushroom, himself the stalk in the shadow of its cap, should probably not be left out of that far reaching equation.[2]

Allegro associated 'shade' with GIG, no doubt a reference to the underlying symbol MI. That said, he began with the Hebrew version of the name Jesus and worked backwards, whereas I have so far found very few direct links between Sumerian and Hebrew.[1] But then, my research has been focused entirely on Sumerian, linking forward mainly to Greek and Latin, whereas

Allegro knew both Aramaic and Hebrew. Nevertheless, the Greek Iesu for Jesus is a close enough match and just as relevant as the Hebrew, if not more.

In all probability, Sumerian JES and JESSU were transformed into their alphabetic forms and carried forward into later languages, their origins carefully hidden from public scrutiny, twisted into newly minted stories, one of which involved a man called Jesse who had a tree growing out of his side. It's only thanks to the recovery of the clay tablets and now the analysis through the monosyllabic method of translation that the knots tied in the writings transmitted by persecuted Gnostic monks - and perceived by John Allegro in his study of their written legacy – begin to cede, the truth at last tiptoeing out of its murky cave and into the light of day. Have I got it absolutely spot on? Have I missed something out? Anything is possible. There is so much material that has yet to be understood, and the old mycelium threads take their time, unravelling slowly in many directions. There is always more. But was Jesus a mushroom? Yes indeed.

Of course, that begs the question: was Jesus only ever a mushroom by a tree? Or did that name over time become synonymous of magic – as well it might – and then of those who produced magic? In other words, did JES and JESSU become the epithets of prophets thanks to the pre-existing spiritual qualities attached to the name? Did a prophet called Jesus exist at the beginning of our era, having taken his name - as others had taken theirs - from that forgotten source? Jesus as a mushroom does not rule out Jesus as a man. But at least we can form an opinion as to which came first.

Jesus And Sophia

The next step on the ladder of understanding is to look for meaning behind the phonetic form JESSU derived from the combination of GEŠ with MI. They are found in the lexical entries with the revelatory breakdown into three words GE-ES-SU[1] here below.

Sophia, who takes her name from Sumerian SU, is the female figure of earthly wisdom within the Gnostic tradition – knowledge of the material realm. Sophia is a concept and not a goddess. The original Gnostics might not have known of or, if they did, had any interest in gods or goddesses as we understand them. Briefly, Sophia has been presented as the twin of Jesus. At the same time, she is held responsible for toppling the original form of perfection, a theme reminiscent of Eve's sinful reputation in the garden but on a considerably less material, more obscure plain. Sophia's responsibility for plunging us all into this sometimes-dismal three-dimensional world is one extremely plausible explanation for the given meaning of 'sink' that accompanies symbol SU. It also carries the equally relevant meanings of 'skin', 'body', 'flesh' and 'omen'.

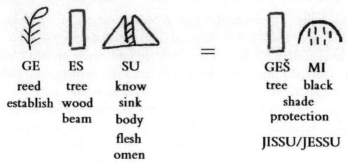

GE	ES	SU		GEŠ	MI
reed	tree	know	=	tree	black
establish	wood	sink		shade	
	beam	body		protection	
		flesh		**JISSU/JESSU**	
		omen			

Branch of the Tree of Knowledge   Jesus

Jesus – Tree – Sophia

Fortunately, there remains in us earthly beings a 'divine spark' which is another way of understanding Sophia who embodies that 'knowledge'. SU is virtually identical to ZU, a pyramidal form with the given meaning 'know'. If knowledge of the other-worldly realm is found in the flesh of a mushroom, then it is feasible that a reference to knowledge of the workings of this material world is hidden within those solid pyramidal forms. SU or ZU? To sink to Earth or to fly up to the knowledge? Both are of the utmost importance in this quest for truth. The wisdom is in the pyramid wherein resides Sophia. What more can I say?

I have translated GE-ES-SU here above to 'Jesus and Sophia', the twins, the brother and sister on either side of the tree, a linguistic rendering which is strangely reminiscent of the figures of Adam and Eve in their garden. But of course, there is every reason to understand this duo as emanating from the heart of the wood, equivalent to the Egyptian myth of the rediscovered body of Osiris (p.150), i.e. to be read from the central word GEŠ out to left and to right, as with the riddle of Abraham and Sarah (p.56). That twist results in:

Out of GES come the branch (the offspring) and the knowledge.

GI/GE, the reed, is the founding symbol of 'genesis' (p.67). This is the reed stylus with which the first words were written and has the given meaning 'to establish'. In the beginning was the word… I begin again:

From GES, the tree, the written knowledge.

Or perhaps '*In GIS was established the knowledge*'. The key to the mystery of the tree lies in its heartwood which, I suggest, lies in Egyptian lore.

178

Sssssssshhhhhh....

Does the Brotherhood exist?

That, Winston, you will never know. If we choose to set you free when we have finished with you, and if you live to be 90-years old, still you will never learn whether the answer to that question is yes or no. As long as you live, it will be a riddle in your mind.[1]

Last but not least, MUŠ and BU have at least one other unacknowledged sibling. Hindu Shesha is among the sis-terhood of snakes, hiding under the guise of Sumerian ŠEŠ:

SES	MUŠ	BU
Brother	**snake**	**snake**

ŠEŠ, also known as ŠIŠ/SIS/SES, qualifies as onomatopoeic, a word reflecting the hissing sound of the snake. There could not be a more obvious phonetic form. However, it has the given meaning 'brother', its snake-like nature occulted by Sumerian lexicons - as is that of BU. Why was that? There is another mystery here; by what quirk did this symbol become the source of 'brother' rather than 'sister'?

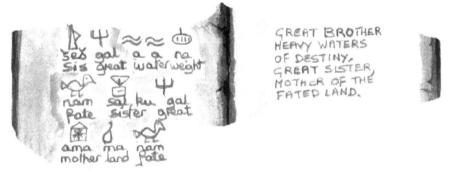

Lines 172 to 174 of *The Story of Sukurru* confirm that there is no mistake. The lines twice refer first to a male figure and then to a female.

ŠEŠ-GAL appears to be a masculine title of great prestige, twice placed in opposition to SAL-KU-GAL, a combination which translates to 'Great Seated Female' giving 'Great Sister'.

179

The Great Brother is followed by A-A, the flowing waters, implying synonymity with AB, the Father of Anunnaki fame, who is also AD of the Adda seal and commonly known as Enki. In A-A, a reference to flowing waters as is BU/PO the snake and the river, we find proof of his snake-like quality or, at the very least, his close acquaintance with snakes.

ŠEŠ-GAL is found on this line in the company of NA-NAM, translated to 'destiny' but also reading 'stone of destiny' or 'weight of destiny'. Along with MU, the name and renown, and MUŠ, the snake, ŠEŠ, the brother, must be taken into consideration as one of the original words serving to form the figure we know today as Moses. MU-ŠEŠ appears a number of times in transliterated texts as inverted ŠEŠ-MU, the 'renowned brother':

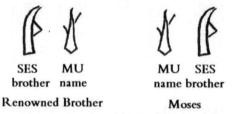

SES	MU		MU	SES
brother	name		name	brother

Renowned Brother   **Moses**

Why would the name of Moses be so intimately linked to the snake? Perhaps it was thanks to his magic staff offered to the prophet by God, a piece of black wood which could be perceived as either a rod or a snake, which with one stroke sent water gushing from a stone, a snake which, when wound around the staff and held up, could provide eternal life, a snake which represented a river, the two rivers of Mesopotamia, all rivers everywhere...

Was SES-MU, the renowned brother, an epithet for someone who provided snake oil, not only curative (p.166) but also the oils through which to perceive magic, taking on the qualities of the snake; the upward thrusting, the virile movement, magical renewal, the shedding of one's earthly skin, rebirth through baptism in the living waters of the rivers? Was Moses a shaman?

SES has another meaning, one that it shares with MAR: bitterness. (p.164) Below is a representation of the lexical entries which show them together, and with some of their given meanings:

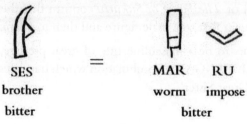

SES	=	MAR	RU
brother		worm	impose
bitter		bitter	

Imposing a worm? The only parasitic worm in Mesopotamian history comes from Nineveh and yet it isn't found in any orthodox Sumerian translation. That worm feeds on the kikayon, the unidentified shady plant of Jonah and leads to his bitter complaint to God. Bitterness is also the driving force of Greek Momus (p.141) when he writes his obsequious message to SES-GAL, the Great Brother, in *The Story of Sukurru*. SES-GAL as 'great bitterness' is another possible translation of that epithet. A bitter Moses descends from his fiery mountain, breaking the tablets of wisdom in a fit of pique, grinding up the Golden Calf and forcing the brew down his unruly brethren's throats (p.63). Then again, bitter complaining is not unknown during the hero's quest in *The Path To Sky-End* (p.88). Without a doubt, there is an underlying theme of bitterness snaking throughout these superficially unrelated stories.

Who Were They?

The mysterious snake head[1] in the Museum of Sanliurfa in Turkey is the oldest evidence of a snake cult in existence ca. 8500 BC. That head was found at Nevali Cori, a site similar to and close to Gobekli Tepe. The face no longer exists. Given the otherwise pristine state of the skull and snake, it's possible that the features were deliberately destroyed.

How old is Moses? No-one knows but, in the absence of any verifiable information, this could be his sculpted head, taken at some point in time from its central niche in a sacred stone chamber and smashed in such a way that the only remaining features are the ears and that highly evocative snake creeping up the back of the skull. We will never know the truth, but I suspect that he had the prominent T-shaped brow and nose seen on other heads found at nearby Gobekli Tepe, the Tau emblem of the magician, symbol ME of the spirit and the magic. Were the perpetrators of the damage to the face too scared, too superstitious to attack the snake? And why has biblical Moses been portrayed more than once with a pair of horns? No firm explanation has been offered for that attribute.

Again, Moses has no fully justified time frame. He could be a figure from a lost pre-Ice Age civilisation of which only the vaguest of remnants survived. Already, his name, given here in its original Sumerian, predates all other mentions by millennia. MU-SES, the Age of the Snake, the Name of the Brother. SES-MU, the Renowned Snake, the Renowned Brother. MUŠ-EŠ₂, the snake and the rope. A snake or a rope? A magician. A shaman.

The Story of Sukurru comprises evidence of the origin of the Exodus narrative during which Moses obtains and breaks the tablets of wisdom, a fact which places that myth at 2600 BC at the latest, some one thousand years earlier than currently accepted.

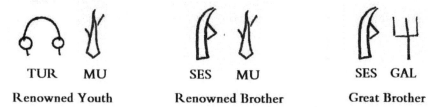

TUR MU	SES MU	SES GAL
Renowned Youth	**Renowned Brother**	**Great Brother**

The character in the scene is TUR MU, which translates to 'the renowned youth' and he is a scribe as attested by the song about clay tablets chosen especially for him on a subject which impacts heavily on his emotions (p.109). TUR MU, the renowned youth, is not the same as SES GAL, the Great Brother, also present in another section of the text. TUR MU is the offspring, the young hero embarking on a quest during a flood, having more in common with biblical Noah than with Moses according to our knowledge of the myths from later sources. Perhaps SES MU, the Renowned Brother, and the closest phonetic form to Moses, is not the same as SES GAL, Great Brother. But who knows how the stories in Genesis started out or when? Or why?

On Her Fine Shoulder

The snake or lizard figurines found at Ur in southern Iraq and dated to ca. 4500 to 4000 BC, the pre-writing period known as Ubaid, appear out of place, unique in the history of Mesopotamia. But not if they are seen as a link between the snake-headed figure from the 9th millennium site of Nevali Cori and the Sumerian writings of ca.3350 BC.

This snake-headed female is adorned with a combination of three Sumerian symbols; SAL, the female, ŠE, the seed, and NINDAxŠE, the seed funnel (p.83). Reading those words into the carvings on her body might indicate a reptilian origin for humanity. But that is not the only possibility. It might be

that this was intended as a fertility talisman. Another figurine from the same period is breast-feeding a baby and they both have snake heads. Apart from that singular feature, mother and child are more evocative of cult images of Madonna and Child that exist today in our churches.

Another possibility is that she is the same snake goddess as Egyptian Wadjet whose Greek name is Buto (p.140). Ancient Egypt can't be left out of the equation where sacred serpents and heads are concerned. The cobra insignia on the headdress of the young pharaoh Tutankhamen is far from the only example of a snake on the forehead of Egyptian rulers. Tutankhamen's snake sits next to the head of a vulture; snake and bird, again a reminder of the ouroboros beasts. Despite the immense gap in time, it is reasonable to perceive a parallel between the stone head found in southern Turkey and the Egyptian wadjet emblem; the serpent, this time a cobra, rising up above the forehead.

The excessively broad, square shoulders of the Ubaid snake lady are adorned with a number of round blobs, fitting the description given in the final line of *The Story of Sukurru*:

Linking Earth and sky with her fine thread, the seeds of soft stone knotted on her fine shoulder.

I took that concluding line, also found at the end of other texts, to be a reference to the cosmic Matriarch as the great weaver of planets and stars. This is the place of NU, the knot, also seen on the shoulder of the female figure on the Egyptian Narmer palette (p.196). The squared shoulders of the snake lady fit with ZAG as 'shoulder', also a boundary. Symbol ZAG takes the form of a bow used to tie garments at the shoulder. Given with AN, it has the meaning 'horizon' and with KUR indicates the summit of the mountain, the place where all the elements of the sky touch Earth, the place where the 'stones' of the sky are placed on Her thread before continuing on their circular journeys. The Zagros mountain range springs easily to mind, stretching from the Mediterranean coast of Turkey and across the region once known as Mesopotamia, joining with the Taurus mountains, birthplace of the twin rivers Tigris and Euphrates. These are also the high places where the oceans and rivers of the sky meet and join with rivers on Earth.

There are a couple of clay tablets from the Uruk III archaeological period, ca.3200–3000 BC, which carry a symbol looking for all the world like a silhouette of the Ubaid figure in profile, yet another variant of symbol SAG, the 'head'. This example from the Uruk III period ca.3200–3000 BC looks like a snake with a suspicion of a forked tongue protruding from its mouth. It is unusual, not resembling the other pictographic forms of SAG.

On this tablet, it sits to the left of two words; HI 'to mix' and AMAR, the 'calf' and 'offspring', an evocative combination if a reptilian lineage for

mankind were under discussion here which it is not... But an open mind is still a prerequisite of this investigation. The three symbols were placed alone in a corner of the otherwise blank reverse side of this unusual tablet. The obverse appears disordered, poorly written compared to other tablets of the period. AMAR is also intriguing in that it looks very much like a capital M from a far later alphabetic language, but the obvious explanation is that the lower half of the symbol was inscribed with less force. It is more shallow but still apparent. The snake-head as SAG with HI, to mix, and AMAR, the calf? Moses grinding the Golden Calf and force feeding it to the population? That's what the Bible tells us.

GREAT FISH
IN THE

SEA

The One Of The Whale

And Dhul Nun -- when he went forth enraged and thought that We would have no power over him; then he called out in the darkness, 'There is no god but Thou. Glory be to Thee! I have done evil.[1]

An Egyptian monk named Al Misri is said to have been an important religious figure within Sufism, an ascetic monk in the style of Saint Anthony of Egypt who is shown here under his T-shaped emblem and in the company of his faithful pig. Al Misri acquired the title Dhul Nun as an honour linking him to the more ancient figure of Yunus, also known as Jonah, the Hebrew prophet. Arabic Nun is the fourteenth letter of that alphabet and translates to 'great fish' or 'whale', the acknowledged translation of Dhul-Nun being 'the One of the Whale'.

Latin nonna, with the meanings 'elder' and 'tutor', is the source of the modern-day nun, a woman who devotes her life to religious practice. Nun is also given as a pagan priestess in etymological dictionaries. It was the root word for both the masculine and feminine nonnus and nonna, while 'monk' derives from 'monos' meaning 'alone' and refers directly to the ascetic form of spiritual practice whereby the person lives frugally and in meditative isolation.

Arabic 'nun' links directly to the Arabic name Yunus and to Hebrew Jonah, and also to Sumerian NUN through the 'great fish' (p.35). Latin nonnus confirms the enduring tutorial, religious aspect that ties into the otherwise not obviously related notion of a 'great fish' or 'whale'.

Al Misri was said to be an alchemist. He died in Cairo at the end of the 1st millennium AD. The details of his life are sketchy and somewhat unrealistic. For example, a story about him on a sea voyage where fish appeared with jewels in their mouths is as unlikely as that of his namesake who spent three days and nights in the belly of a whale. But it highlights the fact that fish played a particularly active role in the stories of the ancient world. Another one on the theme of fish, narrated by Plutarch, has three fish swallowing the penis of Osiris (p.149). The 'One of the Whale' along with Latin nonnus also equates to Greek Oannes, fish god and tutor. Oannes who was said to have appeared out of the Erythraean sea, is another prophet identified with biblical Jonah. Around and around we go. A reminder:

→ Sumerian NUN is the equivalent of HA-A, the lost fish (Sumerian King List),

→ Arabic 'nun' has the meaning 'whale' and 'great fish',

→ Dhul Nun is an Arabic epithet given to a monk, the One of the Whale, a nod to biblical Jonah.

→ Nabi Yunus is the Arabic name for the Hebrew prophet Jonah,

→ Oannes is the Greek name for the fish god and wisdom teacher as indicated by Berossus.

→ Yunus, Jonah, and Oannes are all phonetic forms of the same original name.

→ Latin nonna has the meanings 'elder' and 'tutor', becoming 'nun'.

With all of the above in mind, justified connections can be made across the board leading back to the original premise for the monks' titles:

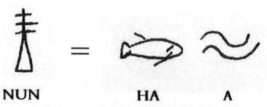

NUN   HA   A

The One of the Whale   **Disappearing**

The Tutor

Yunus

Jonah

Oannes

According to the ancient accounts, Jonah and Oannes follow quite different paths, but both appear out of a fish and both arise out of Mesopotamian stories, one from Nineveh as documented in the bible and the other from the sea beyond Babylon as told by Berossus. Again, we find that opposition between north and south, between Nineveh and Babylon, as with the name of the Chaldeans (p.52) and Abraham (p.56). And again, there is no sign of either of them in the translated Sumerian tablets which predate everything written about them elsewhere – unless we accept that those translations are wrong, that Jonah and Oannes are one and the same, and that both stories are to be found in NUN and HA.

HA, the fish, has a number of synonyms of which JIR which is also PIS and PUS, origins of 'fish', Pisces and Poseidon. JIR/GIR has other given meanings which are of great significance (p.200). They all belong to the same family.

The Kid

Saint Anthony of Egypt was a very real, if enigmatic ascetic monk living in

Egypt in the early 1st millennium AD, and Al Misri is also thought to have lived around the end of that era. Arabic Al Khidr, on the other hand, shares more characteristics with Mesopotamian Musarus Oannes and with the original Dhul Nun said to be the same as biblical Jonah. They are all three attached to fish in one way or another. He can also be equated to Egyptian Thoth, Hermes Trismegistus, Moses, and Abraham, all of whom stretch back into the murky depths of time, in that not one of them can be safely pinned down and given even approximate dates of birth and death or indeed proven beyond doubt to have ever existed on Earth.

Nevertheless, there is a fair amount of intriguing information about Al Khidr. The various accounts provide a strange and fascinating picture of someone who was both present and absent, who appeared and then disappeared only to reappear in a different place, at a different time and in a new guise, a person one might meet more than once during a lifetime and yet not recognise until long after the fact. Al Khidr became the patron saint of the Andalusian Sufi mystic and poet, Ibn Arabi, (born 1165 AD) and is generally portrayed riding the water on the back of a large fish, an Arabic 'nun'.

A relevant point in this linguistic study is that, while Dhul Nun, the One of the Whale, is found in the NUN of Anunnaki, Khidr is phonetically close to KID, the symbol that most often gives the final 'ki' sound to that phrase and which has yet to be examined. Now is the time:

One of the given meanings of KID is 'mat', a definition somewhat borne out by the pictogram and by the many examples of it collocated with GI, the reed, giving GI-KID, the reed mat, a woven mat. But GI/GE can also be read as 'staff': perhaps the staff of Khidr with which he prods his fish vessel. Other given meanings of KID beside 'mat' include 'ghost', 'wind' and 'fool'. The presence of wind suggests a 'reed sail' as an alternative translation for GI-KID. Sails made of woven reeds were common in antiquity,

Enlil Is Nibru Is Enlil

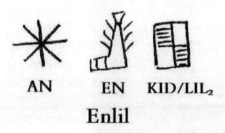

Read as LIL$_2$, KID is notably the hidden symbol behind another well-known Sumerian name: Enlil. That name, invariably preceded by AN, symbol of the sky, appears approximately 1,250 times in the ETCSL corpus,[1] far and away the most cited of all the Sumerian proper names, and considerably more

190

common than Enki from AN–EN–KI who clocks in at around 450 mentions or the various forms of the Anunnaki gods who manage less than 200. Enlil is generally thought to have been some kind of storm god during the Akkadian era, ca.2300 BC.

Looking at these three symbols together through the unorthodox monosyllabic translating method, KID is potentially a qualifier of EN, the Lord. Using conventional lexicon meanings, EN–KID translates to 'Lord on the Mat', 'ghostly Lord', even 'foolish Lord', or taking them separately 'the Lord and the Fool'. Preceded by symbol AN, all of them are celestial, 'in the sky', or at the very least lightweight and floating above ground or water...

EN in this case is the same figure as all others of that name. EN is ' the One' of 'the beginning and the end', the 'Lord' with or without qualifiers. EN is even an essential element of PA/HENDUR, the enduring bond represented by the ouroboros (p.125). Another well-known name that conceals the presence of the lord is Akkadian Suen derived from EN–ZU: 'the Lord to know', 'One who knows the Lord', or 'the One of Knowledge', 'Lord of Knowledge', potentially progressing to 'the ultimate teacher'. With its prefix AN, EN–ZU might give 'the ends of the sky to know' or 'the Lord with knowledge of the sky'. Suen is cited about 220 times in the texts and is closely linked to SIN, meaning 'three' and name of the Akkadian moon god. Without a monosyllabic approach, none of this would be public knowledge.

Nibru appears 163 times as a place name in the ETCSL list of proper nouns. It comprises three symbols, EN–KID–KI:

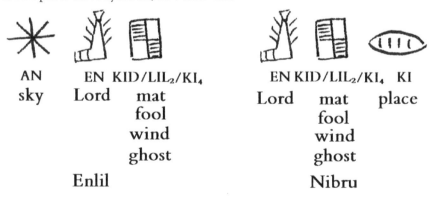

AN	EN	KID/LIL₂/KI₄		EN	KID/LIL₂/KI₄	KI
sky	Lord	mat		Lord	mat	place
		fool			fool	
		wind			wind	
		ghost			ghost	
	Enlil				**Nibru**	

Taking KID to be a woven sail and, from there, to the verb 'to sail', we might read 'the celestial sailing lord' and 'the place (or city) of the sailing lord (or the lord on his mat)'. Taking KID to be a 'fool', we might read 'In the sky, the Lord and the Fool'.

Enlil appears to have been lord of a place also called Enlil, better known as Nibru. To put it another way, it is impossible to know that Enlil and Nibru when read in translated texts are products of the same two original symbols EN-KID. Those two symbols appear together considerably more frequently than all other 'names', proof that they were of major importance in Sumerian texts.

I can only presume that these were the sources used for Zechariah Sitchin's ghostly and dangerous twelfth planet Nibiru. Below is a breakdown of the name given in the lexical entries opposite EN-KID:

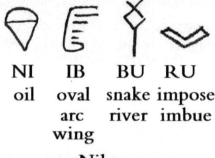

NI	IB	BU	RU
oil	oval	snake	impose
	arc	river	imbue
	wing		

Nibru

To be fair, Sitchin's theory of Nibiru as a distant undetected planet circling the cosmos on an orbit dangerous for Earth is difficult to rule out completely. The Sumerian texts are multi-layered, and context is all important. A possible translation to 'ghostly Lord' from EN-KID and 'thick cloud' from NI-IB without further context have an ominous ring while IB is given as 'oval' in the lexicons. The translations to 'ark' and 'wing' is the result of context and the visual form of the symbol. Neither is the image of a winged planet out of the question. Then again, the foolishness of Greek Icarus and the melting of his wings come to mind, particularly as RU also means 'to fall'.

Make for yourself an ark of gopher wood; make rooms in the ark and coat it with pitch inside and out. (Genesis 6:14)

Lines 111 and 112 of *The Story of Sukurru* shown below constitute a continuation of the instructions given to Noah. The KID/LIL of Enlil is present and also the NI-IB of Nibru. KID is translated as 'fool' while NI-IB, 'Oil on the wing' or 'oil on the ark', is a reference to the waterproofing of the ark of Noah in that context (p.65-66). Someone is being taken for a fool, encouraged with mealy-mouthed praise to waterproof every element from the outside, including the door. In the transliteration, the fool is given as LIL, a symbol close to LIL₂/KID and having the same meaning of 'fool'. Not finding a corresponding pictogram for LIL, I put its equally foolish cousin KID in its place.

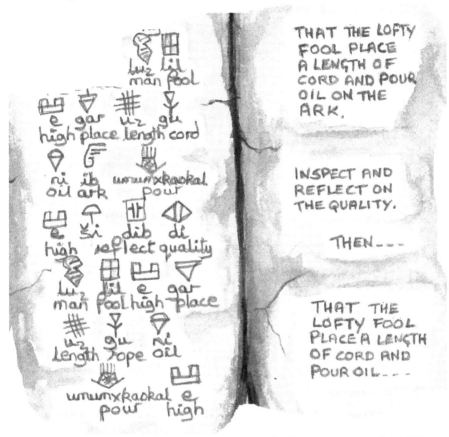

Perhaps by looking more closely at KID, including as source of Al Khidr, more sense can be made of the word, although the evasive nature of that ghostly figure does not bode well for a satisfactory conclusion.

Green Mat, Red Carpet

Muhammad al-Bukhari, an Islamic scholar writing in the 9th century AD, suggested that the name Khidr came about because the ground over which the holy figure passed became green thanks to his presence; Arabic 'khidr' means 'green'. That interpretation offers a perfect match for Sumerian KID, the reed mat, which one would also naturally expect to be green. Joining up some invisible dots, this connection leads to the integration of another figure in an ever-broadening range of possibilities: the Green Man of the Celts, yet another figure of immense but vague antiquity, naturally related to fertility and growth inferred by the colour. But there are enough players already on this board. The Green Man, however relevant, must watch from behind his leaves. Osiris is also given as being green.

According to the ETCSL corpus of proper nouns, there are ninety cases of Anunna with added KID in known tablets and ninety without:

→ AN A NUN KID NE is found 17 times in 13 different texts.

→ AN-A-NUN-NA-KID-NE appears 73 times in over 40 texts.

→ AN-A-NUN-NA-KID-NE-ER, ER being 'to go', 'to wander', is added to 5 of the above.

→ AN-A-NUN-NA: 90 versions do not incorporate KID at all.

| AN | A | NUN | NA | KID | NE | ER |

It may be that these variations were the result of copying and recopying an important phrase over hundreds or even thousands of years. However, Mesopotamian scribes were skilled and careful. It rather goes to show that the AN-A-NUN-NA and the KID were intimate but not inseparable.

KID   NE

In the examples given above, KID, with its strange assortment of given meanings – 'mat', 'ghost', 'wind' and 'fool' - is invariably partnered with NE, symbol of fire, burning and renewal. Together they might translate to 'the fiery mat', 'the new mat', perhaps even 'the red mat or carpet' for the colour of fire. With the addition of ER in five examples, KID-NE-ER becomes 'on a red carpet to err'.

I am a mortal, a man; I cannot trample upon these tinted splendors without fear thrown in my path.

Aeschylus, a Greek tragedian, wrote those lines in 458 BC in a play about Agamemnon, King of Mycenae, who, on his return from the Trojan wars, modestly turns down the invitation to walk into town along a red carpet.

Thus, it appears that a red carpet was uniquely associated with godly figures once upon a time and too good for mere mortals, a theme that continues into our less obviously spiritual times, its original significance long lost. And surely the king was no fool. He associated the red carpet with fear.

A Ghostly Vision

Both green and red can equate to renewal, the green for nature and red for regenerating fire. If we accept that symbol KID is at the origin of the Arabic proper name, KID-NE also translates to 'renewal/rebirth of Khidr'. That translation corroborates the view of Al Khidr as immortal after drinking the waters of eternal youth, becoming green again.

The other meaning of KID as 'ghost' given in Sumerian lexicons might also fit the bill of Khidr as someone who was adept at appearing and disappearing unexpectedly. In one version of the story of Al Khidr, the waters he drank were from 'the river of life'. The concept ties in with others, most notably Greek Hebe's potion, the little that is known of the Ancient Greek Eleusinian mysteries. (p.169) and the eternal youth who appears out of the analysis of the symbols stemming from Genesis (p.86). The red colour of the hibiscus flower also comes to mind in that context. The brew is red and the renewed life is green. Then again, the amanita muscaria mushroom is also a brilliant red and might be seen as carpeting the ground, its potent and dangerous qualities instilling both fear and a form of flight.

So, despite the long white beard sported in the images, Khidr has attained immortality while staying forever young – which, of course, implies that he is still around, lurking somewhere in ghostly form before his next appearance out of…out of where exactly? KID-NE-ER, the wandering red ghost?

If I were to stray further afield, I might point to the regeneration of the kidney, a recently discovered attribute of that red bean-shaped organ that lies in a particularly inaccessible position in the human body, hidden and therefore ghostly. Of course, it would be unexpected to see the origin of its name in Sumerian KID-NE-ER… and unthinkable that its capacity for regeneration were known about before now, let alone thousands of years ago.

Nevertheless, an extremely ancient fascination with kidneys is documented and it does fit well with that curious and hitherto unexplained bundle carried proudly forward by the fourth standard-bearer on the Egyptian Narmer Palette[1] behind NAR, a sleep-inducing fox, a 'renard' as the French would call it, also of Sumerian origin (p.110).

The word 'kidney' is of unknown source, first found in 14ᵗʰ century Old English kidenere – a word that came out of nowhere and for no apparent reason. Neer is 'kidney' in several languages.

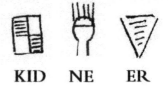

KID   NE   ER

ER has given meanings which include 'to plunder', 'to exude', 'to go', 'to carry' to which I have added quite reasonably 'to err' and 'to wander', bearing in mind Plato's character, Er, who was the Greek celestial wanderer par excellence. KID-NE-ER as 'the wandering kidney' sounds a little far-fetched but 'carrying the kidney' becomes perfectly reasonable thanks to that quite explicit Egyptian image. The notion of a Sumerian kidney was certainly worth a little research:

A person has two kidneys, one of which counsels him to do good, and the other counsels him to do evil. And it is reasonable that the good one is on his right and the evil one on his left, as it is written, "The heart of the wise man is to his right, and the heart of a fool is to his left." [1]

From KID To Kid

While studying the text known as *Enki's Journey to Nibru*, it came to mind that the KID in the combination AN EN KID, from which both Enlil and Nibru are derived, might also refer to the young goat carried by Enki in numerous seal images. It's true that, unlike the majority of my findings, orthodox Sumerian lexicons give no indication whatsoever of any connection between the two, i.e., 'Kid', a young goat, does not appear as a meaning of KID in any dictionary, but the idea can be defended. Beyond the obvious phonetics, the Lord between sky and earth, always translated to Enki, often holds his kid under one arm, an offering with which to seduce the cosmic Matriarch. The superficially humorous line 16 is translated and illustrated (with a detail from an existing seal) with that in mind. Does symbol KID have more than one significant meaning? It seems so.

In context, the house is also a vessel in the sky, the ship in which Enki sails. NUN is given here as 'otherworldly' from NU-UN, 'not' and 'land' or 'people', 'not of the land', 'not of the people'. It is also an example of KA-NUN, source of Greek kanon (p.68) used in context.

The problem in identifying KID as 'kid' the young goat, is how to link it – if at all - to Al Khidr, the Arabic prophet on his fish. It is more easily linked to the notion of 'kidney' in that the animal is obviously intended as an offering. Then again, it may be that the animal acquired its name because the owner of it was a fool. There exists a solid link between Al Khidr and fools.

One possible link between fish and the young goat lies in astronomy/astrology, more specifically with the constellation of Capricorn:

while Jensen says that in Babylonia the Goat and Fish, both complete, were occasionally used together for the constellation. (…) [1]

Jensen says that " the amphibious Oannes of the Persian Gulf was connected with the constellation Capricornus " [2]

Berossos is reported by Seneca to have learned from the old books of Sargon that the world would be destroyed by a great conflagration when all the planets met in this sign. (…) [3]

That last quote also refers to the constellation of Capricorn and again brings to mind the danger that exists according to Zechariah Sitchin's books in the form of a ghostly planet destined to reappear at some unknown point in time. Is there a link to be made between Sumerian KID and Capricorn's goat, between the KID of Enlil's NI-IB-RU and Sitchin's Nibiru? If there is, it is a ghostly one. I can bring nothing more to the table in that regard, at least for the moment. But just imagine having the 'old books of Sargon' to read on a rainy Sunday afternoon. I wonder how Sargon acquired them.

Fool Of God

Finally, there is the irrefutable, unshakeable link between Arabic Al Khidr and Sumerian KID through the meaning 'fool' attested in Sumerian lexicons as dating from the Old Babylonian period ca.1800 BC:

In this dialogue Khidr asks the 'fool of God', "Oh perfect man, will you be my friend?" And the reply from the one, in the Way of God, is, You and I are not compatible, for you have drunk long draughts of the water of immortality so that you will always exist, and I wish to give up my life.

That quote comes from the Mantiq al-Tayr , an allegorical poem by Attar (AD 1145-1221) and it throws up the intriguing possibility that Attar's work was at least partially based in some extremely ancient Sumerian texts, a thought that had already crossed my mind when reading The Conference of the Birds, another long allegorical poem with Hermetic overtones and Sumerian connections. KID, the fool, is a precious piece of an ancient puzzle binding Sumerian Hermeticism to the Sufism attested in the much later Islamic period.

According to this account, Al Khidr is not himself the fool, indicating that the Sumerian KID is related to the notion of foolishness in the same way as Enki's kid. It is not the animal that is foolish but the hero for attempting to carry it up to the cosmic Matriarch along with his ego. My theory is that, thanks to the Sumerian fable, the kid goat became forever attached to its master's folly. But I could be wrong.

Always Three Times

Ibn Arabi claimed to have met Al Khidr three times. On one occasion he came across the prophet walking on water and talking in a strange language. On another, he saw Khidr make a prayer rug fly into the air, an achievement that naturally conjures up the image of a magician and again of KID as the mat, the flying carpet.

No direct mention of Al Khidr is made in the Quran. However, Islamic scholars believe that this is the figure who appears in Sura 18 and who is followed around and hassled by Arabic Musa (biblical Moses). The section begins with mention of a fish destined to be eaten for supper but which, forgotten, comes to life and escapes back to its river – a lost and disappearing fish and thus a promising start.

But when they reached the junction between them, they forgot their fish, and it took its course into the sea, slipping away.[1]

Moses, who has the uneasy role of the fool in this story, is allowed to walk with Al Khidr on the condition that he ask no questions.

He said, "Then if you follow me, do not ask me about anything until I make to you about it mention."[2]

However, given the inexplicable acts carried out by Khidr during their journey, Moses can't resist.

So they set out, until when they had embarked on the ship, al-Khidhr tore it open. [Moses] said, "Have you torn it open to drown its people? You have certainly done a grave thing."[3]

Khidr rebukes him for his forgetfulness.

So they set out, until when they met a boy, al-Khidhr killed him. [Moses] said, "Have you killed a pure soul for other than [having killed] a soul? You have certainly done a deplorable thing."[4]

Khidr responds by reminding Moses that he is showing himself to be incapable of patience.

So they set out, until when they came to the people of a town, they asked its people for food, but they refused to offer them hospitality. And they found therein a wall about to collapse, so al-Khidhr restored it. [Moses] said, "If you wished, you could have taken for it a payment."[5]

And so we discover that Al Khidr was a competent builder. That is the point at which they part company, but only after Khidr gives his reasons for his actions: The boat was sunk to prevent it being taken from its poor owners by a king. The boy was killed to prevent him becoming a disappointment to his parents. The wall was rebuilt to hide the treasure left in it for two youngsters by their father so that they would not find it until adulthood. Perhaps they all appear valid reasons to some, but to others they continue to be questionable. Was a riddle intended and, as with so many others, the keys lost in translation?

A metaphor in the final act of Khidr is a possibility - a wall reconstructed to last until adulthood – or a riddle constructed to be slowly unravelled, its truths discovered only after lengthy enquiry, forever hidden from those unwilling to make the effort or too impatient to follow a trail to its destination. Where is the wall? Is it still standing? How many times has it been rebuilt? Does the treasure still exist?

Circling The Oceans

Jirjīs al-Nabī is yet another Arabic prophet of no confirmed origin or existence. This one, like Dhul Nun and Al Khidr, is interesting for both his name and elements of his story. Jirjis is said to have been executed by the King of Syria, with no approximate date or name given, and to have miraculously resuscitated three times at which point he took to cursing all and sundry, which is hardly surprising. [1]

Jirjis, which can be read as JIR-JIS, the fish and the tree, is of Sumerian origin:

JIR / PIS

JIR, given as 'fish' and 'to do something three times', also brings to mind the three acts of Al Khidr listed above. JIR has a number of interesting phonetic forms:

As already mentioned, it's the source of our word 'fish' through PIŠ/PEŠ and the name of the constellation of Pisces from Latin piscis. This is Poseidon, god of the sea, through PUS.

As phonetic KIR, it's one source of Greek kirkos, the circle. I suggest that, read as GIR, it's also the source of our word 'green'. Apparently, Arabic Jirjis translates to George, and it has been suggested that this mysterious prophet is in fact the same figure as Saint George. All of this leads me to add the prophet Jirjis to the long list of names and mysteriously fishy characters originating from one pagan source, the same source as that of NUN-KI and HA-A-KI, the first city of the antediluvian Sumerian King List.

Sailing The Skies

yet for most of this we should probably look to the Desert, where the stars would be as much required and relied upon for guidance as on the trackless ocean, and so necessarily objects of attentive interest and study. Indeed, Muljammad told his followers, in the 6th Sura of the Kur'dn : God hath given you the stars to be your guides in the dark both by land and sea.[1]

One of the first points made in the introduction to *Star Names and Their Meanings* is that it was not only sailors who navigated by the stars. Not all expanses are wet. Guiding stars would have taken on a variety of identities according to the environment of the watcher. Crossing huge swathes of desert on the routes between east and west, swaying along on lofty camels with no boundary stones, no signposts to show the way, nomadic merchants with little or no attachment to the sea would also have needed to identify the elements of the night skies in order to survive. Perhaps the sky was divided up into dry land for the sheep (who share their symbol LU with the source of 'luminous' and 'lunar') and other animals, and into oceans, lakes and rivers for the fish.

but she (Andromeda) seems to go far back of classical times, and we probably must look to the Euphrates for her origin, with that of her family and Cetus.[2]

201

Neither astronomer nor mathematician and sadly no great swimmer, I have been skirting around the celestial ocean for some time in this investigation, sorely tempted to look away while Cetus, the Great Whale, and AB-GAL, Father of the Great Sea, Sage and Apkallu, stared me down. My reluctance to dive into the sea of this Sumerian puzzle stems from the tangled web of ancient astrological references from different cultural sources and their mythologies, confused and confusing. Trying to match them to their origins in the equally complex Sumerian language is a daunting task. But that is the direction in which these swirling oceans have been ineluctably pulling me. Like Moses behind the ghostly Al Khidr, I have no choice but to shut up and keep up if I want the answers to my questions.

Ancient astronomy/astrology is such a broad subject that I will only dip respectfully into its peripheral waters and hope that will suffice to bring some clarity. As discussed in the section 'Egyptian Genesis' (p.90), the name of Harran, homeland of the Sabian stargazers, the astronomers who were also said to be magicians, can be taken one step further than its epithet 'Churning millstone in the sky'. Symbol HAR/HUR, also the name of the Great Sphinx of Giza (p.92), can be broken down into HA and AR. A reminder:

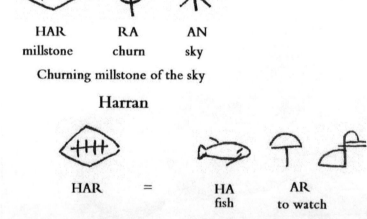

HAR	RA	AN
millstone	churn	sky

Churning millstone of the sky

Harran

HAR	=	HA	AR
		fish	to watch
		ŠI	RI
		to see	gather

On the celestial millstone, watching the fish.

Phonetic AR, comprising two symbols, is not given as 'to watch' in orthodox lexicons. Nevertheless, read individually, ŠI, the 'eye', coupled with RI, the 'collecting', 'gathering' bird, give 'the eyes to gather' leading to 'to watch'. This is one source of the name Sirius and founding symbol of the Archons, the biblical watchers. It can also read the 'eye of the bird', perhaps Noah's bird watching for land or the waterbirds keeping an eye out for food. Context is everything but fish appear to be essential to the cosmic theme.

I have already attempted to link KID to Khidr and then to the kid goat through the constellation of Capricorn coupled with the sound of the name. Now, I find another celestial path that must be followed to see where it leads; linking KID to Ketus. Cetus, the Whale, from Greek ketus, is one of the most ancient constellations according to *Star Names and Their Meanings*. The following comments are noteworthy:

The biblical school of the 17th century of course saw here the Whale that swallowed Jonah; and commentators on that great astronomical poem, the Book of Job, have said that it typified the Leviathan of which the Lord spoke to the patriarch. (…) Although an old constellation, Cetus is by no means of special interest, except as possessing the south pole of the Milky Way and the Wonderful Star, the variable Mira.[1]

That sounds promising, relatively straightforward even; the south pole of the Milky Way and a 'Wonderful' star (recently) named Mira. A variable star is one of fluctuating luminosity that can be observed from Earth.

Its period, fixed by Bouillaud in 1667 as 333 days, is now given as 331 but this is subject to extreme irregularities, — at various times it has not been seen at all with the naked eye for several years consecutively, — and its maxima and minima are even more irregular.[2]

According to the modern record, it was a German pastor, David Fabricios, in 1596 who established that Mira not only increased significantly in brightness over a short period, but also disappeared completely only to appear again in cycles of around eleven months. Add to that its classification as a red giant, a star in the process of burning itself out, and it is not impossible to interpret Mira as a KID-NE-ER, the wandering and even ghostly red planet of Cetus.

Sir William Herschel wrote of it in 1783 as being of a deep garnet color…[3]

What might be the effect of observing such a strongly fluctuating light in the night skies? Presumably, it wouldn't have been of great use as a navigational tool. Did the astronomers of old discover by chance that it sat inside the constellation of an imaginary whale or was the whale imagined around the star? A couple of possibilities come to mind:

Whales have a similarly fluctuating particularity whereby all the air contained in their lungs is propelled in one violent outburst from the nose as they surface to breathe. Since the nose is situated on the top of the snout, this results in impressive jets of water reaching, for some species, up to forty feet in the air. Then there is the equally unusual phenomenon of ambergris, a solid waxy substance produced in the digestive system of sperm whales. Known as whale vomit, it has always been considered precious, used in the ancient world as an incense and a medicine. The Arabs called it 'anbar'. Still today, a lump of ambergris found by chance along the seashore merits a mention in the media and spells certain riches for the lucky finder. Could the occasional discovery of the precious substance and/or the irregular spouts of water from the nostrils of whales have been taken as metaphors for the activity of Mira? Perhaps. Perhaps not. It's a suggestion.

The constellation of Cetus is situated along the great, winding river Eridanus, in a region of the sky once known as the Water or the Sea. Again, according to *Star Names and Their Meanings*:

Capricornus, Cetus, Delphinus, Eridanus, Hydra, Pisces, and Piscis Australis, all the watery shapes in the early heavens, with Argo and Crater, are in this neighborhood; some of whose stars Aratos said " are called the Water"; indeed in Euphratean astronomy this region of the sky was the Sea, and thought to be under the control of Aquarius. [1]

QUID Is The Question

KID

Searching for other etymological links with Sumerian KID, I came across Old English 'quid' which is given as a source for the first syllable of 'kidney', (p.196) a word of otherwise unknown origin. Old English quid had the meaning 'belly, womb, stomach'. It is equated with 'cud',[2] the name given to food regurgitated into the mouth and chewed again by ruminating animals like cows, a digestive process not dissimilar to the gizzard stones used by certain birds of which the now extinct dodo.

The ambergris vomiting phenomenon of the whale again comes to mind, although it's still not clearly established if that substance is vomited or excreted anally. The next obvious phonetic link with KID is Latin quid, a neutral accusative singular form of 'what', a questioning. Consolidating:

→ Ketus, the whale, (Greek)

→ Cetus, constellation of the Whale containing a fluctuating red giant, (Latin)

→ KID-NE, the red ghost, the new-born fool (Sumerian)

→ Khidr, disappearing wisdom teacher who is eternal and walks on water, (Arabic)

→ Kidney, dual, regenerating, red bean-shaped organ, centre of moral choice and indicative of foolishness, (English)

→ Quid, the questioning, linked to Kidr through the questions of Moses, the fool, (Latin)

→ Quid, the stomach (Old English)

→ Quid to Cud (from Sumerian TAR/KUT), the regurgitated contents of the stomach, resin (Old English/English)

→ NUN, the foremost (Sumerian)

→ Nun, the whale, linked to Greek Ketus, also the whale (Arabic)

→ Dhul Nun, the One of the Whale, an ascetic monk, (Arabic)

→ NUN-KI, also HA-A-KI, City of the Disappearing Fish. (Sumerian)

→ NUN-ME, sage, magician, also Great Father, the Apkallu. (Sumerian)

The Stone Whale

Cetus, the Whale or Sea Monster... has been identified, at least since Aratos' day, with the fabled creature sent to devour Andromeda, but turned to stone at the sight of the Medusa's head (Algol) in the hand of Perseus. [1]

It's one thing to get ever closer to the full meanings of NUN and KID individually but another to get to the bottom of the phrase: AN-A-NUN-NA with or without KID-NE. Thanks to Greek mythology and to

Ketus/Cetus, a concrete link can be made between NUN, the Arabic whale, and NA, the stone:

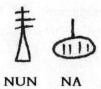

NUN   NA

Then again, the problem with a stone whale is that it can only be explained in terms of a strange story about a maiden held captive on a rock, ogled by an ugly sea monster and saved by a handsome prince in winged sandals, a hero with a blood-dripping snake-infested head in his hand. Superficially, it confirms NA in this context as a qualifier of NUN, but what can be done with a stone whale once we have it in hand?

The earliest images of Cetus date to the 6th century BC when it was painted onto a Greek vase. Bearing in mind that Ketus/Cetus is not just any whale but, according to the Greeks, a veritable sea monster, it comes as no surprise that it has two front paws, shown in the image (p.201). On the old celestial maps, the paws of Cetus dangle across the river Eridanus, infringing on its boundaries, creating a bridge. Why would a whale, of stone or of flesh, be portrayed with paws? Where did that image originate?

An Arm Or A Leg

The Greek name for the celestial river Eridanos stems unsurprisingly from Sumerian ERIDA, also given as ERIDU, phonetic forms of symbol NUN. This corresponds to the transliterated form found as 'eridug-ki' (p.31) in the antediluvian King List. Thus, NUN can be read as the celestial river Eridanus while also named as a disappearing fish and potentially a whale. NUN as source of the name of the river Eridanus leads to new combinations. The lexical entries break down Erida and Eridu as follows:

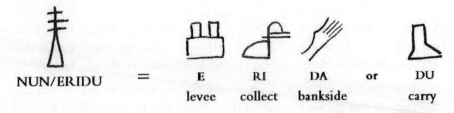

NUN/ERIDU	=	E	RI	DA	or	DU
		levee	collect	bankside		carry

water collection by the riverside

E is given as 'levee' in the lexicons, an elevated construction or natural feature linked to the containment of water, and a symbol of height. It's probable that RI, symbol of the 'collector' bird, is source of 'river', yet another word of unknown origin.

Another clue comes from the Sumerian lexical lists where NUN/ERIDA appears under the enigmatic and inverted guise of DA-URU. URU is also read as ERI and RI_2 and is usually understood as 'city'. The meaning of the two together is 'to be eternal', a fitting attribute of the celestial river but perhaps overstated for a city on Earth:

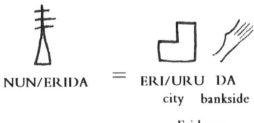

NUN/ERIDA = ERI/URU DA
city   bankside

Eridanus

to be eternal

The original symbol URU/ERI remains eternal, whatever name is given to it. That is the secret to decoding the original language: go back to the pictogram wherever possible. Find the image as it was in the beginning. In one case from the Uruk IV archaeological period, the name has been attributed to what is quite obviously a complete three-step pyramid – shown here.[1]

URU is given as the Akkadian name for the city of Uruk, an important archaeological site in southern Mesopotamia that once sat alongside the river Euphrates and possessed an imposing three-step 'ziggurat' built during the Uruk III period, ca.3200-3000 BC. That said, symbol URU was not solely the name of that place – perhaps not the name of that place at all. Given the above analyses, it appears to have been a generic term having a deeper meaning. Another phonetic form of URU is ALA which potentially became Latin ala, the 'wing'.

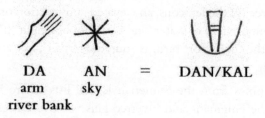

DA   AN   =   **DAN/KAL**

arm   sky

river bank

The arm of (pointing to) the river in the sky.

According to the lexical entries, DA, the arm, joined with AN, the sky, becomes DAN, the 'arm in the sky' or 'the arm to the sky'. If DA represents the banks of a river, DA-AN translates to 'river in/of/to the sky', the celestial river. And with DAN/KAL, we are once again within the realm of the Chaldean astronomers (p.51-52). Is the arm also that of Cetus, the whale?

I propose that the constellation Eridanus, the cosmic river, next to which lounges for eternity the long-armed stone whale of the constellation Cetus, touched down where the Euphrates and the Tigris began, in the Taurus mountains not far from Harran. In fact, the Eridanus is a never-ending and circular river. Some part of it touches down where all rivers flow on Earth while its snake-like body continues to turn in the sky. It flows and twists and turns back on itself, the bird-headed snake biting its own tail: a never-ending knot, the BU/PO which is both river and snake (p.139). The three-tiered pyramid known as URU - but also ERI - was constructed as an earthly link to the eternal Eridanus as are all the tall manmade structures, the standing stones, the obelisks, the nuraghes, towers and pyramids of a lost civilisation. Those of the NUR, the measurers, the creators of the norm, in turn created by the Nuns of Anunnaki fame.

The Mesopotamian rivers have a mysterious bird at their heart (p.127) while symbol GU₂/TIG, like the DA of the Eridanus, can be read as 'bank', a riverbank according to the Sumerian lexicons.

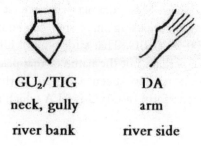

GU₂/TIG   **DA**

neck, gully   arm

river bank   river side

The Old Euphrates

The Akkadian composite name for the Euphrates river is Buranun, shown as UD-KIB-NUN in lexicons while the phonetic form appears in the lexical lists as BU-RA-NUN.

As shown here below, the river Euphrates originally had five signs to its name or two sets of three. Again, BU, the snake, is the founding symbol of Greek potamus, the river, and figures in the middle of the name Mesopotamia, the 'land between the rivers'. As 'po' is a generic term for any river and stems from the snake, the Mesopotamian snake can be said to writhe along every stream in the world. UD, the sun, appears as the first word, equivalent of BU. Together, the sun and the snake can be read as TAM-MUS, a cross-confirmation of the relevance of Tammuz, he for whom the women wept (p.140).

UD/TAM   KIB   NUN
sun   ring

BURANUN
Euphrates

BU/MUŠ   RA   NUN
snake   churn

KIB is represented by two GEŠ, two wooden beams, brought together as a cross, a crossbeam. Its main given meaning is 'ring' and it is also listed with words such as 'strength' and 'force' with an implication of competitivity. KIB gives the origin of Arabic 'kiblah' with the meaning 'which is opposite' and used to indicate the direction in which Muslims pray. At its origin, this would have been in the direction of the sun, the ultimate godlike entity in the Sumerian pantheon: UD-KIB, the ring of the sun.

Opposite KIB we find RA with the given meaning 'thresh' to which I have long since added 'to churn' extending the symbol easily into the churning, rotating movement of the celestial millstone but also, as with the Egyptian version, an epithet of the sun god. Old Norse kippa meaning 'to pull' or 'to snatch' might also stem from KIB/KIP.

Line 131 in *The Story of Sukurru* has the rising sun (UD) discover an intruding vessel (another given meaning of KAL/DAN) on its ocean. Snatching the ship's rope, it launches into a cursing scene.

In that story, the vessel is destined to follow the sun wherever it leads, attached by a rope. I suggest that these are age-old references to the counting of time according to the movements of the sun and the moon. DAN, the arm pointing upward, perhaps in the form of a sundial, a gnomon.

Both UD-KIB, the ring of the sun, and BU-RA, the churning river/snake are followed by NUN. The analysis shows that there is some concept linking the movement of the sun with the churning of the river. The NUN of the Anunnaki and of the Euphrates is the place where the counting begins. See the Latin kalends, ides and nones (p.69).

KIB is also phonetic GIB and the symbol of crossed beams gives the origin of the gibbet, the cross to which people were attached for crucifixion according to accounts in other languages. This is also the source of the jib, triangular foresail of a ship, and originally the T-shaped wooden poles to which the sail was attached. This is the beam to which Odysseus was tied on his homeward journey to avoid being influenced by the sweet songs of the Sirens. Perhaps after all, that is the ultimate meaning of the names of the Euphrates: the river which guides homeward.

The River Birds

The birds are the masters of flight, tasked with carrying in their beaks the cord of the Matriarch and on their backs the returning soul. It's with the help of the bird in flight that mankind can hope to return to the womb, to complete the circle, to be reborn. The Tigris is represented on the earliest tablets by a bird while its magnificent wing is portrayed next to GEŠ, the tree (p.132). Is the ring-collared bird on Pillar 43 at Gobekli Tepe the earliest version of this bird shown by other, later generations as an eagle? Clearly, it's not an eagle or a swan but there are numerous birds in the Sumerian lexicon. The river birds appear twice in *The Story of Sukurru* carrying the rope: on line 139 as DAR, the 'speckled bird', and line 161 as A-HU, the water birds.

DAR
speckled

The instructions whispered to Noah on line 65 of *The Story of Sukurru* from behind the reed façade include the words KA-SIG translated to 'soft voice'; SIG, with the given meaning 'weak', potentially gave 'cygnus', the whispering of the mute swan,[1] a song of death and eternal life, perhaps paired with NU, the knot of gnosis, and NUS, the egg of rebirth (p.174). In Greek, the swan is kyknos, strangely close to Greek gignos-kein and Sumerian KIK/GIG.

The ropes of the ship and the umbilical cord of the Matriarch are one and the same. They have been seized by the sun and the hero's ship is forced along to its home in the west, homeward bound, to the cleft in the mountain, to a cavernous place, to death. A return to the womb?

Riddle Of Odysseus

From their pictographic forms through to the alphabetic forms adapted from their accompanying phonetic values, the Sumerian language and its riddles have never ceased to exist and to fascinate. That is not an outrageous suggestion. The Sator enigma is the most prominent example of the transition of both words and enigma from symbol to alphabetic form. Another must be the hero mentioned by the equally enigmatic Greek author Homer: Odysseus.

I stumbled on the riddle of Odysseus while translating *The Story of Sukurru*. The name appears in the context of the celestial homeward path. The hero's vessel has just started out on its epic journey across the skies. It has yet to experience the heat and rage of the Exalted Sun but already the two children, a boy and a girl, are being snatched by a bird with great knowledge. Is this the original story of the children of Medea? Is this the story of Jason or Odysseus or both at the same time?

Three words on line 124 make up the name: ZU-E₂-ZU, 'to know' and 'house' or 'temple'. The two ZU surrounding E₂ comprise the riddle, the palindrome. You can go backwards or forwards to arrive at the temple. The temple is at the centre of all knowledge. Pictographic ZU, 'to know' takes the form of a pyramid, in this case two pyramids which between them convey all the knowledge of the home of the boy, of UŠ: foundation, the founding.

Confirmation of the enduring nature of the Odysseus riddle exists in Greek on the Siren vase in the British Museum where it's written UZ-E-UZ above the figure of the hero tied to the mast of his ship. The inscription on the Siren vase follows the line of the vessel's ropes and the following word in the Sumerian version is also 'rope'. In Sumerian, 'rope', 'to seize' and 'native' are three meanings taken from a pictogram of a piece of rope. The etymology of the name Odysseus is unknown and that inscription on the Siren vase remains unmentioned in the Museum's website text despite its presence in front of the bound hero's nose. The numerous instances of unexplained labelling on Ancient Greek artefacts have led to lengthy studies of the so-called 'nonsense' inscriptions. No-one had considered a Sumerian origin.

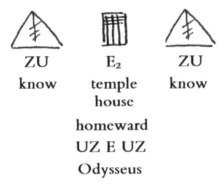

ZU	E$_2$	ZU
know	temple	know
	house	

homeward

UZ E UZ

Odysseus

My translation to 'home of ZU' was chosen to fit with the overall context (the bird ZU, specialist of the skies). The figure tied to the mast of a ship is a scene confirmed elsewhere in *The Story of Sukurru* and highly reminiscent of Jesus crucified.[1] OD/UD, the sun, and ZU-E$_2$-ZU a central temple of knowledge…

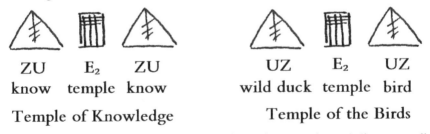

ZU	E$_2$	ZU		UZ	E$_2$	UZ
know	temple	know		wild duck	temple	bird

Temple of Knowledge   **Temple of the Birds**

In Homeric terms, ZU-E$_2$ translates simply to 'home to know', 'homeward', 'homeward bound'. However, Sumerian UZ is given as a 'wild duck'. In Ancient Egypt, it could be termed a goose. UZ, the duck or goose, stems from two symbols, ŠE, the seed, and HU, another word for 'bird'. Alongside symbol GA, UZ is given as 'cella', the inner chamber of a temple, and also intriguingly as 'treasure'. Given the obviously deliberate mirroring of sounds between *The Story of Sukurru* and the Greek vase showing Odysseus, mention of the following two anecdotal discoveries is perhaps relevant to the subject in hand:

- In 2020, a small stone chest was discovered at Deir el–Bahari, an important burial site on the west bank of the Nile, opposite Luxor in Egypt. It contained the skeleton of a goose and the egg of an ibis, individually wrapped in linen. There was also a small wooden box wrapped in four layers of linen. Shaped like a shrine, the box is inscribed with the name of the pharaoh Thutmose II who died in 1479 BC at the age of sixteen. No explanation has yet been found for the existence of the stone chest in that place or its contents.

- Another intriguing discovery made in Egypt in 2008 involves a discreet tomb full of mummified birds on the Giza plateau behind which researcher and author Andrew Collins along with two other explorers rediscovered a vast cave system, previously mentioned on a map by 19th century explorers and then lost again.[1] The caves appear to lead towards the pyramids. Could there be a link with the Odysseus riddle? This is, after all, the lost world of Hermes Trismegistus who is also Egyptian Thoth.

THIS   IS

THE

WAY

The Magic Stone

Always without desire we must be found,
If its deep mystery we would sound.
But if desire always within us be,
Its outer fringe is all that we shall see. [1]

These phrases from the Tao Te Ching reflect a spiritual quest, a self-examining, the meditative silence of the ascetic monks alone at the mouths of their cave dwellings in barren desert settings, staring out at the night skies, those who have no possessions other than the clothes they wear, a staff for wandering and, in the case of Saint Anthony of Egypt, a pig for company.

'But if desire always within us be' is reminiscent of the story of Moses full of desire to advance quickly and to have the behaviour of Khidr explained to him before the master has spoken. To name something is to create a reference distinguishing it from everything else around. Even posing a question, as Moses does, means that the thing, the concept being questioned takes on a form, becomes a word, a noun, a name:

NA   ME

The Magic Stone

The Name

NA-ME is given in the lexicons as 'someone' and 'anyone'. In truth, this is the Philosopher's Stone, the lost Stone of the Magician. The Magician's Stone is the Name. What's in a name? ME, the spirit and the magic, is also given numerous times as the verb 'to be': NA-ME, 'to be stone', 'to be heavy', 'the heaviness of being'. Those special and rare collocations where NA is suffix - EDEN-NA, NUN-NA - are coded references to the original meaning, the most enigmatic of all alchemical references. A weightless name rises as does a weightless stone. Forget your name and the ego (p.128) attached to that name in order to become weightless.

The 'named' fits with symbol NUN as 'foremost', and as 'noun' while the 'nameless' also fits with NUN as 'none' through NU-UN, 'no-one' and even 'noon' when the shadow is absent, disappearing and reappearing. The nameless and the named are one. A name can be read at two levels: the spiritual and the physical. It can be read as earthly or cosmic. It can be read or not read. ME is or is not a name (See the riddle p.220).

When the work is done, and one's name is becoming distinguished, to withdraw into obscurity is the way of Heaven.[1]

One final monk appears in this investigation, this time out of ancient China; Lao Tzu, alternatively Laozi, Li Er, Li Dan and a few other possible names, said to be the author of the Tao Te Ching, Book of the Way and the Virtue. Lao Tzu is an epithet translating to 'Venerable Master'. Again, there is no record of a living person of that or those name(s) and no date can be safely attributed. It's suggested that he once conversed with Confucius in the 6th century BC, but there is no concluding evidence of that either. The most ancient fragment of his writings dates to the 3rd century BC. Clearly, someone wrote down the Tao Te Ching but who? And when? And why?

Lao Tzu commonly portrayed riding along on a water buffalo, an unlikely steed, calls to mind the acrobats leaping into the sky on the horns of the bull, an ancient Sumerian concept carried forward into the Minoan culture but also manifested in rock paintings from deep antiquity.[2]

That image also evokes symbol GIR₃ (p.57), the Sumerian bull's head in profile which, associated with KA, the 'word', has the given meaning 'path'. See where this is leading…

KA   GIR₃
Word of the Bull
The Way

KASKAL
Crossroads of the Beer
Chaldeans of Harran

It was a border guard who stopped Lao Tzu as he was riding off on his water buffalo never to return and requested that he write down his words of wisdom before leaving China. The presence of the border guard in that story evokes the Sumerian KAL/lamassu, the stone bull men who were always on duty at the temple gates and perhaps elsewhere, available for heavy labour but also to question and to call out the names of those who were passing through and, in later Roman times, the kalends, the calling out of the arrival of the new moon. KAL, source word of Chaldean (p.52), has the phonetic value DAN, the 'arm showing the sky' (p.208), while Lao Tzu also had the name Li Dan. Is that coincidence? Perhaps.

Sinking Down

For as Jonah was in the belly of the huge fish three days and three nights, so the Son of Man will be in the heart of the earth three days and three nights. (Matthew 12:40)

Jonah has long since disappeared from view. Who remembers the complete story of the prophet who was swallowed by a whale? How many priests use the tale to bang home the need to repent our sins? And what is a prophet?

Given as Nabi in Arabic, the prophets of old were unique among men in that they had a direct line to the Lord, interceding on His behalf - as did Jonah at Nineveh - to warn of great calamities and retribution on those who were not acting out their lives according to the divine will. The prophets were placed between sky, otherwise known as heaven, and Earth, between the lightness of the air and the weight of the stone: AN-NA, perhaps even between the lightness of air and the heaviness of the beer, NA-BI, where BI gives the source of Greek bios and 'to be'. NA-BI can also be read as the 'two stones' where BI is given the unorthodox meaning of 'binary': Two stones of prophecy there are.

Rising Up

In the same way that the sun at the winter and summer solstices hesitates for three days and nights before resuming its journey across the horizon, both Jonah and Jesus were held captive in cavernous dark places for three days and nights. In the next chapter of the Book of Matthew, we read more words from Jesus:

He told them another parable. "The kingdom of heaven is like leaven that a woman took and hid in three measures of flour, till it was all leavened." (Matthew 13:33)

The Hebrew word for 'leaven' is given as phonetic zumé. I propose that it was taken from the Sumerian, ME ZU, 'the Magic to know', also present in the name Mesopotamia, and that the source of the Hebrew word goes far beyond a basic cookery reference. Yeast or leaven is a magical ingredient. It transforms the flour into risen and en-lightened bread, an alchemical process. The following five symbols appear together in the form of a short but far-reaching proverb:[1]

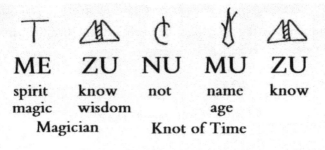

ME	ZU	NU	MU	ZU
spirit	know	not	name	know
magic	wisdom		age	
Magician			Knot of Time	

Your spirit to know,
your name not to know.
In ME, there is no self.
To know ME, forget your name.
To know ME, renounce your fame.

ZU, the pyramid form with the given meaning 'know' indicates a specialisation. In this case, ZU-ME or ME-ZU translate to 'the person who has knowledge of the magic' and becomes 'The Magician'. Add to that NU-MU-ZU and find 'The Magician whose name is unknown'. Four translations are given here. All are correct and this riddle can be usefully matched to the Sumerian concepts of name and ego.

It was inscribed on one of the numerous tablets of Sumerian 'proverbs' written in the style of the Old Babylonian period, ca.1900-1600 BC, and, based in just five words, is a game that keeps on giving. It can also be usefully compared to the writings of Ibn Arabi, a master of Sufism,[2] and to a number of verses in the Bible (p.153). At the same time, this is the 'Meso' of Mesopotamia: between the two, in the middle, taking the meaning of that region's name to a whole new level: the Magicians' land between two rivers.

T-shaped ME, known later as 'tau', is key to the understanding of many sections of the ancient texts. There is more to be gleaned from it than the apparent simplicity of a modern translation into 'magic' and 'spirit'. It appears three times in the three-word phrase between the word 'eye' in *The Story of Sukurru*, (p.158) where it indicates through both word and appearance that this is a straightforward reference to the pineal gland, the so-called third eye situated near the centre of the brain, a hormone-producing, light-sensing organ which has been scientifically linked to out-of-body experiences.

Of course, to claim that the Sumerian word ME was used in the full sense of 'pineal gland' would be to suggest that, in the 4th or early 3rd millennia BC or even earlier, there existed a group of people with scientific knowledge far beyond anything we have so far imagined for them.[1] And of course, to suggest that Saint Anthony of Egypt carried that T-shaped staff and kept that faithful pig as signs of his affiliation with an already age-old Gnostic sect founded in the kind of knowledge that comes through rituals involving consumption of hallucinogens would amount to a considerable dose of heresy. Nevertheless, foraging pigs are known to serve those who make use of the mushrooms that they find. And although it's difficult to imagine the pair searching for mushrooms in the sands of the Sahara desert, why else did the great saint have a pig as companion? And why is the Sumerian word for 'pig', ŠAH, also given with the meaning 'servant'?[2]

The Book

This humorous and barbed proverb[3] on a tablet from the Old Babylonian period ca.1900-1600 BC, confirms that there was just one figure who had the authority to go up to the sky with his questions and to bring back the book, the Tao, containing the answers for the benefit of a noisy rabble below.

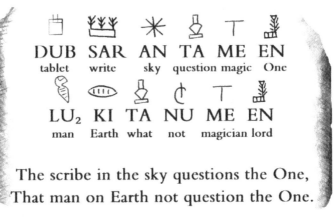

DUB SAR AN TA ME EN
tablet write sky question magic One

LU₂ KI TA NU ME EN
man Earth what not magician lord

The scribe in the sky questions the One,
That man on Earth not question the One.

LU₂-KI, 'man on Earth' gives the origin of Norse Loki, the quarrelsome character who drank in the company of Odin and other gods. He is said to have goaded one of them and then insulted a goddess who attempted to intervene to calm the situation in what can only be described as a fairly typical scene of drunken brawling in a tavern.

Who then is the scribe in this proverb? Enoch brought back a great deal of information in his book, a text which did not make the grade as a biblical text but which was important to the Gnostics at the beginning of our era. They hid it among the Dead Sea Scrolls inside a cave – alongside a copy or two of the Book of Jonah. Or was this a reference to Moses who was handed the tablets by God on a mountain? We're told that his followers were particularly undisciplined and looking elsewhere than to God for answers. They were the worshippers of the very unusual Golden Calf discussed in the context of Marduk (p.63). Was it Greek Sisithrus, another name for Noah, who was charged, according to Berossus, with writing and hiding the history of Earth before the flood? (p.260)

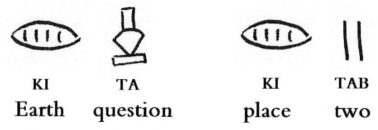

KI	TA	KI	TAB
Earth	question	place	two

Kitab, which is Arabic for 'book', comes from from Sumerian KI-TA, 'place', 'Earth' and 'question', which translates to 'the place of questioning' but also 'Earth to question' or potentially even 'the key to the question'. KI is given as 'place', 'ground' and 'earth' in lexicons. My understanding is that it was used alone as a reference to planet Earth. KI/KE as the source of 'key' is also likely. It is the phonetic mirror of IK/EK which has the given meaning 'door' and 'to open'. TA is the question. KI-TA: 'What is the place of Earth?'

There exists an alternative, or rather an additional source of Arabic kitab: KI-TAB, the place of the two, the place of duality. Symbols KI-TAB are found together in several lexical entries, preceded by GAR, 'to measure' and followed by symbol BA, 'below' or 'less', resulting in 'the measure of the pair below'. KI-TAB also translates to 'two keys'. There are various contexts into which those symbols might fit; the 'tab-ernacle, the two 'tab-lets of stone... Arabic kitab suggests that a great cosmic guidebook was written down somewhere, no doubt incorporating a riddle or two.

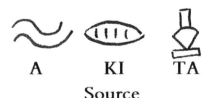

A   KI   TA

Source

A-KI-TA is given in orthodox Sumerian lexicons as 'source'.

Turning The Word

The oldest known versions of the term kabbalah take it not very far back to the 12th century AD and to Jewish mysticism, but with a sense of harking much further back to age-old oral mystical teachings, Hebrew kabbalah means 'received tradition' and Arabic qabala also involves the reception of knowledge from the past. In truth, both take their source in Sumerian:

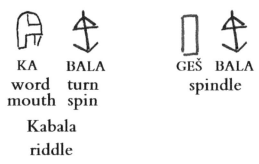

KA   BALA
word   turn
mouth spin

GEŠ BALA
spindle

Kabala

riddle

KA-BAL/BALA, the turned word, is best expressed as 'riddle'. It should not be a surprise to find that the word derives from a language that appears to have been largely invented for the purpose of spinning… BAL/BALA used with GEŠ becomes the 'wooden spindle'.

And not just any old weaving spindle. This is Plato's spindle, the wooden pole on which the entire cosmos turns:

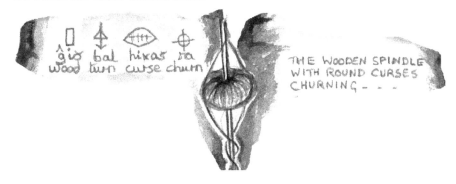

THE WOODEN SPINDLE WITH ROUND CURSES CHURNING - - -

On line 227 of *The Story of Sukurru*, the spindle is followed by HAR-RA, the churning millstone, also written as phonetic HUR, and source of the name Harran - potentially also source of the most ancient name given to the Great Sphinx of Giza: Hor/Haur (p.92). A translation as 'the spindle - the central wooden pole - of the millstone churning' would have been equally acceptable, the choice being made to continue in the more humorous style. Line 227 is the final line of the Solstice Riddle in which the KA of KA-BAL also appears.

From these ends is extended the Spindle of Necessity from which all the revolutions turn. Plato, Republic, Book X.

BAL/BALA gives the source of the first syllable of Greek 'palindrome' with its meaning 'recurrence'. A palindrome is a game in which words can be read both forwards and backwards with the same result, one example being the word 'tenet' central to the Sator Square (p.82). BAL is the rotation, the turning of the word, the riddle. [1]

AN	BAL	KI	BAL	AN	BA	KI	AN	BA
sky	rotate	Earth	spindle	sky	divide	place	upper	lower

The spindle of the universe turns, dividing Earth from sky.

AN-KI is given as 'universe' in the lexicons. The repetition of three AN in this nine-symbol proverb indicates the reference to MUL, three-star symbol of the well-known Babylonian astronomical tablet, MUL APIN.

Thanks to its positioning in the Solstice Riddle (p.290) and again in this proverb, it is safe to assume that the Sumerians used BAL as a means of encoding astronomical information. Was it meant to be seen as a light-hearted game of linguistic hide-and-seek or was there some deeper, potentially darker reason for the secrecy? Who knows?

THE MOUTH

OF THE
WHALE

Measure The Mouth

Arabic nun, the great fish, along with the epithet Dhul Nun, the One of the Whale, provide a convincing phonetic link to the Sumerian NUN, confirming that, if not himself a whale, then a monk and tutor with some interest in or link to the greatest mammal on our planet. There is a Sumerian word for 'whale' which has been missed in the orthodox Sumerian lexicons: BAL meaning 'to turn', 'to spin', 'the spinner', and BAL-E-EN 'lofty spinning of the Lord', leading directly to both 'whale' and 'baleen', nouns of otherwise unknown origin. I will insert a clear caveat at this point. There is nothing in the 'official' Sumerian lexicons to support this suggestion. It is mine alone.

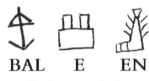

BAL   E   EN

baleen whale

The high spinning Lord

The baleen whale has a filtrating comb in its mouth in place of teeth, so no immediate chewing. It might swallow you whole but that's another matter. There is a minute chance of surviving like Jonah if the great fish decides to spew you up before its digestive juices go to work… possibly leaving time to sit in the dark interior and to reflect on one's own small size. The mouth of a whale is worthy of consideration. It can catch and eat huge quantities of small fish at one go, a useful feat for a mammal which lives in water but must take its oxygen from the air above, an animal that lives both above and below. Watch its breath-taking spin as it shoots up out of the sea; impressive enough to be dubbed 'Lord Baal', one might say.

The whale doesn't normally dine on humans. Jonah was an exception and, on reflection, got spat out like a dirty lump of ambergris. Perhaps the grumbling and bitterness of the prophet – or the grovelling - in the depths of the whale's stomach was perceived by the great beast as a pain that needed eliminating. Bitterness is a theme that appears more than once in the Sumerian texts. One of the suggested reasons for the 'belly of the whale' in that story has been that it equates to a womb,[1] the emergence from the mouth of the whale being a metaphor for rebirth, that of the initiate in some Eleusinian or cabalistic ritual. A mind-altering experience situated inside a cave comes to mind. KA-BAL tells us that, at some very early point in time, the link was made between the mouth of a whale and the spinning of words to form a riddle, to encode a secret. Was Jonah's story a riddle?

There comes a time when a leap of faith is the only way forward, the only path. In the introduction to this book, it was made as clear as crystal that nothing would be conjured out of my imagination, passed off as fact without explanation, or in any way unjustified and unjustifiable, and so it must be said:

→ KA-BAL is not given as 'riddle' in Sumerian lexicons, although it does appear as 'translate' and can be read as 'the turned word'.

→ BAL is not given as 'whale'.

→ BAL-E-EN does not appear opposite 'baleen' in those lexicons, although the three symbols do appear together more than once, notably in the context of a riddle (p.230).

It is only through my own translations – of which that riddle - carried out according to the unorthodox monosyllabic method, that those sources re-emerge into the light of day. Another potential example is found in AN BAL KI BAL, the four opening words of the riddle on p.224, which might also read 'Celestial whale and Earthly whale' or 'The whale between sky and Earth' (dividing the above from the below). Should they be ignored because lost along the way as the entire story of Mesopotamian Jonah and his whale have been lost from the equally Mesopotamian corpus of literature? BAL as whale is as fully justified here as possible from the material in hand. Not only do I take responsibility for the baleen whale but will add other unorthodox meanings into the mix for good measure:

→ BAL as the source of 'wall'.

→ KA-BAL: the words on the wall.

→ BAL and EN as direct source of Greek palin, first word of 'palindrome', meaning 'back' and 'again', and given as 'from PIE root'.

The caveat is firmly in place. The reader of this must decide for themselves.

After reflecting on the following riddle, I typed two words into a search engine: 'Giza Whale'. With no previous knowledge of any link between whales in general and the site of the Great Pyramid of Giza in particular, it was my findings in the process of preparing this book that led me to that rewarding search. Whether or not the information can be linked to the Sumerian puzzle (which I now officially dub The Riddle of the Whale) is, like my other suggestions and theories, for the reader of this to decide.

Whale Valley

Only some 150 kilometres south-west of the Giza plateau, Wadi Al-Hitan, known as Whale Valley, has in recent years been listed as a World Heritage site. The region contains fossils of whales eighteen metres in length, some completely intact and preserved by the dry heat of the Sahara desert. They swam around the place in a shallow sea some forty million years ago. While Wadi Al-Hitan is unique for the quantity and quality of the whale fossils, it is also fascinating to note that these early species were found to have both front and back feet. The great fish had once walked and, in that, they are strangely reminiscent of the 16th century Cetus with its front paws lolling across the Eridanus river (p.201). They also evoke all those images of fish gods with human arms and legs, sometimes portrayed with the open mouth of the fish appearing above a human head - in the manner of the Pope's headdress…

Fossils such as the whales of Wadi Al-Hitan must surely have come to the attention of humans thousands of years ago, here in proximity to Giza and in other locations too. It is completely safe to say that the long sinuous lines of vertebrae and other bones have been lying in that valley throughout history, not for thousands but for millions of years, and it is reasonable to imagine that at least some were discovered and studied long before the Great Pyramid was erected nearby, and that they were known even before the rocky mound of the Sphinx was whittled down, her own front paws stretched out to face the rising sun, stretched out to touch the former bank of the river Nile.

How were those massive skeletons perceived by ancient cultures? Did the concept of evolution have a place in their teachings? Were they deeply religious, profoundly superstitious? Did they equate whales which had feet and arms and were lying on dry ground with the whales that seafarers had surely seen in Mediterranean waters and elsewhere? Is it reasonable to assume that their skeletal remains were not unknown? Were the people who passed through the Wadi Al-Hitan land dwellers with no knowledge of the sea, uninformed of the existence of such sea creatures? Surely not all of them. Did they notice the feet and toes, the flipper hands with fingers and wonder how that could possibly have happened? A whale with human features or a man inside a whale? Hebrew 'balah' has the meaning 'to become old' and 'to waste away' but also 'not' and 'nothing'. Is that coincidence? Perhaps. A passage from Allen's *Star Names and their Meanings* concerning the constellation of Cetus, the whale, adds a layer to that mystery:

Equally veracious additions to the story, from Pliny and Solinus, are that the monster's bones were brought to Rome by Scaurus, the skeleton measuring forty feet in length and the vertebrae six feet in circumference; from Saint Jerome, who wrote that he had seen them at Tyre; and from Pausanias, who described a near-by spring that was red with the monster's blood. But the legend in which Cetus figured seems to have been current on the Euphrates long before our era...

Cetus, however, has been the usual title from the days of Vitruvius, varied by Cete with the 17th-century astronomical writers, although the stellar figure is unlike any whale known to zoology. The Harleian and Leyden Manuscripts show it with greyhound head, ears, and fore legs, but with a long, trident tail ; the whole, perhaps, modeled after the ancient bas-relief of Perseus and Andromeda in the Naples Museum. It is found thus on the Farnese globe, (...) [1]

The suggestion here is that the natural mound which became the Great Sphinx of Giza was originally sculpted to correspond to some extent to the impressive creatures found lying nearby and that its paws extend towards the Nile in the way that those of celestial Cetus hang over the banks of the eternal river Eridanus.

I also suggest that the Magicians of Harran were in awe of the great stone creature which the equally great magician Hermes Trismegistus, founder of their civilisation and language, was responsible for bringing into existence. He was responsible for naming it HAUR and HOR, from HAR/HUR, the millstone, the watching fish - which also gives the source of Old Norse 'har' which had the meanings 'fish', and 'shark', and also 'high' and 'proud' for no otherwise obvious reason. Therein lies the primary reason for the Harranian tradition of pilgrimages to Egypt.

And I see in the following riddle yet another link between the Sumerian language and the whale, between the whale and the monuments of the Giza plateau. But of course, all of this is theory: the idea that BAL is source of 'whale' and that there was once a whale or some strange four-legged hybrid creature in place of the Sphinx as we know it today. It might also be that that the riddle refers uniquely to long lost structures and to great stones of Mesopotamia. I give my opinion. Nothing more. As with any self-respecting palindrome, a constant back and forth between the words and their fundamental meanings is the winding path leading to truth. If the maze of information here spins heads, that's what it was designed to do. Truth spirals upwards. The reader of this was forewarned.

Riddle Of The Whale

Confirmation of KA-BAL as source not only of 'riddle' but also 'the mouth of the whale' comes in the first line of this riddle.[1] Given meanings alongside my offerings with some of the possible interpretations of the first line are shown here. The full riddle is given below (p.232) with further clues:

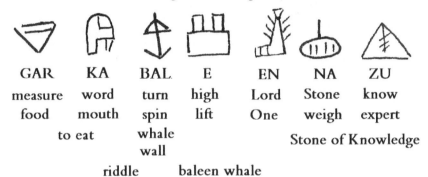

GAR	KA	BAL	E	EN	NA	ZU
measure	word	turn	high	Lord	Stone	know
food	mouth	spin	lift	One	weigh	expert
	to eat	whale				
		wall				

riddle		baleen whale

Stone of Knowledge

Eaten by the lofty whale, the weight of the Lord to know

Measure the words on the wall of the one architect.

Measure the riddle of the Baleen Whale and the Lord of the Stone.

'Eaten by the whale' is a reasonable suggestion for GAR-KA-BAL followed by 'the Lord'. Jonah, once inside the whale, might find there the stone known as ambergris. KA with GAR, as GU₇, have given meanings 'to eat' and 'to consume'.

NA-ZU give the 'stone specialist', the mason or architect. But it might be a reference to heaviness; 'weight to know', perhaps the person in charge of the scales, someone like Osiris weighing hearts at the moment of death.

Then again, 'measure the mouth of the whale' might be a veiled reference to some astronomical event, for example the monthly disappearance and reappearance of the moon, constantly swallowed and regurgitated. See NUN as the halfway house in that regard (p.69). The complete Riddle of the Whale is posted here below. I have done my best with it but there is always the possibility of something missed, some word unturned or turned the wrong way, some tale lost to time, a wall destroyed and beyond rebuilding. Between what is written above and what is written below, all the known elements are provided. Other sections of this book might provide further clues. It's a question of looking at everything with an open mind and within a variety of possible contexts.

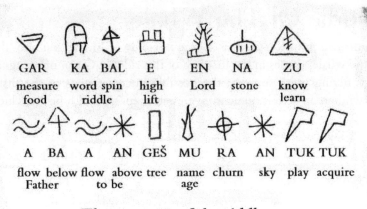

GAR	KA	BAL	E	EN	NA	ZU
measure food	word riddle	spin	high lift	Lord	stone	know learn

A	BA	A	AN	GEŠ	MU	RA	AN	TUK	TUK
flow below Father	below	flow above to be	above	tree	name age	churn	sky	play	acquire

**The measure of the riddle
of the Stone Whale (and Lord) to know,
Flowing below, flowing above
On the renowned Tree
The music of the skies is played.**

GAR: To measure the word but also to give the measure of the music.

KA-BAL: The turned word and mouth of the whale. A potential link to Baal and Baalbek can be considered.

EN: Baal is linked to EN, the Lord, through both Hebrew and Akkadian sources (p.24). BAL is also given as source of Baal through Akkadian belu.
A-BA: See p.23.

AN: Appears twice and surrounds three symbols. That positioning might be significant.

GEŠ: The wooden beam used by the king of Byblos as a pillar for his palace and which contained the body of Osiris (p.150). See index of symbols p.265.

MU: MU is also phonetic MEHIDA.[1] See index of symbols p.265.

RA-AN: The churning of the sky, Two words found in the name Harran (p.52). I posit that RA is one epithet of the sun as 'churner' and an element of RA-NI, 'churner of the night', the moon, source of Hindu rani, 'queen'.

TUK: Given as 'to play a musical instrument' and 'to acquire', it is possible that the double symbol indicates that both meanings are to be used, never forgetting that LUL, the musician, is also NAR, the fox and trickster, source of 'narcotic' (p.110)

LOST STONES

Riddles, Riddles, Riddles

There are unsolved mysteries still lurking in the original versions of the pictographic and cuneiform Sumerian writings, a multitude of intriguing riddles and messages still waiting to be solved and understood. The most commonly recurring enigma since I began this journey has been that of the number three, symbol EŠ/SIN. Quite a few potential reasons for the importance of that number come to mind: for example, the three days and nights of the winter and summer solstices when the sun, the great deity of the ancient world, hesitates in its course along the horizon before turning back, ensuring continuity. The fertility of the earth was in the balance, in jeopardy, and the solstices were the subject of special festivals and rituals. One explanation for the mouth of the whale might be that it was a metaphor for the mouths of caves and other manmade stone structures into which the sun would be swallowed, its light hitting the deepest spot of the place at the time of the sun's rising on the winter solstice, the moment of rebirth from that womblike place. Anything that could be done - rituals, offerings, supplications - to avoid a permanent sinking of the great planet was undertaken during those three days and nights.

Of equal importance in the counting of time and the fertility of both land and people, whichever calendar system dominated at any period, the three phases of the moon gave the name of the later moon god SIN. Roman kalends, nones and ides were all taken from Sumerian concepts and words, becoming the three expressions of those cycles. It is said that the astronomers of Harran worshipped the god Sin. I would contest both words 'worship' and 'god' in that regard. The mindset of the Sabians, who first recorded the celestial movements, was not what those words in their modern setting imply.

The Solstice Riddle across lines 223 to 227 of *The Story of Sukurru* is annexed on p.290. It takes the form of an acrostic where the words KA-BAL, the riddle, and GEŠ-BAL, the spindle, are intertwined, read vertically and horizontally. Symbol NI was deliberately placed three times over three lines of text, and in sixth position each time, potentially linking to the 666 of the biblical quotation in Revelation, and the 666 talents of gold received by King Solomon every year. NI has the given meaning 'oil' to which I have added 'night'. NI is also an element of phonetic NITA/UŠ, the phallus, first syllable of Egyptian Osiris, and third syllable of AMA-NITA. The feminine SAL, symbol of the vulva and 'chamber' of 'salvation', is also present three times in first position in the Solstice Riddle. On the fourth line, SAL appears directly above GEŠ. After three nights, from SAL the birth of a sun, a son, from within the Tree of Life.

NI NI NI, SAL SAL SAL… three nights, salvation. Reference to an acrostic of this type is made in the City of God (Augustine of Hippo, 5th century AD):

For Flaccianus, a very famous man, who was also a proconsul, a man of most ready eloquence and much learning, when we were speaking about Christ, produced a Greek manuscript, saying that it was the prophecies of the Erythræan sibyl, in which he pointed out a certain passage which had the initial letters of the lines so arranged that these words could be read in them: Ἰησοῦς Χριστος Θεοῦ υἱὸς σωτηρ, *which means, "Jesus Christ the Son of God, the Saviour." (…)*
(…)Lactantius also inserted in his work the prophecies about Christ of a certain sibyl, he does not say which.

The three days and nights spent by Jonah in the belly of the whale are not coincidental. Nor are the three days and nights that Jesus spent in a cave before his resurrection. The visiting Magi with their three gifts of precious oils and gold at the time of the birth of Jesus continue the endless theme of the three, the Holy Trinity also. The story of the prophet Jirjis has him resuscitating three times (p.200) while three measures of flour are necessary for the leaven to work its magic in the biblical verse of Matthew 13:33 (p.219).

In the antediluvian King List, a potential key to an unknown riddle comes in the form of three words inserted into the names of three rulers (p.260, notes to line 26). And finally, the 'tris-me-gis' of Hermes Trismegistus, the Three Times Great, where 'tris-me' correspond to the ME-EŠ of line 36 (p.73). Or should it be MI-GIŠ, the shady tree?[1]

Connecting The Stones

Approximately six thousand years separate the T-shaped stones of Gobekli Tepe (photo p.233) from the first words appearing on Mesopotamian clay ca.3500 BC. Was Sumerian the language once spoken in the place? Was it used to communicate during the rituals carried out there? In all logic, the answer should be yes. Those people spoke. They communicated. And there are tantalising links to be found in the pictographic writing. GU₂/TIG is one of them (p.123). This unidentified yet eloquent T-shaped word,[2] seen on more than one tablet, is

236

another. And they are not alone. Sections of *The Story of Sukurru* refer to the traditions of that culture, the most obvious example being the description of three baskets in the context of a ritual (p.289). The reader of this has a great deal of evidence in hand, enough to decide for themselves.

There are few close and obvious associations to be made between the phonetics and meanings derived from Ancient Egyptian hieroglyphs and those of the Sumerian language. Perhaps Egyptian Nu, also Nun, will be an important exception. Egyptian Nun is father of the gods, one of a group of eight deities, but also the watery abyss, an underground stream, the primordial waters, chaos. The meanings attributed to Egyptian Nu/Nun are difficult to grasp. In that, it has a lot in common with Sumerian NUN. Unsurprisingly, the indisputable links between Sumer and Egypt come about through the Greek: the snake of the sun, for example. Sumerian Tammuz and Egypto-Greek Buto are either one and the same or intimately connected by their common language source (p.140). The same can be said of Egyptian Osiris found primarily through Sumerian UŠ/OS and found again at the heart of GEŠ, the Sumerian tree.

Magicians Of Mesopotamia

On the last and greatest day of the feast, Jesus stood up and called out in a loud voice, "If anyone is thirsty, let him come to Me and drink. Whoever believes in Me, as the Scripture has said: 'Streams of living water will flow from within him.'" (John 7:38)

ME-ZU, they who practise the magic, reside between the rivers of above and below. The magic of ME-ZU connects Earth to the otherworldly realm through the living waters, the streams and rivers. ME is the spirit which might be termed 'holy' and became the Tau; ME-ŠI, the Spirit Eye, the third eye, which gave 'Messiah' in later languages and became the emblem of Saint Anthony of Egypt.

The Gnostics, the GIG-NUS, knew the 'troublesome' nature of fungi and their mind-altering properties. From those people come the evocative names of the agaric, the amanita muscaria, the cannabis and thorny acacia plants. The Gnostics and the Magicians were one and the same. The living waters were those of the rivers that they tamed to irrigate and render the land fertile - and those of the brews prepared by the shamans of the times, the ŠA₃-BI, the Beer-Hearts. Water and beer. They were the Agari, measurers of the flow, specialists of snakes and bitter medicines (p.166), people who lived along riverbanks where plant-enhanced baptisms were carried out, the rites of passage into adulthood and beyond.

ME–ZU of BU–TAM: the Mesopotamians, Magicians of the Snakes, of the Rivers and of the Sun. Their words show them to have had the knowledge of seafarers. They were the masters of the 'knot', the ship's rigging secured, the curved movements of the stars measured, masters of the knowledge that generates maps, enabling long voyages and Homeric adventures at sea. These were people who had the intellectual capacity to develop the concept of the ouroboros – as long ago as the carvings on the stones of Gobekli Tepe. They are the people we unthinkingly term Anunnaki or Apkallu. Does it matter? Probably not. Whoever believes in ME... Did they practise their magic within the stone circles of Gobekli Tepe?

The great Nun is shown with water flowing below his feet, sometimes from above his head, sometimes from his shoulders or from pots held out in front of him - pots flowing into other pots, curiously reminiscent of the dripping Egyptian Karnak clock but earlier, far earlier. I suggest that their knowledge of water was far-reaching, that it included more delicate, complex concepts of 'flow', of circulating energies, of monuments placed not only in patterns corresponding to visible celestial elements but also to mark the spots where the cosmic and earthly energies naturally come together along ley lines and at points where underground streams converge. They were the boundary stones of Hermes, between visible and invisible, integrating celestial calculations, the keys to the knowledge of the lost civilisation. Around and around we all go.

Last Gnostics

AN–A–NUN–NA: Upward and downward flowing stone guide, the original purpose of which was to enable navigation on the serpentine Eridanus, right up to the front paws of Cetus, and from there to observe the movements of the sun, the moon and the stars, and to transcribe them in a book of knowledge or rather two parallel books: KI–TAB, a dual book of knowledge, KI–TA, knowledge of Earth and AN–TA, of the sky (p.221).

KI	TA	+	AN	TA	=	KI	TAB
Earth	question		sky	question		places	two

Book of Sky and Earth

Arabic kitab was the book of the 'People of the Book', an epithet once associated with the Sabians of Harran, supposedly as a ruse to save them from the wrath of an Islamic overlord. I found the Sabians under their epithet of SHA-BI, Beer-Hearts, in the oldest of the Sumerian literary texts and no more solid origin has been given for that name. These were the first scribes and masters of the riddles, founders of all the later Gnostic groups, of which the Mesopotamian Mandaeans, the only Gnostic sect still in existence today.

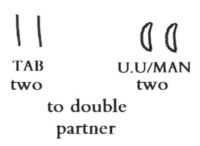

TAB   **U.U/MAN**
two   two
to double
partner

The Mandaean rituals centre on baptism in living water, in rivers, cascading down through mountain gullies, where the lively fish appear and disappear, rituals which are for them forever associated with the river Jordan and with John the Baptist whom they revere. The root of their name is Sumerian MAN, symbol of duality, of companionship, a symbol which contains an underlying and intriguing sense of rivalry between two elements or people. MAN is the equivalent of phonetic TAB, the two of the Kitab, the Place of the Two. The tablets, the tabernacle…

Where It All Began

Heaven's utmost deep Gives up her stars, and like a flock of sheep They pass before his eye, are number'd, and roll on.[1]

From the earliest of mankind's movements across this earth and its waters, the planets and stars have served as guides, their positions memorized. The places were recorded by one means or another, visible or invisible boundary stones, and gradually built upon, each light in the night sky given its own name according to the perspective and knowledge of the voyager. Perhaps the stars became sheep herded by a great shepherd or fish swimming in a beer-coloured sea, all disappearing from sight at dawn. NUN was the greatest fish of them all, as is the whale in the Mediterranean and everywhere else of course. On Earth, in its role as observatory, it was made of stone and associated with the NUR and NER, those smaller fish who became the Greek Nereids, sea nymphs and daughters of Nereus, god of the sea.

Latin nonna is the legacy of the tutor, a wise ancestor sitting at the centre of ANUNNA and, like Moses, conjuring water, the original elusive alchemist and their magical stone, their NA-ME (p.287-288).

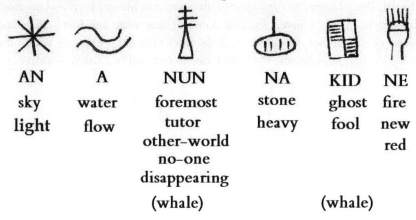

AN	A	NUN	NA	KID	NE
sky	water	foremost	stone	ghost	fire
light	flow	tutor	heavy	fool	new
		other–world			red
		no–one			
		disappearing			
		(whale)		(whale)	

What was the original meaning behind the ceremony of baptism? Disappearing under water like a lively fish escaping from a net. Rising out of the water, saved as the whale is saved each time it breaks surface to breath, or saved as the man disappearing into its belly and then vomited up helpless but far wiser on some desolate seashore, reborn? John of the Living Waters? [1]

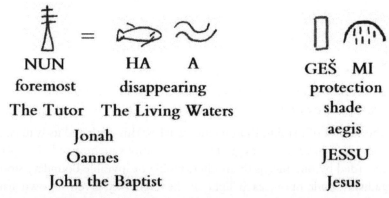

NUN	HA	A		GEŠ	MI
foremost	disappearing			protection	
The Tutor	The Living Waters			shade	
Jonah				aegis	
Oannes				JESSU	
John the Baptist				Jesus	

It has been suggested more than once that Jonah, the Hebrew prophet, who was both swallowed by a great fish and given shade by a kikayon plant, could be equated to Oannes, the Mesopotamian fish god who appeared out of the sea to teach and then disappeared back into the water every night. Strangely, neither one appears in conventional translations of the Sumerian texts written in the language of their supposed region of existence between the two Mesopotamian rivers. So here they are at last, resuscitated. The link between John the Baptist and Jesus is made numerous times in the Bible. With the words of Jesus comparing his plight to that of Jonah (p.11), another compelling link can be made, a trio of names. At the same time, Gnosticism and Jonah's mysterious plant kikayon share the same source word in GIG-NUS which, in turn, is linked to the original name of Jesus through the Sumerian symbol MI, source of 'mycelium'.

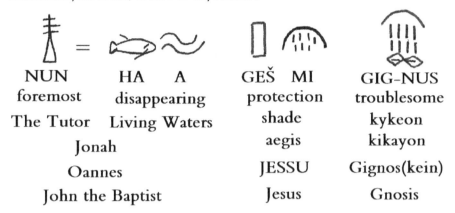

NUN	HA A	GEŠ MI	GIG–NUS
foremost	disappearing	protection	troublesome
The Tutor	Living Waters	shade	kykeon
Jonah		aegis	kikayon
Oannes		JESSU	Gignos(kein)
John the Baptist		Jesus	Gnosis

All of the above stem from logical and fully justified analyses, largely grounded in given meanings found in orthodox Sumero-Akkadian lexicons. In other words and if it still needs to be said, nothing here can be dismissed as fanciful. Sumerian was a monosyllabic language but that doesn't mean that whoever devised it was fixated on the one narrow and overriding subject of the amanita mushroom central to a fertility cult as the analyses in John Allegro's book strongly suggest. I have pulled together some of the oldest strands of the language, but the river runs deep and the work is far from complete. There is always more to be found, to be dug up, resuscitated.

In the course of this investigation, some interlocking themes have shown themselves; love and bitterness, bitterness and foolishness, ego and self-knowledge, perfection and music, the enduring cosmic bond and cycles of time. I invite the reader to go back and forth over the symbols, the extracts from the Sumerian writings and the notes, the meanings given in external lexicons, and then come to their own conclusions on the subject of Jonah, John, Jesus, Gnosis and, of course, my theory concerning the great Whale.

As for the ancestral home of the Anunnaki identified through NUN-KI and found in the opening lines of the antediluvian King List, also see the new and unabridged translation of that text beginning on p.245 and the notes to lines 1 and 2 on p.251-252. Even if this new perspective doesn't bring all the answers to all the questions, it provides a fair amount of new food for thought.

Land Of Kalam

Not of which land? Was the Nun originally a stranger to this land? A foreigner arriving in a vessel, crossing the seas after some great disaster so old that we have lost the thread, the trace? A foreigner arriving in a vessel descending from the sky or appearing out of the ocean? Annoyingly, the question of their ultimate source remains unanswered – at least for the time being. Kalam is one name of the land and its people. The early tablets show it in a variety of ways, with only the vertical pole and arrow - probably a standard, a flag-pole - remaining constant. The lexical lists give the breakdown of KALAM:

KA	LAM		KALAM/UN
word	flourish	=	people, land

United by the Word

The given meanings 'to flourish' and 'to grow' are self-explanatory. According to the history books and the biblical tale, Sumer/Kalam was part of the land between two rivers which, at some point in time, saw the construction of the mythical Tower of Babylon and from there the destruction of a unique and unifying language.

KALAM is source of Greek kalamos, the stylus. A word on wood, paper, papyrus, or another fragile medium could not survive the millennia separating us from the Sumerians. But that doesn't mean that no materials other than clay were ever used to relay their thoughts, their stories, their knowledge. Did the presence of clay dictate the development of the language or was it just one of several media, the most primitive, the last rather than the first, chosen for its endurance, for its availability and the negligeable cost of its transformation? Used to copy and to perpetuate rather than to invent? Was it the only medium to survive great catastrophes, and thoughtless or deliberate purges? The reader of this must, just one more time, decide for themselves what is plausible or implausible in all of the above, what is shown to be true through this investigation and what is not. It's not the absence of proof that makes a lost body of work an impossibility; a compilation on an unknown medium at the time of the first Sumerian tablets and earlier. If entire cities with their pyramids, their ziggurats, their nuraghes could crumble to dust within the space of a few thousand years, anything is possible. We have no idea of what has been lost and must respectfully treat as precious all the words that have miraculously survived.

THE

ANTEDILUVIAN

KING LIST

Unabridged

The Sumerian King List

(1) NAM LUGAL   AN TA LAGARgDU   NE A BA

The great ruler a mound to the sky established, fire to carry below.

(2) NUN KI NAM LUGAL LA

(3) NUN KI ID LU ŠI LUGAL

In the City of the Nun, the great ruler the light suspended, that its strong wing be seen.

(4) MU 28800 NI AK

28,800 years passed.

(5) ID LAL₃ GAR MU 36000 NI AK

The honeyed wing was measured.
36,000 years passed.

(6) 2 great rulers

Two great rulers.

(7) MU BI 64800 TUM AK

A total of 64,800 years was their legacy.

245

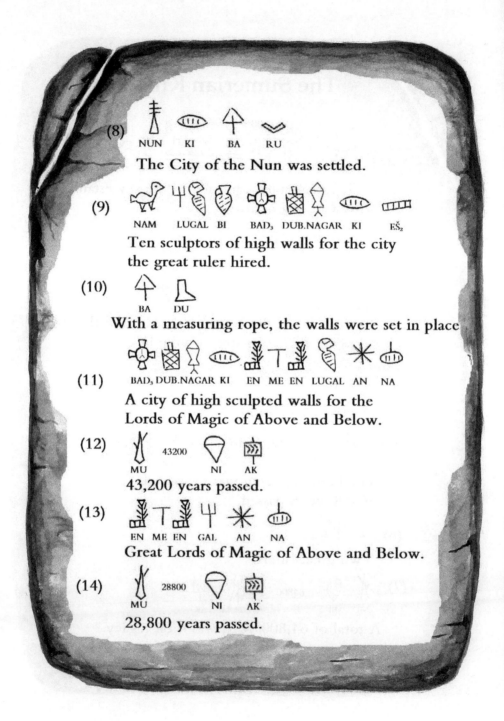

(8) NUN KI BA RU

The City of the Nun was settled.

(9) NAM LUGAL BI BAD₃ DUB.NAGAR KI EŠ₂

Ten sculptors of high walls for the city
the great ruler hired.

(10) BA DU

With a measuring rope, the walls were set in place

(11) BAD₃ DUB.NAGAR KI EN ME EN LUGAL AN NA

A city of high sculpted walls for the
Lords of Magic of Above and Below.

(12) MU 43200 NI AK

43,200 years passed.

(13) EN ME EN GAL AN NA

Great Lords of Magic of Above and Below.

(14) MU 28800 NI AK

28,800 years passed.

246

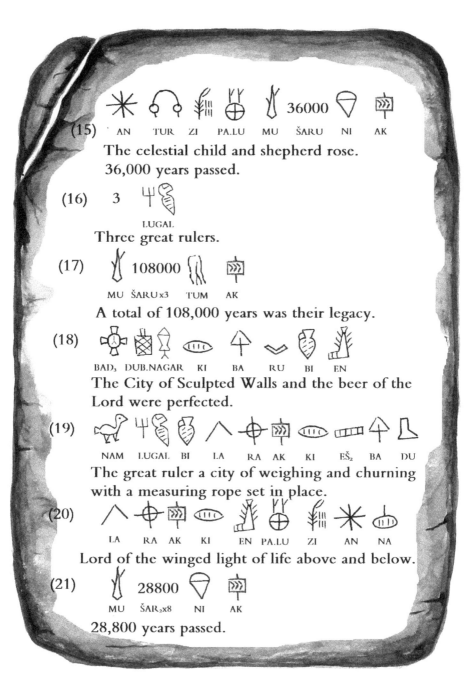

(15) AN TUR ZI PA.LU MU ŠARU NI AK

The celestial child and shepherd rose.
36,000 years passed.

(16) 3 LUGAL

Three great rulers.

(17) MU ŠARUx3 TUM AK

A total of 108,000 years was their legacy.

(18) BAD₃ DUB.NAGAR KI BA RU BI EN

The City of Sculpted Walls and the beer of the
Lord were perfected.

(19) NAM LUGAL BI LA RA AK KI EŠ₂ BA DU

The great ruler a city of weighing and churning
with a measuring rope set in place.

(20) LA RA AK KI EN PA.LU ZI AN NA

Lord of the winged light of life above and below.

(21) MU ŠAR₂x8 NI AK

28,800 years passed.

247

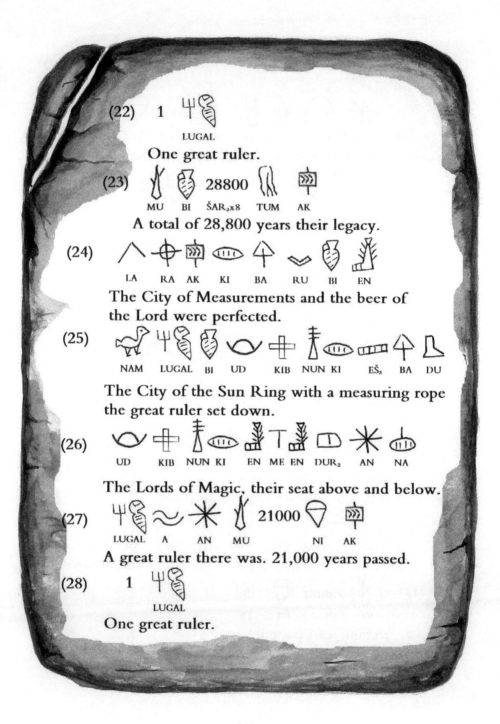

(22)　1　𒈗
　　　　LUGAL

One great ruler.

(23)　MU　BI　ŠAR₂×8　28800　TUM　AK

A total of 28,800 years their legacy.

(24)　LA　RA　AK　KI　BA　RU　BI　EN

The City of Measurements and the beer of
the Lord were perfected.

(25)　NAM　LUGAL　BI　UD　KIB　NUN KI　EŠ₂　BA　DU

The City of the Sun Ring with a measuring rope
the great ruler set down.

(26)　UD　KIB　NUN KI　EN ME EN　DUR₂　AN　NA

The Lords of Magic, their seat above and below.

(27)　LUGAL　A　AN　MU　21000　NI　AK

A great ruler there was. 21,000 years passed.

(28)　1　𒈗
　　　　LUGAL

One great ruler.

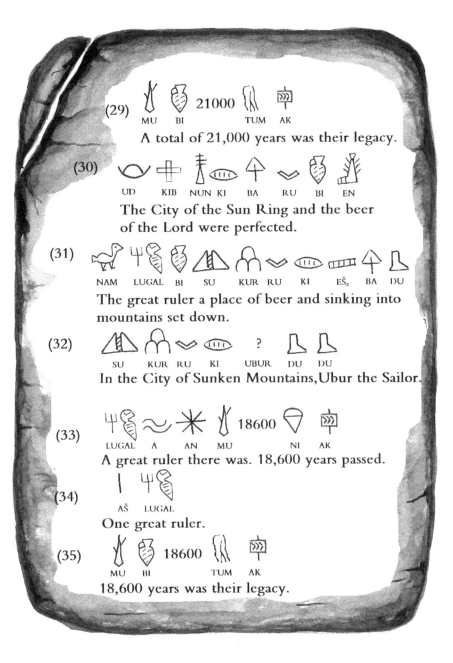

(29)

MU   BI   21000   TUM   AK

A total of 21,000 years was their legacy.

(30)

UD   KIB   NUN KI   BA   RU   BI   EN

The City of the Sun Ring and the beer
of the Lord were perfected.

(31)

NAM   LUGAL   BI   SU   KUR   RU   KI   EŠ₂   BA   DU

The great ruler a place of beer and sinking into
mountains set down.

(32)

SU   KUR   RU   KI   UBUR   DU   DU

In the City of Sunken Mountains, Ubur the Sailor.

(33)

LUGAL   A   AN   MU   18600   NI   AK

A great ruler there was. 18,600 years passed.

(34)

AŠ   LUGAL

One great ruler.

(35)

MU   BI   18600   TUM   AK

18,600 years was their legacy.

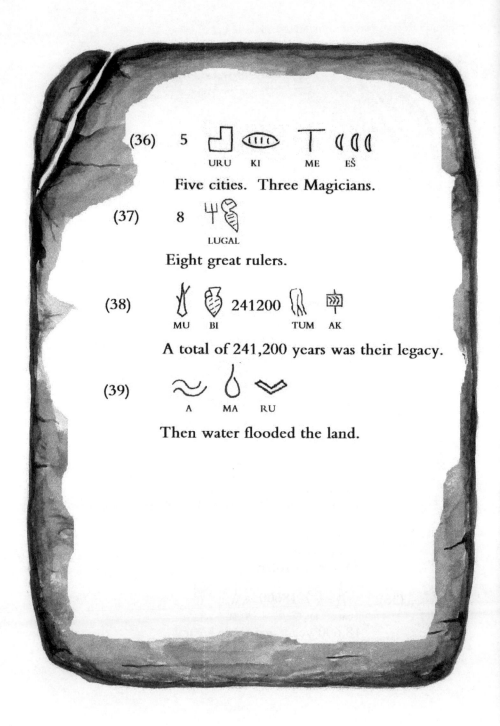

(36) 5 URU KI ME EŠ

Five cities. Three Magicians.

(37) 8 LUGAL

Eight great rulers.

(38) MU BI 241200 TUM AK

A total of 241,200 years was their legacy.

(39) A MA RU

Then water flooded the land.

King List Notes

Lines I and 2.

The key to unravelling the meaning of this first line lies in the fifth word which is transliterated as unassuming 'ed₃' in the orthodox version and has the main given meaning 'to go up or down'. That enigmatic reference hides two original words: LAGARg and DU. They can be seen together on tablets from the ED (Early Dynastic) IIIa archaeological period, ca.2600-2500 BC as shown here. (CDLI ref. P010060, Coll. Oriental Institute, University of Chicago.)

The style is increasingly abstract but still the original 'mound' of LAGAR with added striations (g=gunu) is quite plain. LAGAR alone is given as 'mound' but with the interior lines, it becomes only 'priest'. I suggest that the added figure of a priest does not detract from the existence of the mound and that the lines across the symbol are referencing an action in relation to that mound. Going up or coming down? Why the choice? Perhaps both, giving 'going up in order to carry down'.

Below it sits DU, the foot, with given meanings that include 'to bring', 'to carry', 'to stand', 'to be assigned to a task', and 'to establish'.

The next symbol is NE hidden behind its alternative form of 'de₃' in the academic transliteration. NE is essentially the 'fire' and the renewal, the rebirth. Thus, there is a mound, something carried, established, (or renewed) and fire. A Zoroastrian slant begins to appear. The Iranian based religion is often symbolised by an altar with a perpetual fire at its summit and it also lays emphasis on Asha, the concept of truth and cosmic order (p.47). If there is indeed a link, then it is this much earlier Sumerian text that indicates the source of Zoroastrian traditions and *The Story of Sukurru* that takes them further back, to the first half of the 3rd millennium.

The mound was left unmentioned in the original translation. Was it the mountain of Hephaestus, the mythical smith who lived and worked at the heart of a fire-breathing volcano? Or was it a mound in the style of a pyramid/ziggurat/nuraghe constructed to reach the sky?

The appointed hour was approaching when man in his turn was to go forth into the light of day; and Prometheus, not knowing how he could devise his salvation, stole the mechanical arts of Hephaestus and Athene, and fire with them (they could neither have been acquired nor used without fire), and gave

251

them to man. Prometheus and Epimetheus (Protagoras 320b–323a), Plato's Myths

Prometheus is yet another name that has gone unnoticed by the translators of Sumerian, a name concerned with fire and the sun through PIR/UD, with ropes and magic through UM-ME-TE, potentially with meteors if ME-TE gives the source of that word. UM-ME-TE appear together on line 68 of *The Story of Sukurru*, section in which mankind's fate is being decided.

The first line of the King List ends with A-BA, 'water' or 'flow' and 'below' or 'without', becoming ABA, the Father. The second line begins with the name of the first city, NUN-KI. At this point, the analysis of NUN (p.287) is complete except for one more phonetic form and a crucial lexical list entry:

GU	RU	UD	=	GURUD/NUN-KI
cord	impose	sun		to throw down
	Guru?			to place

This is where a cord to the sun was first placed.

Line 3. Alulim

A₂/ID-LU-ŠI/LIM.

ID is 'wing', 'time' and 'strength'. LU is both 'sheep' and 'light'. (LU as 'light' is explained in *Before Babel*, p.11.) ŠI, the 'eye' and 'to see': 'the light wing to see', 'the wing of light to see', 'the strength of the light to see'.

LU-ŠI, the light to see, is an obvious Sumerian source for the name 'Lucifer' given in bible dictionaries as 'light-bringer', 'light-bearer' and 'brilliant star'. Both the sound and the meanings are a match. Lucifer is said to be an epithet of the king of Babylon stemming from a name given to Venus, the morning star:

How art thou fallen from heaven, O Lucifer, son of the morning! how art thou cut down to the ground, which didst weaken the nations! (Isaiah 14:12)

If the bible sources can be matched to the far earlier King List, the name on line 3, Alulim is that of an 'illustrious prince', a son. At the same time, the *Manuel d'Epigraphie Akkadienne* lists LU-LIM as a name of Saturn.

On p.109 of *The Sacred Mushroom and the Cross*, John Allegro suggests that Jesus is the underlying reference in Isaiah 14:12, and that the verse is likening the fall of the king of Babylon to the ephemeral nature of a mushroom's life.

His reasoning involves another verse from Revelation which links Jesus to the morning star:

I, Jesus, have sent My angel to give you this testimony for the churches. I am the Root and the Offspring of David, the bright Morning Star. (Revelation 22:16)

Whatever the truth of that matter, this first ruler of the Sumerian King List gives the source of the name Lucifer but perhaps also of the following line in Revelation where LU as 'sheep' is still young, just a lamb:

And the city has no need of sun or moon to shine on it, because the glory of God illuminates the city, and the Lamb is its lamp. (Revelation 21:23)

ID as source of the Roman ides is in itself an indication of strong light when the moon is full, i.e. 'strength of the ides'. (p.69)

Line 5. Alalĝar

A₂/ID-LAL₃-GAR

Repetition of ID, the strong wing. LAL₃ is given as 'syrup' in lexicons. GAR, the measuring: 'the strength of the honey to measure'. Does this phrase reference the source tale of Greek Icarus who flew too close to the sun and was killed when the wax holding his wings together melted? That would also provide a reasonable explanation for the preceding Alulim as the son who saw the light, perhaps indicating that they were one and the same, which would demolish the notion of the antediluvian list as succeeding reigns of kings. Then again, ID can be understood as 'time' and another meaning of GAR is 'bread', potentially giving 'a time of bread and honey'.

So you were adorned with gold and silver, and your clothing was made of fine linen, silk, and embroidered cloth. You ate fine flour, honey, and oil. You became very beautiful and rose to be queen. Your fame spread among the nations on account of your beauty, for it was perfect in the splendor I bestowed on you, declares the Lord God. (Ezekiel 16:13-14, Jerusalem's Unfaithfulness)

Lines 7, 17, 23, 29, 35 and 38

MU-BI is translated as an indication of the passage of time, as 'years'. Another way to read it while still using conventional lexicons is 'Renown/name/age of the beer'. And of course, the Sabians and Chaldeans were the master brewers, carrying the beer at their heart.

TUM/DUM, appearing four times, is visually a torso from waist down and legs. Main given meanings are 'back', 'rear', 'inheritance' which I have extended to 'legacy'. It is probable that this is the source of 'dome' through Greek doma and also 'tomb' through Greek tymbos, given as 'burial mound' and 'tomb', and interesting to note that TUM is used as final syllable in the wording of 'ziggurat' (p.115). It also has the given meaning 'cross-beam'.

Lines 8, 18, 24 and 30

BA-RU have the given meanings 'below' and 'to fall'. The orthodox translation of the King List has this as the indication that a city falls, to be replaced by the next. 'To fall' and 'to drop' can also indicate arriving from a higher place, being set down below, perhaps brick by brick. BA as 'below' with RU, 'to set in place', leads to the idea of a place in heaven (above) being copied by a place on Earth (below). It is possible that each city is 'settled' or 'perfected' before the text moves on to the next name. It is interesting that 'baru' in Malay has the meaning 'recently made or created'.

At the same time, line 8 gives NUN-KI as the first city to be linked to BA-RU. With the strong possibility of the City of the Lost Fish being the same as Plato's Atlantis which sank beneath the waves, then 'dropping below' fits the bill only too well.

Lines 9, 11 and 18. Bad-tibira

BAD₃-DUB-NAGAR

BAD₃ is a composite symbol of EZEN with either BAD, meaning 'remote' and 'open', or AN, the sky, at its centre. That combination is given as 'wall', 'fortification', 'high' and the number 'ten'. EZEN is also phonetic HIR/HER, with the meanings 'to bind' and 'boundary'. Analysis of HIR/HER/EZEN is carried out in *Before Babel* (from p.231) in the context of the name Hermes. Below are two variations on the same symbol and with the main given meanings:

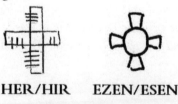

HER/HIR   EZEN/ESEN

bind, boundary, festival, song

It is interesting to note in this context of city names that Jerusalem can be read as Greek Hierousalem, potentially taken from the same source as Hermes, HI-ER, which is listed opposite HIR/HER in the lexical lists.

EZEN/ESEN from that same source is potentially the origin of the Essenes, a group of Gnostic monks with close ties to Jerusalem whose existence had been undocumented until the discovery of the Dead Sea Scrolls in 1947. Overall, BAD₃ indicates a fortified place which was open to the sky and surrounded by high sculpted walls: that of the Essenes of Jerusalem?

TIBIRA is given as 'sculptor'. It comprises DUB, the tablet or cylinder seal, and NAGAR, the 'carpenter', indicating someone carving a wooden tablet, or the place where that tablet was made. However, NAGAR is also found in the lexical lists with URUDA, meaning 'copper', perhaps a copper scroll... TIBIRA breaks down to TE-BI-RU which I suggest gave rise to Hebrew 'tebeth', the tenth month, from mid-December to mid-January. TE/TEN is the 'tether', the binding, and the four Ts of 'tenet' on the Sator square (p.82). 'Ten' is also one meaning of BAD₃ (see above) while EZEN/HIR is given as 'festival' and 'song'. Pulling all the elements together, this analysis implies that the name of the second city on line 9 of the King List has its root in winter solstice celebrations, taking place within the boundaries of high sculpted walls and that a mysterious tablet is to be found there.

Overall, the name has a slight whiff of Hiram, the mythical architect of Solomon's Temple in Jerusalem, but also the name of a king of Tyre. Hiram is mentioned in a number of strange stories, taken from both Freemasonry and the Bible.

Now Hiram king of Tyre sent envoys to David, along with cedar logs, carpenters, and stonemasons, and they built a palace for David. (2 Samuel 5:11)

The Hiram stories tell of the building of temple walls, hidden passwords, knowledge of the secrets of the masons and even murder.

KI-EZEN (also EZEM/ESEM) is given as 'locus' and might be at the origin of the Kurdish word 'qesem' meaning 'oath': KI-EZEM, the Place of the Oath? A recent discovery in Israel of contents in a cave named as Qesem indicates human occupation some 420,000 years ago. How old is that place name? EZEN is reportedly repeated three times in the antediluvian King List. See note to line 32 which casts some doubt on that assumption, at the very least indicating that it was not the same case in all copies of the original list.

One important symbol that has been completely occulted by the orthodox translation and which is repeated four times in all is EŠ₂, the 'rope'. Found after KI, the 'place' on lines 9, 19, 25 and 31, one possibility is that it is installed to anchor the place on Earth to an otherworldly partner. The rope is an essential part of the ship's rigging. It is given as 'to seize' which is what probably led to the notion in the orthodox translation that each city was seized and destroyed. But the rope has a multitude of uses not least of which measurement. Then, of course, there is the umbilical cord, the most important binding rope of them all. Also see RI, the bird, with EŠ₂, the rope, as source of RIS/RES/SAG, the head (p.169). On line 9, 'to hire', another of its given meanings; was used: the hiring of the ten sculptors.

Line 11. En-men-lu-ana

EN-ME-EN-LU₂-AN-NA

EN, the Lord and the One, surrounds ME, the spirit and the magic (which is also the central symbol signifying the pineal gland between two symbols of the eye). The central LU₂, man, is sandwiched between the One of the Spirit, and AN-NA, 'above and below', 'light and heavy'.

The repetition of EN might or might not signify a plural. It might also be an indication of circularity where One meets One (alternatively one 'end' meets the other 'end) through the magic, never forgetting that the symbol ME gives the source of 'measurement'. This is a Lord of Measurement.

ME also gives the source syllable of Greek methy, the wine, and English mead, both having magical properties. Ultimately, ME as 'me' can best be understood through the prism of a precursor to Sufism. See the proverb p.220. That is where the small word which we so freely use on ourselves began. 'Lords of Magic' seemed the most fitting translation here, with a caveat concerning the singular or plural. It might well be a title given to those astronomers who had the unique skills to forecast and to predict, but the brewers and shamans can't be ruled out of that picture.

Line 13. En-men-gal-ana

EN-ME-EN-GAL-AN-NA

Only the central symbol GAL differs from that of line 11 where LU₂ takes fourth position. GAL has the given meaning 'great'. I believe it to also be the source of the 'galley' ship and even the name of the rooster, the Gallois. Both GAL and ME/ŠIP, pronounced 'ship', are symbols that I regrettably can't prove to have that meaning.

ME-EN is given opposite MEN in the lexical lists. MEN is a composite symbol showing EN, the lord, inside MAL, the basket, potentially translating to 'the lord in his vessel'. Given as 'pure' and 'a type of crown', MEN can be compared to AMA which is AN, the sky, also inside MAL, giving the name of the cosmic Matriarch. Men? Men in magical vessels? I suggest that ME-EN and ME-NE give the source of Greek mene, the 'moon' and the 'month'.

Is this the source of Greek Endymion, the figure said to have been both the son of Zeus and a shepherd? Pliny the Elder suggested that he was an astronomer and the first human to observe the movements of the moon. (*Naturalis Historia* Book II.IV.43.) Was Endymion Sumerian EN? See the riddle (p.81) in which EN-DIM₂ appears twice: Lord and Architect.

Line 15. dDumuzid

AN-DUMU/TUR-ZI SIPA

Given here as AN-TUR-ZI, where ZI, 'to rise' and 'life', is the source of Greek Zeus. Preceded by symbol AN, in orthodox translations this should logically be the name of a god and might translate to 'Celestial Rising Son' where DUMU/TUR has the given meaning 'child'. In the King List, it's written 'Dumuzid, the shepherd'.

SIPAD, given as 'shepherd', stems less often from SI.PA than from symbols PA.LU, the 'wing' and the 'sheep' or 'light', potentially giving 'the wings of light'. These are the two symbols given in their later cuneiform style by scribes who were probably copying the King List from earlier examples. In this case, the pictographic signs are visually eloquent. PA, also 'sceptre', can be seen as a pair of wings placed above the circular LU that is both 'sheep' (the given meaning) and the 'light' (my own deduction):

PA.LU

The Shepherd

My suggestion is that PA.LU, the wings above the stone of light (LU as the source of lunar, the light of the moon), were the words used to describe the original well-documented Egyptian winged stone (shown here on the underside of one of the great gates at Karnak in Egypt, photo Ian Faure). See Janus and the alchemical rebis (p.25) for another, later image of the winged stone.

257

PA is also phonetic HENDUR and primary symbol of the ouroboros (p.125). ZI before PA.LU might give 'the enduring/eternal light of life':

I am the light of the world. Whoever follows me will never walk in darkness, but will have the light of life. (John 8:12)

A lot rests on the true interpretation of symbol TUR/DUMU, given in the lexicons as 'small' and 'child' but also 'discernment' and 'sagacity'. Visually, TUR is, in some cases, very like a torc, a type of metal necklace found at various European sites and from different periods of history. This 'celestial son of Zeus' perhaps gives the source of Greek Heracles whose myth involves a long period of atonement, twelve labours, and marriage to Hebe, celestial queen bee who mixes the beer...or Apollo, or Hermes, or Dionysus, or some combination. Zeus had numerous sons. In all cases, with AN as prefix, the reference is celestial. See Greek Endymion in the notes to line 13.

Lines 19, 20 and 24. Larag

LA-RA-AK

LA indicates the balance, the scales and the weighing, with RA, the churning, and AK, the action. Followed by EŠ₂, the measuring rope, it is possible - but not written in stone - that this interpretation is correct. Lara was a name given to 'household deities' in the Roman culture, the source unknown. Larag is another name repeated three times in this antediluvian section of the King List. Potentially, the name refers to the hanging and the churning action of the planets and stars, being one way of describing the science of astronomy.

Line 20. En-sipad-zid-ana

EN-PA.LU-ZI-AN-NA

Truly, truly, I tell you, I am the gate for the sheep. All who came before Me were thieves and robbers, but the sheep did not listen to them. I am the gate. If anyone enters through Me, he will be saved. He will come in and go out and find pasture. (John 10:8-9)

Again, the shepherd appears next to ZI but in a different position, giving 'the Lord' from EN and 'the Shepherd' from PA.LU. This could read 'The Lord and Shepherd' or 'EN/The One on the wing of light rises' where ZI is used as verb, in which case it begins to sound distinctly Enochian. See the notes to line 15. PA.LU followed by ZI might read 'the risen Shepherd'.

This is the third name ending in the mirrored phonetic forms AN-NA which are 'sky' and 'stone' and can be read as 'light and heavy', 'above and below'. Given as 'upper' in the lexicons, there are four examples of the duo in the King List.

There is the obvious inference in the above bible quote that Me is more than just 'me'. The word in that passage is translated to English from Greek 'ego'. Our word 'ego' comes through Greek and Latin from two Sumerian words; E_2, the temple, followed by GU_2, also DUR, the gulley and the umbilical cord. (See p.128 and the notes to that page.) Sumerian 'ego' is found in an irrefutably relevant context in the literary text known as Enki's Journey to Nibru. The following analysis is entirely based in orthodox lexicon meanings:

E_2	GU_2,	=	egó	=	I, me	=	$\top$
Temple	Gulley		(Greek) (Latin)		(English)		ME
							Magic to be

Temple of the Enduring Bond and of the Magicians

Temple of the Navel (and of the Stone Bowl)

Gobekli (Turkish)

Portasar (Armenian)

Through analysis of GU_2 and KAK, the peg holding the circle of the snake firmly in place, we find BUR/PUR, the stone bowl, source of the Armenian name for the place. This long overdue re-translation of the language of Mesopotamia, mother tongue of Greeks and Romans, through its original monosyllabic elements brings the T-shaped emblem of Saint Anthony of Egypt firmly home to its source in the T-shaped stones, the NA of the ME, the magical stones of the Magicians, in Gobekli Tepe ca. 9600 BC. See PA.GAN on line 44 of *The Story of Sukurru. If anyone enters through ME, he will be saved.* Saved from what? From himself?

Line 26. En-men-dur-ana

EN-ME-EN-DUR₂-AN-NA

This is the third instance of EN-ME-EN and, in each case, a different word is inserted before the same two final words AN-NA. Together they give:

$$LU_2, GAL\ DUR_2$$

Is this a code? DUR_2 is almost identical and, according to the lexical lists, interchangeable with KU. The main given meanings are 'cleft' and 'sit' or 'seat' with meanings related to 'foundation' and 'founding': The Great Seated Ruler? The Great Man who cleaves? Great Ruler and Founder? Could this

259

be Lord Baal? (p.24) The *Manuel d'Epigraphie Akkadienne* cites LUGAL as both Belu, an epithet thought to be that of Baal, and preceded by MUL, as Regulus, brightest star in the constellation of Leo.

What was meant by placing those three symbols in fourth position of the six-symbol names of three otherwise identical kings? Note that the symbols LU₂-GAL are otherwise given together, transliterated as 'lugal' and translated as 'king' throughout the voluminous list.

Lines 25, 26 and 30. Zimbir

UD-KIB-NUN-NA

UD-KIB-NUN-NA-KI are the cuneiform signs which appear on the Ashmolean prism. Found opposite UD-KIB-NUN-KI in the lexical entries, ZIMBIR is given with BURANUN in the list of names of the Euphrates river (p.209).

Another form given there is SIPPAR, name of a Babylonian city on the eastern bank of the Euphrates, a name which breaks down to ŠIP-PAR, 'Magic/Magician of the Sun' but also according to my own interpretation of ŠIP: 'Ship of the Sun':

SIP   PAR
ME   UD
magic   sun
Sippar
Ship of the Sun

After Euedoreschus some others reigned, and then Sisithrus. To him the deity Cronus foretold that on the fifteenth day of the month Desius there would be a deluge of rain: and he commanded him to deposit all the writings whatever which were in his possession, in the city of the Sun in Sippara. (L.P. Cory, *Ancient Fragments*, 1832: Berossus ca.290 BC, sourced from Eusebius (ca. 260-339 AD) *Chronicles* 5.8., from Abydenus ca.200 BC.)

Upon some of the boundary stones of Sippara (Sepharvaim of the Old Testament), a solar city, Sagittarius "appears sculptured in full glory." (Richard Allen, Star-Names and their Meanings, 1899, Sagittarius, The Archer, p.354)

Zimbir/Buranun/Sippar is the third of three cities in the list to be mentioned three times. Also see the riddle of Odysseus (p.212-214). Also see the notes to p.2 concerning the vessel carrying a scribe.

The three different names, apparently all pertaining to the same city and/or to the river Euphrates, are presented as multi-syllabic and inherently meaningless. That presentation dissimulates the fundamental linguistic link between the sage who is NUN-ME (generally read 'Apkallu', p.28) and the secret knowledge to be found in Sippar which can be read as both UD-KIB-NUN and ME-UD. My guess is that the secret knowledge had to do with the movement of the sun and, more generally, with astronomical calculations.

Lines 31 and 32. Šuruppag

SU-KUR-RU

Sukurru is the final city mentioned in the list before the flood. SU can be understood as 'knowledge' but also the 'sinking' which might or might not be relevant to the flood story: the 'sinking of/into the mountain to impose' is one potential literal translation. The Gnostic concept provides a more philosophical reference via the falling of Sophia (p.177), with SU qualified by RU which carries the meaning 'to fall'.

KUR, a word portrayed as three mounds, is given as 'mountain', either singular or plural, but also 'underworld', never forgetting that this is the source of Greek Kore, also Persephone, (p.169) the maiden who is kidnapped just after having plucked a narcissus (see NAR p.110) and dragged under the water by Hades.

and by what trick did the strong Host of Many beguile you? (...) we were playing and gathering sweet flowers in our hands, soft crocuses mingled with irises and hyacinths, and rose-blooms and lilies, marvellous to see, and the narcissus which the wide earth caused to grow yellow as a crocus. That I plucked in my joy... Homeric Hymn to Demeter (*Hesiod, the Homeric hymns and Homerica*, Trans. H. G. Evelyn-White 1914)

Does this lead to an equivalence between Gnostic Sophia and Greek Kore, between SU and KUR? It seems so:

SU	KUR	RU
sink	mountain	fall
Sophia	Kore	

RU has a number of given meanings of which 'to lay down', 'to set in place'. See the notes to lines 8, 18, 24 and 30.

And so on to more rueful sinking, this time in the company of Nabi Yunus, the prophet of Nineveh and the One of the Whale. A translation of Sukurru

261

as 'Sinking in the mountains' is a reasonable suggestion in light of his thanks to God:

> *The waters engulfed me*
> *to take my life,*
> *the watery depths closed around me,*
> *the seaweed wrapped around my head.*
> *To the roots of the mountains I descended,*
> *the earth beneath me barred me in forever!*
> *But You raised my life from the pit,*
> O LORD my God!
> (Jonah's Prayer 2:5-6)

But, if Jonah's name is to be found alongside that of Oannes, the disappearing fish god, in the name of the first city, NUN, how could he also be referenced in the fifth and final city, SU-KUR-RU? Unless, of course, the timeline and perhaps even the fundamental message(s) of the antediluvian King List are not as straightforward as we have been led to believe. According to *The Story of Sukurru*, Sumerian Ubara Dudu appears to have more in common with biblical Noah who was NU-A, 'not in the water' (p.55). Jonah's trials in the belly of the whale, like those of Saint Anthony fighting devils in his desert cave, might be interpreted as a particularly gruelling baptism of an earth-bound fool - accompanied by mind-altering substances - before rebirth and enlightenment. Jonah's prayer ends:

> *Then the Lord commanded the fish, and it vomited Jonah onto dry land.*

How did the great fish get close enough to the dry land to perform that trick? The remarkable Valley of the Walking Whales in Egypt, a place from which the sea receded many millions of years ago, comes to mind.

Line 32. Ubara-Tutu

UBUR-DU-DU

This ruler presents us with two possible versions of his name to compare:

Sumerian King List	The Story of Sukurru
UBUR DU DU	UBAR TU TU

The strong phonetic similarity between them doesn't mean that they are interchangeable at will. Only a Mesopotamian scribe could enlighten us about their choice of symbol, and we have none on hand. One thing is sure. We have two distinct pieces of information about the king of Sukurru/Shuruppak who is said to have reigned there for 18,600 years. They are not the same, but they are certainly related in some way. While UBUR's main given meanings are 'breasts' and 'nipples' with an underlying theme of 'milk', UBARA is a composite symbol of EZEN (see notes to lines 9, 11 and 18) with KASKAL, the crossroads and the beer, at its centre. See the word used with its phonetic forms HER and KIRIS on p.293.

It's interesting to note that ubur-ubur means 'jellyfish' in Malay. Of course, a Malaysian ubur-ubur does not a Sumerian jellyfish make, but this isn't the first time an astonishing link can be made, one that goes beyond a quasi-perfect phonetic match, between Sumerian and Malay (p.166). UBUR's outline, closely similar if not identical to that of SUHUR, the carp, seems to indicate that it was meant to visually portray a fish. The tail fin is still apparent even at this stage in the evolution of the Mesopotamian language, the linguistic skeletal remains of the lost original pictogram. A quick glance at those ever-useful Sumero-Akkadian etymologies known as the 'lexical lists'

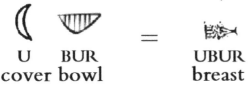

U BUR
cover bowl

UBUR
breast

brings up the possibility of finding a monosyllabic origin to UBUR: one result is U, the 'cover', with BUR, the 'bowl'. That meaning plays into the fact that the word UBUR is found primarily on stone bowls and other vessels at the earliest period of its known existence. Now imagine trying to describe the shape of a jellyfish's body: an upside-down bowl or its matching cover? There can be no absolute proof that this was the original intention but still… a linguistic and visual mix of different sea creatures?

DU and TU are both concerned with the act of carrying. DU has the given meaning 'to carry' extended to 'sailor' when two feet are present, while TU,

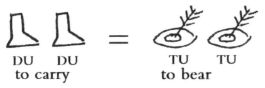

DU DU
to carry

TU TU
to bear

its pictographic version being a curious mix of what appears to be an egg yolk pierced by a feathered arrow, has the given meaning 'to bear'. TU is concerned with the womb as carrier and refers to the foetus borne in and born from the womb. This is the word translated to 'birth' in *The Story of Sukurru*. The young son is carried off from his ship by the Bird of Knowledge and left to reflect on his birth inside her nest of straw along the Milky Way. What became of him? Line 247, its opening words already mentioned on p.176, ends as follows.

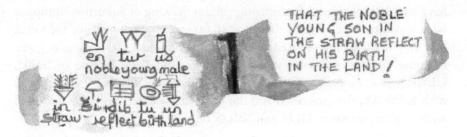

Considering that this study relates to the name of a great king on the antediluvian King List, why would he be portrayed with a double epithet of birth or pre-birth? One possible answer which combines UBUR with both DU and TU is that the figure was understood to have been twice born, carried in the womb of a great Matriarch, fed from her breast, and resuscitated or saved in some way, perhaps even made immortal by her milk. The suckling of Greek Zeus comes to mind. One of UBARA's dictionary-given meanings is joy: Born-Again King of Joy! Now there's a fitting title, positively glorious, seen here peeled back to the visual forms that Ubara Tutu might have taken

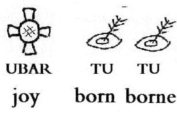

UBAR   TU   TU

joy   born borne

during the earliest pictographic era five thousand years ago. If he had existed…

In *The Story of Sukurru*, UBARA TU TU is followed by KID, a word occurring frequently as a component of Enlil and Nibru (p.191) and equated with Arabian Khidr, ghostly prophet who educates fools. A fool who is a sailor? The fool on a flightless bird? (p.131, 148, 149) The fool whose heart is 'to the left'? (p.196) The fool of God? (p.198) The death of a bitter fool during baptism in living waters or a young fool swallowing a bitter medicine, the bitterness of the amanita muscaria brew, the sharp lesson of the thorny acacia plant? (p.129) Borne and reborn into Gnosis? (p.293)

There are numerous hints at bitterness and foolishness in the Sumerian texts, an intriguing indication of philosophical discourse accompanying the use of mind-altering substances, providing a glimpse into the most ancient of Gnostic teachings. The source of the cosmic bond hidden in Pagan PA/HENDUR along with the flying man on pillar 43 offers up the strong possibility that the tribe of masons and sculptors who created the stone circles at Gobekli Tepe were already philosophising ca.9600 BC. The presence of numerous grinding stones indicates that they also knew how to make beer.

Index of Symbols

GI₄ 38, 77

GIG 131, 170-174, 211, 237, 241, 293

GIR see PIŠ

GIR₃ 57, 59, 218

GU₂/TIG 123-124, 128, 208, 236, 259

GU₇ 231

GUR 115, 120

GURUD see NUN

HA 35-36, 92, 166, 188-189, 200, 202, 205, 240-241

HAR/HUR 52-53, 92, 106, 202, 224

HENBUR see KAK

HENDUR see PA

HER/HIR see EZEN

HI 85-87, 125-127, 184

HIBIZ see HI

HU 92, 121, 124, 211

HUR see HAR

IB 192, 198

ID 65-67, 69, 252-253

IG/IK 32, 115, 222

IM 109

IN 90, 92

IR 194-196, 203

IŠ/SAHAR/ISIS 79

IZ see GEŠ

JIR see PIŠ

JISSU 175-178

KA 2, 32, 37, 68, 113, 128, 211, 218, 223-224, 227-228, 231-232, 235, 242

KAK/HENBUR 32, 81-82, 123-125, 127-130, 259

KAL/DAN 52-53, 64-69, 207, 210, 219

KALAM see UN

KAŠ see BI

KASKAL 49, 52-53, 218, 262-263

KI 23, 31-32, 35-37, 42-43, 70, 72, 99, 113, 196, 200, 205, 221-224, 228, 238, 255, 260

KIB 209-210, 259

KID 27, 190-198, 204-206, 240, 264

KIK see GIG

KIR see PIŠ

KU 32, 90, 259-260

KUD see TAR

KUR 169, 183, 261-262

LA 32, 257

LAGARg 251

LAL₃ 253

LAM 242

LAMMA see KAL

LIL 192-193, 263-264

LIL₂ see KID

LU 252-253, 257-258-259

LU₂ 2, 90-91, 221-222, 255, 259-260

LUL see NAR

MA 40-41, 90

MAH 90

MAL 2, 159, 256

MAN 239

MAR 163-164, 180, 184

ME 2, 28, 70, 72-73, 90-91, 139-140, 158, 181, 205, 217-218, 220-221, 237-238, 239, 252, 256, 259-261

MEHIDA see MU

MEN 256

MES 90

MEŠ₂ 73

MI 131, 165, 171-172, 175-176, 178, 236, 240-241

MU 98, 141-144, 151, 159, 180, 182, 220, 232, 253

MU₂ see SAR

MUL 224

MUŠ 104, 138-143, 151, 166, 170-171, 179-180, 209

NA 27, 80, 84, 86, 110, 180, 190, 205, 217, 219, 231-232, 238-240, 256, 260

NAGAR 254-255

NAM 37, 180

NAR/LUL 32, 38, 109-110, 134, 261

NE 2, 79, 82, 128, 194-196, 203-205, 240, 251

NER see NUR

NI 161-162, 165, 192, 198, 235-236

NI² see IM

NIM 164-165

NIN 105

NINDA₂ 83, 182

NIR see NUR

NITA see UŠ

NU 2, 55, 70, 90, 92, 119, 130-131, 174, 183, 196, 211, 217, 220-221, 262

NUN 27-32, 35-37, 40-43, 63, 65, 68-70, 111, 113, 165-166, 187-189, 190, 194, 196, 200, 205-210, 217, 231, 237-238-241, 252, 260-261

NUR 40-43, 111, 113, 115, 208, 239

NUS/NUNUS 131-132, 171-172, 174, 211, 237, 241

PA/HENDUR 26, 91, 125-127, 132, 153, 191, 257-259, 264

PAN 26

PAP 91, 132

PAR see UD

PI 92, 100-101, 107-110, 151

PIR see UD

PIŠ 172, 189, 200

RA 2, 32, 52-53, 56, 115, 202, 209-210, 224, 232, 257

RI 92, 169-170, 202, 206, 255, 293

RIS/RES see SAG

RU 97, 180, 192, 198, 254, 261-262

ŠA/ARA 56

ŠA₃ 47, 49-50, 114, 237

SAG 2, 26, 80-81, 106, 158, 161, 169-170, 184, 256

ŠAH 221,

SAHAR see IŠ

SAL 105-106, 169, 182, 235-236

SAR 21-22, 24, 95-98, 101, 109, 112-113, 154, 166, 221

SAR₂ 96, 112-113

ŠE 77, 82-83, 86, 90, 182

ŠEŠ 179-182

SI 59-60, 256

ŠI 32, 92, 115, 131, 158-159, 202, 237, 252

SIG 211

SIN see EŠ

ŠIP/SIP see ME

SIPAD 256, 258

SIPPAR 260

SU 177-178, 261-262

ŠU 67

ŠUBUR see ŠAH

SUD 263

SUHUR 263

SUM 90, 92

TA 140, 161-162, 221-223, 238

TAB 222, 238-239

TAL see RI

TAM see UD

TAR 25, 37, 165

TE/TEN 42, 252, 254

TIBIRA 254

TI/TIL 26, 81

TIG see GU₂

TU 263-264

TUK 67, 232, 293

TUM 115, 254

TUG₂ 100, 102-107, 110, 151

TUR 84-86, 182, 257-258

TUR₃ 43

Notes And References

The cover photo shows a group of T-shaped stones at the archaeological site of Gobekli Tepe in southern Turkey (photo Ian Faure).

Sources include:

→ Electronic Pennsylvania Sumerian Dictionary (ePSD) for phonetic values of the symbols, given meanings, approximate dating and quantifying of their appearance on existing tablets, corpus of the lexical lists. Shows computerized examples of cuneiform signs.

→ The Open Richly Annotated Cuneiform Corpus (ORACC), also a University of Pennsylvania project, includes a second version of ePSD.

→ Cuneiform Digital Library Initiative (CDLI), a joint project of the University of California, the University of Oxford, and the Max Planck Institute for the History of Science, for photographic evidence from museums around the world. Includes tablets from all archaeological periods, including original examples of pictographic forms and transliterations.

→ Electronic Text Corpus of Sumerian Literature (ETCSL), University of Oxford, transliterations and translations. Shows only phonetic forms.

→ Lucien-Jean Bord and Remo Mugnaioni, *L'Ecriture Cunéiforme, Syllabaire Sumérien, Babylonien, Assyrien,* Geuthner Manuels, 2002, from pictogram through the different stages of transformation of cuneiform alongside their various phonetic values. It's not necessary to read French to use this book.

→ René Labat and Florence Malbran-Labat, *Manuel d'Epigraphie Akkadienne*, Geuthner Manuels, 1988 edition, showing the evolution of signs, meanings given through later Akkadian, with transliterations and explanations in French.

→ *The Assyrian Dictionary of the Oriental Institute of the University of Chicago (CAD),* 1964, transliterations and meanings given through later Akkadian. Shows only phonetic forms. No images. Available for consultation online.

p.1 [1]Re-translation of the earliest known Sumerian literary text titled *The Story of Sukurru* (aka *The Instructions of Shuruppak*, ETCSL ref.5.6.1.), 280 lines comprising approximately 3,000 words, a text that predates the Epic of Gilgamesh by some five hundred years, at least in terms of the clay on which it was found. *The Story of Sukurru* was published in 2017 and the notes reflect my more limited understanding of some words at that time. In 2020, an explanation of the Solstice Riddle was added.

p.2 [1] Quote from Herodotus (born ca.484 BC) on the boats arriving in Babylon, *Histories*, Book 1, 194. Trans. G Rawlinson; Wordsworth Editions.

[2] ETCSL Sumerian Proverbs Coll.6.1.03, lines 325–326: The riddle entails reading in a circle where the first four symbols, 'the man (who is also a scribe) in the basket' are repeated at the end. The basket is round according to the wordplay but also named as such through the given meanings of NU with UB, 'no corners', positioned at the centre of the riddle. BI, which has both 'beer' and the verb 'to be' as given meanings,

269

also appears at the centre of the vessel. The return of the beer is a theme mentioned in *The Story of Sukurru* and repeated in other riddles, referring to the return of the sun after the winter solstice, bringing the certitude of a new year and a new harvest. At the same time, the riddle refers to the circular journey of the sun and to the science of astronomy written on tablets by a very special scribe. While that might appear to be an excessively large amount of information stored in just a few words, it demonstrates the flexibility of the monosyllabic language and its clever manipulation. The themes are confirmed in other texts.

T-shaped ME is also phonetic ŠIP, pronounced 'ship'. Its primary given meanings are 'spirit' and 'magician'. I have added 'ship', a word of otherwise unknown source, and, through another phonetic form, SIB, suggest that this is also the source of 'sibyl', the female prophet of Ancient Greece. ME/ŠIP/SIP as 'magic', 'ship' and 'sibyl' brings to mind the Greek legend of Jason and the Argonauts. Their ship, the Argo, possessed a magical wooden beam which was also an oracle. Traces of that and other Homeric tales are found in *The Story of Sukurru*.

UB gives the origin of Hebrew 'ob', a bottle made of skin. On line 201 of *The Story of Sukurru*, Noah's ark is described as a 'waterskin' in a cursing scene:

From the sky onto Eden's stony plain that it sink, that the waterskin bearing the noble arm split!

Confirmation of the waterskin as vessel is found in two of the Assyrian bas reliefs that once lined the walls of the Palace of Sennacherib (ca.700 BC). The North West Palace incorporates images of men, in or under water, riding astride or stretched out on inflated waterskins, the ancient equivalent of a rubber buoy. The line from *The Story of Sukurru* also confirms that the sailor doubles as a scribe.

p.5 [1] Sumerian King List on the Weld-Blundell Prism, ca.1800 BC, found at Larsa, Iraq, Ashmolean Museum, University of Oxford. (photo Wiki-Commons)

p.6 [1] Sumerian King List, ETCSL ref.2.1.1. It is possible to read the Kings' names as incorporating 14 symbols.
[2] Berossus, a Babylonian author in the 3rd century BC, writing in Greek. Fragments of his work, including the translation of the antediluvian King List, are known only through second or third-hand accounts, and those later copies potentially influenced by the religious beliefs of their Christian authors.

p.7 [1] Dumuzid also appears in other texts, notably Dumuzid's Dream, ETCSL ref. 1.4.3. See the notes to the King List p.257.
[2] From the Suda, a 10th century AD Arabic compilation which also states: *He wrote philosophical works, poems and histories; Astronomy, or Catasterisms; On the Philosophical Sects; On Freedom from Pain; many dialogues; and numerous grammatical works.*

p.8 Sketch made from De Sphaera Mundi, Sacrobosco, 1550 edition of a 13th century textbook of astronomy.

p.12 [1] Berossus, ca. 3rd century BC, text on Oannes, L.P. Cory, *Ancient Fragments*, 1832 This is an extract from the *Chronicles* of Eusebius (AD 260-339) by Syncellus (9th century AD) through an Armenian translation.
[2] Detail from wall panel, Palace of King Sargon II, Louvre Museum, Paris, France. (Photo Ian Faure)

p.13 Zechariah Sitchin (1920-2010) wrote *The Earth Chronicles*, a series of books based in interpretations of Sumerian, of which The 12th Planet, published in 1976. He posited that the Anunnaki were extra-terrestrial beings and that Planet X was mentioned in the Sumerian writings as being on a recurring orbit with the potential to destroy Earth.

p.15 John Marco Allegro, *The Sacred Mushroom and the Cross*, Introduction, p.xx. (2009 edition)

p.17 Ibid. Introduction, p.xxii

SEAL OF THE FATHER

p.21 [1] Clay imprint from the Akkadian cylinder seal known as the Adda Seal, ref.89115, British Museum, London, England. (photo Wiki Commons).
[2] As discussed in Before Babel, pictographic AD varies quite significantly, one version closely resembling the object held by Ishtar. I likened it to a handheld fishing net but a root clump is more in line with the scene.

p.24 BAL, a different but related symbol, is a better fit for the 'phal' of 'phallus' in my opinion, particularly as BAL is found once with UŠ, symbol meaning 'phallus', in the lexical lists.

p.26 [1]Rebis image from *Theoria Philosophiae Hermeticae*, 1617, Heinrich Nollius (photo Wiki Commons)
[2] *The names of the Philosophers who spoke about the art: Hermes, Agathodaimon and many others... They are remembered for making the head and the perfected elixir.* Ibn an-Nadim, *Kitâb al-Fihrist* (Book of the Catalogue) Ch.10, (p. 849-850 of translation by Dodge) AD 987.
[3] *Coursing beside him in that rapid chase went the dog with sagacious mind, the dog which highhorned Pan, breeder of hounds, offered as a gift to Dionysos, once on a time when he was hunting in the highlands which he loved.* (Nonnus, Dionysiaca 16. 185 ff. www.theoi.com)

p.27 *Enki and the World Order*, ETCSL ref. 1.1.3.

p.28 *Enki and Ninhursaga*, ETCSL ref. 1.1.1.

p.29 [1] Detail CDLI ref. P342526, Uruk V, ca.3500-3350 BC, private collection (anon.)

p.30 [1] Detail CDLI, Uruk IV ca. 3350-3200 BC, ref. P001050, Vorderasiatisches Museum, Berlin, Germany (photo Olaf Tessmer).
[2] Detail CDLI, Uruk IV ca.3350-3200 BC, ref. P000745, Vorderasiatisches Museum, Berlin, Germany (photo Olaf Tessmer).

p.31 Sumerian King List, ETCSL ref. 2.1.1.

p.32 ETCSL Sumerian Proverbs Collection 6.1.06, Lines 276-277.

FISHING AROUND

p.33 Pair of dolphins or whales: detail CDLI ref. P004130, Uruk IV ca.3350-3200 BC, National Museum of Iraq, Baghdad, Iraq. Referenced as ZATU758 with no known phonetic equivalence or meaning, other examples are considerably more abstract. The two heads combine as one while retaining the two vertical lines indicating the mouths.

p.35 Jacobsen, *The Sumerian King List*, 1939, p.58, note 107, p.70, note 5.

p.36 [1] L.P. Cory, *Ancient Fragments*, 1832, Fragments of Chaldean History, Berossus from Alexander Polyhistor (sourced from Syncellius, Chron. 28, from Eusebius Chron. 5.8, AD 260-339). (www.sacred-texts.com)

p.37 This theme is also discussed in *Before Babel The Crystal Tongue*, ch.20 Atlantis and the Fish.

p.39 [1] R.H.Allen, *Star Names and their Meanings*, 1899 (www.archive.org).
[2] I daresay Jensen or another Assyriologist somewhere has long since made the interesting connection between the conventional transliteration NUN-KI for the first city, the HA-A-KI of the Sumerian King List as found on fragment W-B 62 (see note to p.35), and the wording on the astronomical Mul Apin text. (where celestial MUL-HA/KU$_6$, the 'fish', and MUL-NUN are mentioned in the same section.) As above so below?
The Chicago Assyrian Dictionary gives Sumerian HA as later Akkadian nunu and links it to the constellation of Pisces. That entry also makes a number of links to NU-UN and to NU-NU (p.70 and 131), linking back to the lexical breakdown of NUN and thus indirectly confirming the strong connection between HA and NUN.

p.40 [1] Lines 127-131, *The Story of Sukurru*.
[2] *Enki's Journey to Nibru*, ETCSL ref. 1.1.4. The references made to this text are unrelated to the orthodox translation found in the ETCSL corpus. The translated excerpts and comments result from my own findings employing the monosyllabic approach. May the reader of this carry out their own comparison and decide which version of the lines they find more plausible.

p.42 a) NUN.NUN (NUR) over symbol TE. TE/TEN takes the form of two crosses joined at their centres by a horizontal line and has the given meaning 'to approach', a written reference to the joining of two points with a connotation of travel, of distance. TE is associated with the Sator Square and is source of Latin tenet.(p.82).
b) NUN.NUN (NUR) joined by a horizontal line at the apex of the triangle,
c) NUN.NUN (NUR) above GEŠ, rising from a horizontal wooden beam in the same manner as symbol SAR, the garden.

p.43 TUR$_3$ appears on the unfortunately broken line 214 of The Story of Sukurru and can be seen on CDLI ref. P006262, Uruk IV, ca.3350-3200 BC.

IN THE BEGINNING WAS THE CAMEL

p.50 Graham Hancock, *Magicians of the Gods*, Ch.16 Written in the Stars. (Hodder & Stoughton 2016) provides an overview of the region and its history in this regard. Discovered in the late 20th century by a German archaeologist, Klaus Schmidt, the site of Gobekli Tepe consists of huge T-shaped, carved pillars arranged in circles, the earliest of which has been dated to 9600 BC, corresponding to the end of the last ice age. (Cover photo and on p.233) Elements of the carvings on pillar 43 are discussed from p.123.

p.51 [1] Berossus from Syncellus (ca. 800 AD) *Chronicles* 207, taken from Josephus (37-100 AD) (I.P. Cory, *Ancient Fragments*, 1832)
[2] *And he mentions that there were written accounts, preserved at Babylon with the greatest care, comprehending a period of above fifteen myriads of years: and that these writings contained histories of the heaven and of the sea; of the birth of mankind; and of the kings, and of the memorable actions which they had achieved.* (Polyhistor on Berossus, from Eusebius, from Syncellus.) (I.P. Cory, *Ancient Fragments*, 1832)

p.52 [1]Berossus from Eusebius (ca.260-340 AD) (I.P. Cory, *Ancient Fragments*, 1832).
[2] To fully appreciate the importance of the mythological millstone, read *Hamlet's Mill* (Giorgio de Santillana & Hertha Von Dechend, published by David R. Godine).

p.53 [1] An example connecting both KAL and KASKAL to Harran (ePSD Lexical lists):

    ka-as-kal   kaskal har-ra-nu (Sb Voc. II 76)

[2] Berossus from Abydenus (ca.200 BC) from Eusebius. (ca.260-340 AD), from Syncellus (ca 800 AD). (I.P. Cory, *Ancient Fragments*, 1832)

p.56 ETCSL Sumerian Proverbs Collection 4, line 8. See annexed proverb p.291.

p.57 [1] GIR₃ is given as HUŠ on p.175 of *L'Ecriture Cunéiforme* (Bord and Mugnaioni, Geuthner Manuels, 2002) where the drawing takes the form of a mouse peeping out from its hole.
[2] Detail CDLI ref. P002207, Uruk IV ca.3350-3200 BC, Vorderasiatisches Museum, Berlin, Germany (photo Olaf Tessmer).

COGS WITHIN COGS

p.61 Akkadian seal image, Marduk (Photo Wiki Commons).

p.63 ETCSL list of proper nouns (etcsl.orinst.ox.ac.uk).

p.64 Lamma goddess, Larsa, 2000-1800 BC, bronze, baked clay, Oriental Institute Museum, University of Chicago (photo Wiki Commons)

p.65 [1] Copied from a drawing in Adam Falkenstein's list of archaic signs (1936) from tablets discovered at the archaeological site of Ur.
[2] CDLI, ref. P000121, Uruk IV, ca.3350-3200 BC, Vorderasiatisches Museum, Berlin, Germany.
[3]Lines 63, 110 and 206.

p.66 Minotaur on kylix, ca.515 BC, National Archaeological Museum, Madrid, Spain. (photo Wiki Commons)

P.71 Randall Carlson is known for his investigations into the geological events at the end of the Ice Age and his subsequent collaboration with Graham Hancock in that regard. His sacred geometry workshop is in Sedona, Arizona. (www.randallcarlson.com)

p.72 [1] From the alchemical text known as The Emerald Tablet of Hermes Trismegistus, from a Latin copy dated to 1541 (trans. Isaac Newton).
[2] Detail CDLI, ref. P004479, Uruk III ca.3200-3000 BC, German Archaeological Institute, Berlin, Germany.
[3] Concerning ME as 'ship' see notes to line 13 of the Sumerian King List, p.256. As mentioned in *Before Babel*, p.219, KI-ME, is phonetically close to Kemet, an ancient name for Egypt.

p.73 [1] CDLI ref. P384786.
[2] The full name of Hermes Trismegistus is also analysed in *Before Babel*, p.211. The 'tris', meaning 'three', bears a tantalising similarity to our word 'tree'. At the same time, the Sumerian origin of the name is evident in the 'gis', an accurate reflection of GIS/GES, the tree, which also became the French word 'giste', a joist or beam. TRIS-ME-GIS: the three great ships of the Magician?

PERPETUAL GENESIS

p.75 Creation of the World, from the *Nuremberg Chronicles*, Anton Koburger, 1493 Bibliothèque Nationale de Paris, France. (photo Creatuve Commons, Hartmann Schedel)

p.79 The Emerald Tablet. See notes to p.72.

P.81 [1] Riddle: ETCSL Sumerian Proverbs Coll.6.1.02, Seg.B, lines 12-13.
[2] PI with ESEN/EZEN (also HIR/HER) gives the source of Greek piezien 'to press tight', 'to squeeze'. This is the source of piezo- meaning 'pressure' used to name a form of electricity obtained from amber and crystal. (*Before Babel*, p.232). HIR/HER, with the given meaning 'boundary' is the founding symbol of the name Hermes. See EZEN on p254.

p.82 *Before Babel The Crystal Tongue*, Ch. 19. The Sator Templar Connection.

p.83 Detail CDLI, ref. P003500, Uruk III ca.3200-3000 BC, National Museum of Iraq, Baghdad, Iraq.

p.84 [1] Homer, Illiad, Book 4:1-3 (Trans. G. Chapman)
[2] Lexical entry: *gi-en-na genna (DUMU.DIŠ) še-ir-ru (Sb Voc. II 304)*

p.87 [1] Nonnus, Dionysiaca 27. 241 ff (www.Theoi.com)
[2] *Enki's Journey to Nibru*, ETCSL ref. 1.1.4.
[3] The Sumerian theme of taking notes at the time of the flood is reminiscent of the quote attributed to Berossus and concerning an account to be hidden at Sippar (p.260).

p.90 [1] ETCSL Sumerian Proverbs Collection 6.1.05, Seg.D, Lines 22-23.
[2] *Before Babel The Crystal Tongue*, ch.18 Hermes and the Crystal Heresy.
Also see notes to p.240 on the subject of PAP.

p.91 In *Magicians of the Gods*, (p.209, paperback edition 2016) Graham Hancock cites the Egyptologist Selim Hassan in that regard. On p.296 of his book, Hassan is also cited on the connection between the Sabians of Harran in Turkey and the monuments of Giza in Egypt. Concerning the 'em' of Hor-em-akhet, also see the comment on EM/IM/NI$_2$ on p.109 and the notes to that page.
[2] Egyptian head : top left detail CDLI ref. P005573, Uruk III ca.3200-3000 BC, Musées royaux d'Art et d'Histoire, Brussels, Belgium. Given as DARA$_3$, the 'goat', the unique headdress demonstrates that this is a different sign.
[3] AR, composed of two symbols, has no given meanings unless associated with other words. My own interpretation from its two founding words and their orthodox meanings, 'eye' and 'collect/gather', gives it as 'to watch'. ŠI-RI, the eye of the bird, is one source of the name Sirius, Greek Seirios. The others are ŠE-IR, the wandering seed, found on line 186 of *The Story of Sukurru*, and potentially ŠI-UR, the eye of the dog, two words which come together as HUL with a connotation of disaster.

A star that keenest of all blazes with a searing flame and him men call Seirios… (…) and to some he gives strength but of others he blights the bark utterly. Aratus, *Phaenomena* 328ff. (sourced from Theoi.com) Also see notes to p.148.

The Greek noun 'arkhon' has the meaning 'ruler' and 'chief'. As arkhein, it means 'to be first', a fitting description of Sirius rising before the sun just once a year. Another symbol with the same sound is transcribed as AR$_2$ and is one phonetic value of UB. There exists one important lexical list entry which gives HAR opposite HA with AR$_2$. (See p.110 and the notes to that page. See p.289.)

THE GARDEN

P.93 Detail of wall panel, 'Isolated building', Palace of King Sargon II, Louvre Museum, Paris, France (photo Ian Faure).

p.95 [1] Berossus from Apollodorus sourced from Eusebius AD 260-339, (L.P. Cory, *Ancient Fragments*, 1832).
[2] Detail CDLI ref. P004175, Uruk IV period, ca.3350-3200 BC, National Museum of Iraq, Baghdad, Iraq.

p.97 [1] Lexical entry: *šar-ru   LUGAL (CT 18 29-30 i 18)*
LUGAL occurs many times in the Sumerian King List, translated to 'king'.
[2] Manuel d'Epigraphie Akkadienne (Labat).

p.98 Book of the Dead, Judgement Hall of Osiris: one interpretation of the scene gives 'the company which is with SAR' i.e. Osiris (www.sacredtexts.com).

p.100 Lines 150, 173, 260.

p.101 Cannabis is sourced from KA-NA-AB on line 56 which gave Persian 'kanab'. The third eye appears as ME-ŠI-ME twice in this section of text. See page 158.

p.102 [1] The Secret Book of John, Barbelo Appears, Nag Hammadi text, from Coptic, (Trans. M. Meyer. W. Barnstone and M.Meyer, *The Gnostic Bible*.)

p.103 Plato, Gorgias 523 (trans. W. Lamb, Harvard University Press; London, William Heinemann Ltd. 1967.)

p.105 SAL is repeated three times in the Solstice Riddle (p.290).

p.106 [1] *Enki and Ninhursaga* ETCSL ref.1.1.1.

p.107 From an Old Norse poem known as Völuspá (Trans. Carolyne Larrington).

p.109 [1] 'Know thyself' is another way to translate NI$_2$-ZU, an aphorism used throughout antiquity and notably in *Prometheus Bound* where it occurs in a passage of complaint, reminiscent of the complaint of Jonah (p.11) or Momus (p.141) who writes it all down in clay (IM is 'clay'). It tends to confirm that the themes of bitterness and subsequent self-knowledge through rituals involving mind-altering substances and music were born in the Sumerian culture, as was Prometheus himself (p.252), and perpetuated in Greek mythology. Also see p.92 and the notes to that page concerning Hor-em-akhet, the Great Sphinx who watches himself/herself/itself in the sky.

[2] ETCSL Sumerian Proverbs Collection 2+6, Seg.A, Lines 89-95: all seven lines include the three-word phrase PI-EL-LA$_2$.

One lexical entry gives the following combination:

lu2-nundum-pe-el-la2   ša ša-ba-šu qa2-al-la (OB Lu A 341)

LU2 KAxNUN (nundum) PI EL LA$_2$ translates to 'The man on whose lips the perfect pitch is suspended' where Akkadian 'nundum', which comprises KA with NUN, is given as 'lips'. KA-NUN gives the origin of 'canon' through the Greek, the canonical measure of excellence (p.68). PI-EL refers to the number seven, to music, to the Pleiades (a group carved on to numerous seals) and to perfection. It is inherently linked to the word NUN. Perhaps this is where the notion of seven sages was born. It can be said that the perfect pitch is used to seduce and potentially to trick. Hence the presence of NAR, the fox, who is also LUL, the lullaby, in the line from *Enki's Journey to Nibru*. But what does that imply for the biblical scene on the mountain? I'll leave that one for others to decide.

p.110 [1] Given the context, it is not unreasonable to see in UB/UP, the pentagram symbol, the source of Greek 'opos' which gave 'opium'. Another word of unknown origin is 'up'. Also see NU-UB (p.2) and HA-AR$_2$ (p.92).

[2] Pseudo-Hyginus, *Astronomica* 2. 7, 2nd century AD (trans. Grant) (www.Theoi.com)

p.111 Nuraghe Nieddu, Codrongianos, (Photo Gianni Careddu, Wiki Commons.)

p.115 Lexical list example : *u6-nir   zi-ig-gur-ra-tum (MBGT II 149)*

AROUND AND AROUND WE GO

p.117 Line 10, *Enki's Journey to Nibru*.

p.119 [1] Pseudo-Apollodorus, *Bibliotheca* 3. 52 – 55, Greek mythographer C2nd A.D., trans. Aldrich.
[2] Atalanta Fugiens, 1617

p.120 [1]Inscription inside two rings of the document known as the Chrysopeoia attributed to the alchemist Cleopatra of Alexandria.
[2] Kilpeck is discussed in *Before Babel*, Ch.8, Springs, Fountains and Waterspouts.
[3]Servius, 4th century AD, Commentary on the Aeneid of Virgil, Book 5:85.

p.121 [1] Double ouroboros on one of the shrines enclosing the sarcophagus of Tutankhamun, Egyptian Museum, Cairo (Wiki Commons)
[2] Detail CDLI ref. P004228n Uruk IV ca.3350-3200 BC, National Museum of Iraq, Baghdad, Iraq.

p.122 Image from Chrysopoea of Cleopatra (Codex Marcianus graecus 299 fol. 188v) 10th century AD. (Wiki Commons)

p.123 *Before Babel The Crystal Tongue*, Ch.13 The Idigna Bird of the Taurus Mountains.

p.124 [1] The source of Gobekli from GU$_2$-BI, found together on line 189 of *The Story of Sukurru*, is discussed in the notes there.
[2]With the bird's neck as gullet and linked to the concept of the ouroboros in which a potentially bird-headed snake swallows its own tail (p.121), the BU/PO, snake and river of Mesopotamia, becomes a logical candidate for the snake's (invisible) body. This is a circular celestial river (p.208).

p.128 If there is a direct reference to the site of Gobekli Tepe in this line of text, then it is potentially indicating that the place was built (KAK as verb) to include the directions to find NUN-KI, the 'otherworldly place'.
Also see the notes to line 20 of the King List (p.259) for the link between ME and 'ego'. Symbol KULLA on line 14 was the final clincher in identifying E$_2$-GU$_2$ as the source of our word 'ego'. It is analysed in the notes to my ongoing retranslation of *Enki's Journey to Nibru*, re-named *The Path to Sky-End*.:

A builder inscribing his name on the foundation pegs carries out an act born of ego, as will I by adding my name to this text. (…) Visually, KULLA, which has the given meaning 'mud brick', suggests a wall being punctured by a series of nails. This line confirms that the word is used in the context of the Mesopotamian peg-shaped foundation cones (used to illustrate the page) inscribed with cuneiform words of dedication once the construction is completed. But it is noteworthy that the word has come down through the ages and still exists as the kulla, a tall, thin building with slits for windows, situated in valleys and said to have been used as defensive positions in the case of blood feuds (A-NE, the red flow). It is not a coincidence that this leads on very neatly from the preceding 'ego', also a building in a gulley, and, in my opinion, a reference to the fact that 'ego' is expressed by words emanating from the throat or gullet (see KAK). These tower-houses called 'kullas' can still be seen in several countries including Greece. In that context and conforming to the original evocative pictogram, the symbol can be interpreted as a valley with a set of obstacles along its path – to be defeated. It might also be a wall or a smaller item pierced with holes. Ety: Latin colare, to strain, a wicker fishing net, English colander, a strainer, French couloir: a corridor, and couler: to flow, trickle or to sink. (...)

KULLA-BI, mud brick-beer/bi-. The Egyptian purification ritual carried out at the moment of dedication of a new building was known as the 'Strewing of the Besen'. Mud bricks were inscribed with the name of the ruler and buried in the foundations. The construction theme and, most importantly, the overall link between Egypt and Mesopotamia continue in these lines.

See BUR/PUR, the stone bowl, for the etymology of 'pure' through Latin purus meaning 'clean', 'unadorned', 'undefiled' (p.127 and 259). Thanks to this further study of DUR, GU$_2$ and KAK in the context of the alchemical ouroboros symbolism, the deeper meanings behind the sculpted birds on pillar 43 at Gobekli Tepe become not only more evident but also infinitely more thought-provoking than might have been expected.

It also becomes evident that there was a strong connection between Sumerian and Egyptian rituals at the time when both *The Path to Sky-End* and *The Story of Sukurru* were written. There are other tantalising clues to this crossover in terms of architectural mastery in *The Story of Sukurru*, notably line 29 which begins 'A stone temple there will be...'. Bearing in mind that Mesopotamian buildings were constructed using mudbricks, this is a surprising but clear translation of the original word in that text. The word is NA. A 'heavy' building is one possible translation but still...a stone temple is better suited to both Egypt and to Gobekli Tepe.

p.129 Hypostile Hall, Temple of Karnak, Luxor, (photo courtesy of www.touregypt.net)

p.132 [1] Detail CDLI ref. P005210, Uruk III ca.3200-3000 BC, © Ashmolean Museum, University of Oxford, England.
[2] Detail CDLI ref. P005157, Uruk III ca.3200-3000 BC, © Ashmolean Museum, University of Oxford, England.

p.133 [1] Cicero, *De Natura Deorum* 2 :24, 1st century BC, (trans. Rackham),
[2] Aion mosaic from a Roman villa ca.200-250 AD. (photo Wiki Commons)

IN THE NAME OF THE SNAKE

p.135 Sketch of a carved serpent on the Gulgul Gongs, carved wood, East Java, Indonesia, ca. 1900 AD, Metropolitan Museum, New York.

p.137 Sketched from a painted image on an Ancient Greek oil jar.

p.138 [1] *[Zeus] told Paieon (Paeeon) to heal him; and scattering medicines to still pain upon him Paieon rendered him well again, since he was not made to be one of the mortals. As when the juice of a fig in white milk rapidly fixes that which was fluid before and curdles quickly for one who stirs it; in such speed as this he healed violent Ares;* (Homer, Iliad 5. 899 ff (trans. Lattimore) (Greek epic C8th B.C.)

[2] BU, detail CDLI ref. P001324, Uruk IV ca.3350+3200 BC, Vorderasiatisches Museum, Berlin, Germany (photo Olaf Tessmer).

p.140 Tammuz, *International Standard Bible Encyclopedia* (www.biblehub.com)

p.141 Aesop, *Fables* 518 (from Babrius 59) (trans. Gibbs) (Greek fable C6th B.C.) (www.theoi.com)

p.143 [1] Lexical entry: *mu-uš = muš (Proto-Ea 797)*

p.144 J.M.Allegro, *The Sacred Mushroom and the Cross*, Introduction, p.xxiii. (2009 edition)

BONES OF OSIRIS

p.145 Detail CDLI ref. P000487, Uruk III ca.3200-3000 BC, National Museum of Iraq, Baghdad, Iraq. My interpretation of this unique and otherwise unexplained image is that it represents the constellation of Orion, a figure which has been suggested as also being that of Egyptian Osiris.

p.147 [1] *Enki and Ninhursaga*, ETCSL ref.1.1.1, Lines 63-68.
[2] UŠ: CDLI ref. P001261, Uruk IV ca.3350-3200 BC, Vorderasiatisches Museum, Berlin, Germany (photo Olaf Tessmer).

p.148 [1] Lines 195-198 of *The Story of Sukurru* confirm the existence of an original myth involving an orgasm as metaphor for a flood. The principal figures there are GA, the milk, who I take to be the source of both Gaia and the Milky Way, and UR, the dog/lion, who is preceded by ŠI, the eye. See the notes to p.92 for ŠI-UR as a potential source of Sirius. Is this an account of the annual heliacal rising of Sirius and the flooding of the Nile? Written in or before 2600 BC?
[2] Ithyphallic bird-man, Lascaux caves, France, (Photo Creative Commons).

p.149 [1] Detail lower bird and ithyphallic headless man, Pillar 43, Gobekli Tepe, Turkey.
[2] Detail imprint from Sumerian seal.
[3] Plutarch (ca. 46-119 AD), Moralia, On Isis and Osiris, (Trans. C.W. King)

p.151 [1] Ibid.
[2] Lexical entry: *[m]u-uš-tug2 PI = gištug2 (Emesal Voc. II 183)*

p.152 Tree of Jesse, stained-glass, 14th century, St Mary's Church, Shrewsbury, England, (photo Creative Commons).

AMA-NITA MON AMOUR

p.155 Photo 'Amanita muscaria Marriott Falls', by JJ Harrison (CCBYSA3.0)

p.157 [1] J.M. Allegro, *The Sacred Mushroom and the Cross*, Introduction, p.xxiii (2009 edition)
[2] Adapted from an article published on Graham Hancock's website in October 2020 (https://grahamhancock.com/dainesm5/).

p.158 EDEN with SAG: Detail CDLI ref. P000523, Uruk III ca.3200-3000 BC, National Museum of Iraq, Baghdad, Iraq.

[2] *The Story of Sukurru*, line 56, KA-NA-AB. Also discussed in *Before Babel The Crystal Tongue*, (p.167).

p.159 [1] Detail, CDLI ref. P001757, Uruk IV ca.3350-3200 BC, Vorderasiatisches Museum, Berlin, Germany (photo Olaf Tessmer).

p.160 [1] Lexical list reference: ama-nita (Proto-Lu 325a)

[2] This is a drawing of a Sumerian seal said by Zechariah Sitchin to represent the creation of Adam. His imagined caption reads 'My hands have made it', a reference to the otherworldly origin of humans. I have a different take on it but at least we can agree on the place being the Garden of Eden.

p.161 [1] Drawing, CDLI ref. P471688, Uruk III ca.3200-3000 BC, location unstated.

[2] NI: Detail CDLI ref. P001136, Uruk IV 3350-3200 BC, Vorderasiatisches Museum, Berlin (photo Olaf Tessmer).

[3] The Solstice Riddle takes the form of an acrostic, a word puzzle solved by reading both horizontally and vertically. It begins on line 223 and continues through to line 227 of *The Story of Sukurru*. It appears in the context of a shamanic ritual and is discussed in the annexe to the translation. Here on p.290.

p.162 AMA might also be read as a cosmic vessel in the manner of Zechariah Sitchin's understanding of the early Sumerian culture. It would be a mistake to rule anything out without a full investigation and multiple meanings are shown to exist in the language. But I have so far found nothing more meaningful with which to take the subject further down that route.

p.163 AMAR appears after BI-IR on line 181 of *The Story of Sukurru*, potentially translating to 'bitter beer'! They appear together in the context of a cursing scene and, since AMAR is not given as 'bitter' in orthodox lexicons, my translation took it in another direction, but the overall theme of bitterness is nevertheless present.

p.164 Lexical entry: *a-mar-ra   a-gar-ra A.MEŠ ša2-ha-tu   (Emesal Voc. III 69)*

[2] The Solstice Riddle (p.290). See note [3] to p.161.

p.165 Pliny, *Natural History*, Book XXIV, Ch.2.

p.166 *Dictionary of Greek and Roman Geography* (1854, William Smith, LLD, Ed.) (Pliny Nat. 25.9. s. 57; Dioscor. 3.1; Galen, de fac. simp. med. p. 150), (www.perseus.tufts.edu).

THE SECRET REVEALED

p.170 [1] Professor Carl A. Ruck, an authority on the ecstatic rituals of the Greek god Dionysus, has written and co-authored a number of books on the subject of entheogens, notably *Persephone's Quest: Entheogens and the Origins of Religion* written with R. Gordon Wasson, Stella Kramrisch and Jonathan Ott (1988).

P.171 *The Sacred Mushroom and the Cross* (Ch.V Plant Names and the Mysteries of the Fungus, p.40). The Sumerian phrase was GIG-AN-TI which Allegro defined as 'shade of heaven'. However, the phonetic link was not being made between GIG/KIK and Hebrew kikayon but between AN-TI and Greek antimimon.

p.174 J. Isaac Hollandus, Hand der Philosophen (1667) (Alexander Roob, Alchemy & Mysticism, p.300, 2019, Taschen Gmbh)

p.175 [1]*Man his measure to take, man his measure not to take...* Line 184 has both GAR and GIG, with GAR translated there to 'measure' and GIG to 'troublesome'.
[2] MI: Detail CDLI ref. P001243, Uruk IV ca.3350-3200 BC, Vorderasiatisches Museum, Berlin, Germany (photo Olaf Tessmer).

p.176 [1] If a 'mushroom' context is taken into account for JESSU/GEŠ-MI, then 'horn of the soil' would be appropriate for the two following words in that line of text: SI-IŠ. SI, the horn, and IŠ, the soil, are given once in the lexical lists opposite ŠEŠ, brother and snake. It is also an integral element of the original name of Isis through I-SI-IŠ found multiple times opposite IŠ/SAHAR in the lexical entries (p.79). The words MI-SI-IŠ, black-horn-soil, appear together only three times in the entire Sumerian corpus, two of which in *The Story of Sukurru*. They are given together as 'money chest' in the lexicons. Line 176 is the only example of those three words being preceded by GEŠ.
JESSU/JISSU appears in numerous literary texts, of which line 53 of *Enki's Journey to Nibru*, beginning NUN-KI GEŠ-MI-ZU, which might translate to *'In the City of the Nun, the shady-tree specialist...'*
[2] Mayan mushroom stone, ca.1000 BC-500 AD, Guatemala.

p.177 Lexical entry: (gizzu:) gi-is-su (Diri III 58)

p.179 George Orwell, *1984*, Book 3, ch.2.

p.181 Snake head, Museum of Sanliurfa, Sanliurfa, Turkey (photo Ian Faure).

p.183 Female figurine with bitumen headdresses ceramic Ur Iraq Ubaid 4 period 4500-4000 BC (photo Mary Harrsch CCBY2.0)

p.184 Detail CDLI ref. P253961, Uruk III ca.3200-3000 BC, Schøyen Collection, Oslo, Norway.

GREAT FISH IN THE SEA

p.185 GIR: Detail CDLI ref. P006268, Uruk III ca.3200-3000 BC, Schøyen Collection, Oslo, Norway.

p.187 [1] Quran, Chapter (21:87) sūrat l-anbiyāa (The Prophets) (Trans. Arberry)
[2] Saint Anthony of Egypt, Painting by Francisco de Zurbaran (1598-1664) (Photo public domain).

p.189 Al Khidr, 17th century Indian miniature, Albert and Victoria Museum, London (Photo public domain).

p.191 ETCSL List of Proper Noun (https://etcsl.orinst.ox.ac.uk)

p.195 Detail, Narmer palette, ca.3100 BC, Egyptian Museum, Cairo, Egypt (Public domain).

p.196 From the Talmud, a set of ancient texts covering Jewish laws and traditions. Hebrew Talmud means 'learning'. Bull kidneys were used as burnt offerings according to Leviticus 4.

p.197 R. H. Allen, *Star Names and their Meanings*, 1889, (www.archive.org)
[1] p.138
[2] p.139
[3] p.136

p.199 Quran, Surat l-kahf (The Cave), (Sahih International translation)
[1] ch.18:61
[2] ch.18:70
[3] ch.18:71
[4] ch.18:74
[5] ch.18:77

p.200 [1]The very little existing information was found on www.en.wikishia.net.

p.201 [1] R.H. Allen, *Star Names and their Meanings*, p.xiv, Introduction
[2] Ibid. p.32
[3]Cetus from Urania's Mirror, a set of astronomical star chart cards, 1825, (Public domain, restauration by Adam Cuerden).

p.203 [1] R. H. Allen, Star *Names* and their Meanings, p.162
[2] p.164
[3] p.165

p.204 Ibid. p.45
[2] The words 'cud' and 'cut' both derive from Sumerian TAR/KUD/KUT which has the meaning 'to cut' and leads to TAR-TAR, which in turn leads to Tartarus p.38.

p.207 URU: detail CDLI ref. P001596, Uruk IV ca.3350-3200 BC, Vorderasiatisches Museum, Berlin, Germany (photo Olaf Tessmer).

p.211 Dutch engraving, Den singende swaen, The Singing Swan, Reinier van Persijn, 1665 (Photo Public domain).

p.213 That episode also exists on line 44 of *The Story of Sukurru* where the mast is represented by ME, T-shaped symbol of the Magician but also the 'spirit'. It's more fully discussed in Before Babel p.216, with a further link to the third eye (p.158) and to PA-GAN, through symbols NAM ME translated there as 'for his task as spirit'. That the Sumerian text is pagan in origin is beyond doubt. That underlying references to mind-altering substances are omnipresent is also beyond doubt.

p.214 Andrew Collins, *Beneath The Pyramids: Egypt's Greatest Secret Uncovered*, (4th Dimension Press, 2009)

THIS IS THE WAY

p.217 Tao Te Ching, *Sacred Books of the East*, Vol 39, Trans. J. Legge (1891).

p.218 Tao Te Ching, *Sacred Books of the East*, Vol 39, Trans. J. Legge (1891).

[2] Laozi (Photo public domain).

p.220 [1] ETCSL Sumerian Proverbs Collection from Nibru, ref. 6.2.1.
[2] Ibn' Arabi (1165-1240), Sufi mystic, philosopher and poet. The Sumerian riddles and proverbs predate any known religious teachings. Nevertheless, consider the parallel with "*God describes Himself to us through ourselves. Which means that the divine Names are essentially relative to the beings who name them, since these beings discover and experience them in their own mode of being*" (*Alone with the Alone: Creative Imagination in the Sufism of Ibn'Arabi* by Henry Corbin, orientalist and philosopher.)

p.221 [1] The link to the pineal gland is discussed in several section of *Before Babel*. ME also appears three times between two symbols EN in the antediluvian King List. The three-word phrase EN-ME-EN is translated there to 'Lords of Magic'. Was it meant to be read as a plural? On the assumption that the same format as ŠI-ME-ŠI, the spirit between two eyes, is in use, I suggest that it was but consider it unproven beyond doubt.
[2] There exists a link between the Sumerian word ŠAH given as both 'slave' and 'pig'[1] with BA-AL, to dig. It comes in the form of an extremely short proverb from the Old Babylonian period, ca.1900-1600 BC. which I have translated as follows:
The pigs in the house on the water (riverboat) dig and dig...(BA-AL BA-AL)
The only way I have found to interpret this proverb - if it is to be understood as both logical and humoristic – is to consider that Noah has taken a pair of mushroom-foraging pigs (perhaps also servants) on board the ark and that they are busy foraging a hole into the keel. Repetition of BA-AL, to dig, is an indication that this is likely the correct context. Line 95 of *The Story of Sukurru* uses repetition of the word 'enter' to indicate that the animals go 'two by two' into the ark. Hence the importance of having at least one fully translated literary text in hand for comparison and a better understanding of the wordplay. ŠAH/ŠUBUR, the pig, also makes an unexpected appearance in the Solstice Riddle (annexed in *The Story of Sukurru*. Here on p.290).
[3] ETCSL Sumerian Proverbs Collection 6.1.02, Seg.A, Line 76.

p.224 ETCSL Sumerian Proverbs Collection 6.1.01, Seg.B, Line 89.
BA-AL is found with BAL on the lexical lists. (Erimhuc V 28)

THE MOUTH OF THE WHALE

p.225 Image of baleen whale mouth. *On The Genesis of Species*, St. George Mivart, F.R.S. (1827-1900.) London: Macmillan and Co. 1871. (Project Gutenberg. Public domain)

p.230 R. H. Allen, *Star Names and their Meanings*, p.160-161.

p.231 ETCSL Sumerian Proverbs Collection 6.1.01, Seg.A, Lines 44-45.

p.232 MU, given as 'name' and 'year', is source of the first syllable of 'moon' and 'month', but also 'movement' and 'music'. MU gives the source of the nine Greek Muses, protectors of the arts, - again, the number nine, three times three... never forgetting that MU is also phonetic MEHIDA, a word given in a Hebrew dictionary of biblical terms as 'riddle' and 'sharpness of wit'; a major key to something…but to what?

LOST STONES

p.233 Gobekli Tepe, Turkey (photo Ian Faure).

p.236 [1] GIŠ-MI is discussed on p.175-176 as source of 'Jesus'. There exists a lexical entry which gives the three words together in a different order:
mi-eš giš (Proto-Ea 641).
Is GIŠ the origin of 'Giza'? Perhaps. The ultimate source of both Trismegistus and Giza are otherwise unidentified and there are numerous indications of strong links between the Sumerian writings and Egypt.
[2] Detail CDLI ref. P001011, Uruk IV ca.3350-3200 BC, Vorderasiatisches Museum, Berlin, Germany (photo Olaf Tessmer). There are a number of early tablets carrying this T-shaped form. Another tablet from the same era shows two of the T-shaped forms side by side with a circle joining them: I sent that image to Graham Hancock in 2017 and, like me, he was intrigued by the obvious similarity between the tablet and the T-shaped stone circles of Gobekli Tepe. Challenged on that point by archaeologists working at the site, my response took the form of an article on Graham Hancock's website (https://grahamhancock.com/dainesm3/)

p.239 Shelley, Prometheus Unbound, Act IV (1820).

p.240 The source of 'baptism', BAB/PAP/BAP is analysed in *Before Babel The Crystal Tongue*, p.288, (written in 2019 before the more global study made here). The visual aspect of PAP corresponds to the form of the three boat pits on the eastern flank of the Great Pyramid of Giza (p.91).
PAP is portrayed in front of the mouth of a great fish on a tablet from the Uruk III period, ca.3200-3000 BC (CDLI ref. P006268, Uruk III ca.3200-3000 BC, *Before Babel The Crystal Tongue*, p.270).
Sumerian BAB/PAP/BAP has the given meanings 'father' and 'pre-eminent'; John who was Oannes who was Jonah…who was Thoth? The fathers in three ships? (p.72)

Index of Names

(Pages on which their Sumerian sources are identified)

ANUNNAKI

AN   A   NUN   NA   KID

sky   water   foremost   stone   ghost

light   flow   guide   heavy   fool

disappearing   (whale)

(fish)

NUN–KI/GURUD

The cord to the sun (p.252)

NUN–ME
ABGAL

Magician and Sage (p.28)

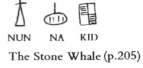

NUN   NA   KID

The Stone Whale (p.205)

NUR (TE)

Nuragic (p.111)

NUN/ERIDA

The eternal Eridanus (p.207)

NUN/AGARGARA

Agaric (p.166)

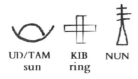

UD/TAM   KIB   NUN

sun   ring

Euphrates (p.209)

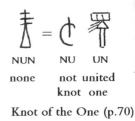

NUN   NU   UN

none   not   united

knot   one

Knot of the One (p.70)

BU/MUŠ   RA   NUN

snake   churn

THE STONE

NUN NA
Guide Stone (The Stone Whale p.206)

NA ZU
Stone Know (The Stone of Knowledge p.231)

NA ME
Stone Magic (The Name p.217)

NU ME
Knot Magic (The Magic Knot p.90)

NUN ME
Guide Magic (Great Father p.28)

KA NUN
Voice Guide (The Canon p.68)

UM ME TE
Rope Magic Tether (Prometheus p.252)

The Measuring Rope

288

THE MILLSTONE

HAR/HUR
millstone
miller
ring

HAR/HUR   **RA**   **AN**
millstone   churn   sky

Celestial Churning Millstone

Harran

HU   UR
flight   dog, lion

HUR

=

HAR/HUR
millstone
miller
ring

Hor

=

HA
fish

ŠI   RI
eye   gather
          watch

AR

Sirius

HA   UB/AR₂
fish   ruin (mound)

corner, recess

HAR

THE SOLSTICE RIDDLE

223.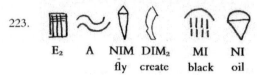

    E₂   A   NIM DIM₂   MI   NI
                 fly create black oil

Temple of the Waters

224.

    SAL ANŠE TAR A   KA   NI
  female ass   cut
  prophetess   tar water

225.

    SAL ŠAH TAR A   TUR   NI
       pig, servant   child
                        three nights

226.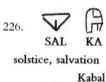

    SAL KA
  solstice, salvation
        Kabal

227.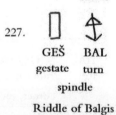

    GEŠ BAL
  gestate turn
    spindle

Riddle of Balgis

Riddle of the Spinning Tree of Life

THE OSIRIS RIDDLE

UD	ŠU₂	UŠ	UŠ	E	A	AB	RA	AN
Sun	sink	male	phallus	rise	water	ocean	churn	sky

UŠ₂	ŠAG₄	BA	GIN₇	GI	A	A	AB	LA₂	EN
Death	heart	less	create	reed	water	water	ocean	order	Lord

By day, the virile sinking and rising
The water of the ocean churns.
Heartless death he created.
With his reed, the floods harnessed by the Lord.

'Heartless death' is a play on the scene of the weighing of the heart at death carried out according to Egyptian lore and mentioned on line 40 of The Story of Sukurru. A humoristic understanding gives death without a heart as the unfortunate result of that procedure. Death is also the unfortunate result of catastrophic flooding provoked by a heartless deity and can be understood, as John Allegro suggested, as a celestial orgasm.

(ETCSL, Sumerian Proverbs, Collection 4, line 8)

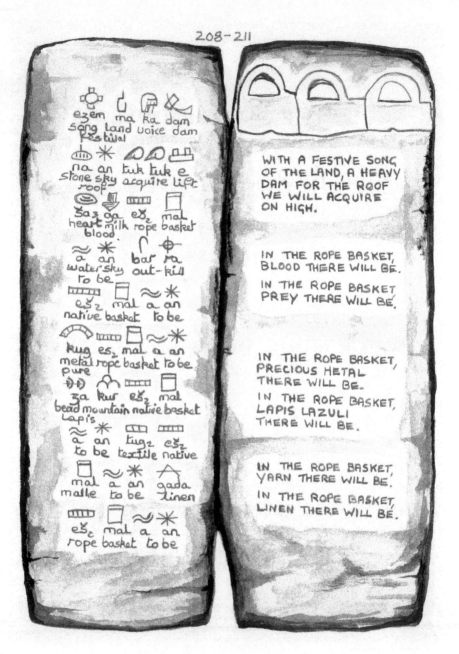

ezem ma ka dam
song land voice dam
festival

na an tuk tuk e
stone sky acquire lift
roof

ša₃ ga eš₂ mal
heart milk rope basket
blood

a an bar ra
water sky out-kill
to be

eš₂ mal a an
native basket to be

kug eš₂ mal a an
metal rope basket to be
pure

za kur eš₂ mal
bead mountain native basket
lapis

a an tug₂ eš₂
to be textile native

mal a an gada
matle to be linen

eš₂ mal a an
rope basket to be

WITH A FESTIVE SONG
OF THE LAND, A HEAVY
DAM FOR THE ROOF
WE WILL ACQUIRE
ON HIGH.

IN THE ROPE BASKET,
BLOOD THERE WILL BE.

IN THE ROPE BASKET
PREY THERE WILL BE.

IN THE ROPE BASKET,
PRECIOUS METAL
THERE WILL BE.

IN THE ROPE BASKET,
LAPIS LAZULI
THERE WILL BE.

IN THE ROPE BASKET,
YARN THERE WILL BE.

IN THE ROPE BASKET,
LINEN THERE WILL BE.

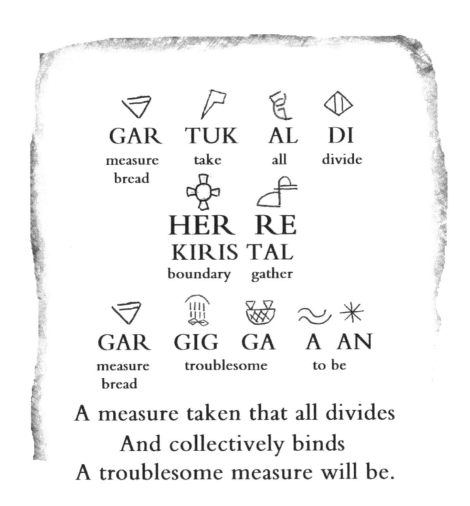

A measure taken that all divides
And collectively binds
A troublesome measure will be.

HER and KIRIS are two phonetic forms of symbol EZEN. With TAL, one phonetic form of RE/RI, they give the source of 'crystal' through Greek krystallos, and 'heresy'. Therein lies the reason for the subtitle of *Before Babel: The Crystal Heresy*. EZEN is source of many things, not least under the guise of its phonetic value KIRIS: Greek khristos, the 'anointed,' origin of Christ. The words GAR-GIG can be read 'bread of gnosis' giving:

> *To take bread that all divides and collectively binds*
> *is to take the Bread of Gnosis.*